Escape from the Doll's House

by *Saul D. Feldman*

In the 1880s, a college-educated woman was viewed with a curiosity bordering on horror, and more than one social critic saw "the identical education of the two sexes . . . a crime before God and humanity." By 1929, women received a substantial proportion of the bachelor's degrees awarded in the United States. By this time, also, the graduate school system was firmly established in American higher education, training those those who aspired toward professional careers. At this higher level of education, however, women received far fewer degrees.

As the author observes in this study of present-day graduate and professional schools, the situation has not improved. In fact, the proportion of doctorates awarded to women has decreased since 1920. But the inferior position of women in graduate education goes beyond underrepresentation. Analyzing massive questionnaire data, Dr. Feldman substantiates a number of patterns of sex-based inequality. finds that female-dominated fields, mostly in the humanities, "not only offer less power, privilege, and prestige, they also offer less in terms of self-image." Even within the same fields, men and women differ in their relationships with professors

(continued on back flap)

(continued from front flap)

and fellow students. These relationships can profoundly affect the performance of students in graduate school as well as their career plans.

The effects of earlier socialization are also reflected in these data. We discover that women enter graduate school with higher grades than men, but are less likely to feel that they are among the best students in their field, and may even say that they will drop out of school because of a lack of ability.

Thus, the author believes that although women are underrepresented in graduate education, merely increasing their number will not solve the more basic problem of eliminating the prejudicial training that women receive throughout their education. The solution to sex-based inequality must be sought not only within colleges and universities, but also within earlier levels of education and in all segments of our society.

Saul D. Feldman is assistant professor of sociology at Case Western Reserve University, Cleveland, Ohio.

Carnegie Commission on Higher Education

Sponsored Research Studies

RECENT ALUMNI AND HIGHER EDUCATION:
A SURVEY OF COLLEGE GRADUATES
Joe L. Spaeth and Andrew M. Greeley

CHANGE IN EDUCATIONAL POLICY:
SELF-STUDIES IN SELECTED COLLEGES AND
UNIVERSITIES
Dwight R. Ladd

STATE OFFICIALS AND HIGHER EDUCATION:
A SURVEY OF THE OPINIONS AND
EXPECTATIONS OF POLICY MAKERS IN NINE
STATES
Heinz Eulau and Harold Quinley

ACADEMIC DEGREE STRUCTURES:
INNOVATIVE APPROACHES
PRINCIPLES OF REFORM IN DEGREE
STRUCTURES IN THE UNITED STATES
Stephen H. Spurr

COLLEGES OF THE FORGOTTEN AMERICANS:
A PROFILE OF STATE COLLEGES AND
REGIONAL UNIVERSITIES
E. Alden Dunham

FROM BACKWATER TO MAINSTREAM:
A PROFILE OF CATHOLIC HIGHER
EDUCATION
Andrew M. Greeley

THE ECONOMICS OF THE MAJOR PRIVATE
UNIVERSITIES
William G. Bowen
*(Out of print, but available from University
Microfilms.)*

THE FINANCE OF HIGHER EDUCATION
Howard R. Bowen
*(Out of print, but available from University
Microfilms.)*

ALTERNATIVE METHODS OF FEDERAL
FUNDING FOR HIGHER EDUCATION
Ron Wolk
*(Out of print, but available from University
Microfilms.)*

INVENTORY OF CURRENT RESEARCH ON
HIGHER EDUCATION 1968
Dale M. Heckman and Warren Bryan Martin
*(Out of print, but available from University
Microfilms.)*

*The following technical reports are available from the Carnegie Commission on Higher Education, 2150
Shattuck Avenue, Berkeley, California 94704.*

RESOURCE USE IN HIGHER EDUCATION:
TRENDS IN OUTPUT AND INPUTS, 1930–1967
June O'Neill

TRENDS AND PROJECTIONS OF PHYSICIANS
IN THE UNITED STATES 1967–2002
Mark S. Blumberg

MAY 1970:
THE CAMPUS AFTERMATH OF CAMBODIA
AND KENT STATE
Richard E. Peterson and John A. Bilorusky

MENTAL ABILITY AND HIGHER EDUCATIONAL
ATTAINMENT IN THE 20TH CENTURY
Paul Taubman and Terence Wales

AMERICAN COLLEGE AND UNIVERSITY
ENROLLMENT TRENDS IN 1971
Richard E. Peterson
*(Out of print, but available from University
Microfilms.)*

PAPERS ON EFFICIENCY IN THE
MANAGEMENT OF HIGHER EDUCATION
*Alexander M. Mood, Colin Bell,
Lawrence Bogard, Helen Brownlee,
and Joseph McCloskey*

AN INVENTORY OF ACADEMIC INNOVATION
AND REFORM
Ann Heiss

ESTIMATING THE RETURNS TO EDUCATION:
A DISAGGREGATED APPROACH
Richard S. Eckaus

SOURCES OF FUNDS TO COLLEGES AND
UNIVERSITIES
June O'Neill

NEW DEPRESSION IN HIGHER
EDUCATION—TWO YEARS LATER
Earl F. Cheit

PROFESSORS, UNIONS, AND AMERICAN
HIGHER EDUCATION
*Everett Carll Ladd, Jr. and
Seymour Martin Lipset*

POLITICAL IDEOLOGIES OF
GRADUATE STUDENTS:
CRYSTALLIZATION, CONSISTENCY, AND
CONTEXTUAL EFFECT
Margaret Fay and Jeff Weintraub

A CLASSIFICATION OF INSTITUTIONS
OF HIGHER EDUCATION

FLYING A LEARNING CENTER:
DESIGN AND COSTS OF AN OFF-CAMPUS
SPACE FOR LEARNING
Thomas J. Karwin

THE DEMISE OF DIVERSITY?:
A COMPARATIVE PROFILE OF EIGHT
TYPES OF INSTITUTIONS
C. Robert Pace

The following reprints are available from the Carnegie Commission on Higher Education, 2150 Shattuck Avenue, Berkeley, California 94704.

ACCELERATED PROGRAMS OF MEDICAL EDUCATION, *by Mark S. Blumberg, reprinted from* JOURNAL OF MEDICAL EDUCATION, *vol. 46, no. 8, August 1971.**

SCIENTIFIC MANPOWER FOR 1970–1985, *by Allan M. Cartter, reprinted from* SCIENCE, *vol. 172, no. 3979, pp. 132–140, April 9, 1971.*

A NEW METHOD OF MEASURING STATES' HIGHER EDUCATION BURDEN, *by Neil Timm, reprinted from* THE JOURNAL OF HIGHER EDUCATION, *vol. 42, no. 1, pp. 27–33, January 1971.**

REGENT WATCHING, *by Earl F. Cheit, reprinted from* AGB REPORTS, *vol. 13, no. 6, pp. 4–13, March 1971.*

COLLEGE GENERATIONS—FROM THE 1930s TO THE 1960s, *by Seymour M. Lipset and Everett C. Ladd, Jr., reprinted from* THE PUBLIC INTEREST, *no. 25, Summer 1971.*

AMERICAN SOCIAL SCIENTISTS AND THE GROWTH OF CAMPUS POLITICAL ACTIVISM IN THE 1960s, *by Everett C. Ladd, Jr., and Seymour M. Lipset, reprinted from* SOCIAL SCIENCES INFORMATION, *vol. 10, no. 2, April 1971.*

THE POLITICS OF AMERICAN POLITICAL SCIENTISTS, *by Everett C. Ladd, Jr., and Seymour M. Lipset, reprinted from* PS, *vol. 4, no. 2, Spring 1971.**

THE DIVIDED PROFESSORIATE, *by Seymour M. Lipset and Everett C. Ladd, Jr., reprinted from* CHANGE, *vol. 3, no. 3, pp. 54–60, May 1971.**

JEWISH ACADEMICS IN THE UNITED STATES: THEIR ACHIEVEMENTS, CULTURE AND POLITICS, *by Seymour M. Lipset and Everett C. Ladd, Jr., reprinted from* AMERICAN JEWISH YEAR BOOK, *1971.*

THE UNHOLY ALLIANCE AGAINST THE CAMPUS, *by Kenneth Keniston and Michael Lerner, reprinted from* NEW YORK TIMES MAGAZINE, *November 8, 1970 .*

PRECARIOUS PROFESSORS: NEW PATTERNS OF REPRESENTATION, *by Joseph W. Garbarino, reprinted from* INDUSTRIAL RELATIONS, *vol. 10, no. 1, February 1971.**

. . . AND WHAT PROFESSORS THINK: ABOUT STUDENT PROTEST AND MANNERS, MORALS, POLITICS, AND CHAOS ON THE CAMPUS, *by Seymour Martin Lipset and Everett C. Ladd, Jr., reprinted from* PSYCHOLOGY TODAY, *November 1970.**

DEMAND AND SUPPLY IN U.S. HIGHER EDUCATION: A PROGRESS REPORT, *by Roy Radner and Leonard S. Miller, reprinted from* AMERICAN ECONOMIC REVIEW, *May 1970.**

RESOURCES FOR HIGHER EDUCATION: AN ECONOMIST'S VIEW, *by Theodore W. Schultz, reprinted from* JOURNAL OF POLITICAL ECONOMY, *vol. 76, no. 3, University of Chicago, May/June 1968.**

INDUSTRIAL RELATIONS AND UNIVERSITY RELATIONS, *by Clark Kerr, reprinted from* PROCEEDINGS OF THE 21ST ANNUAL WINTER MEETING OF THE INDUSTRIAL RELATIONS RESEARCH ASSOCIATION, *pp. 15–25.**

NEW CHALLENGES TO THE COLLEGE AND UNIVERSITY, *by Clark Kerr, reprinted from Kermit Gordon (ed.),* AGENDA FOR THE NATION, *The Brookings Institution, Washington, D.C., 1968.**

PRESIDENTIAL DISCONTENT, *by Clark Kerr, reprinted from David C. Nichols (ed.),* PERSPECTIVES ON CAMPUS TENSIONS: PAPERS PREPARED FOR THE SPECIAL COMMITTEE ON CAMPUS TENSIONS, *American Council on Education, Washington, D.C., September 1970.**

STUDENT PROTEST—AN INSTITUTIONAL AND NATIONAL PROFILE, *by Harold Hodgkinson, reprinted from* THE RECORD, *vol. 71, no. 4, May 1970.**

WHAT'S BUGGING THE STUDENTS?, *by Kenneth Keniston, reprinted from* EDUCATIONAL RECORD, *American Council on Education, Washington, D.C., Spring 1970.**

THE POLITICS OF ACADEMIA, *by Seymour Martin Lipset, reprinted from David C. Nichols (ed.),* PERSPECTIVES ON CAMPUS TENSIONS: PAPERS PREPARED FOR THE SPECIAL COMMITTEE ON CAMPUS TENSIONS, *American Council on Education, Washington, D.C., September 1970.**

INTERNATIONAL PROGRAMS OF U.S. COLLEGES AND UNIVERSITIES: PRIORITIES FOR THE SEVENTIES, *by James A. Perkins, reprinted by permission of the International Council for Educational Development, Occasional Paper no. 1, July 1971.*

FACULTY UNIONISM: FROM THEORY TO PRACTICE, *by Joseph W. Garbarino, reprinted from* INDUSTRIAL RELATIONS, *vol. 11, no. 1, pp. 1–17, February 1972.*

MORE FOR LESS: HIGHER EDUCATION'S NEW PRIORITY, *by Virginia B. Smith, reprinted from* UNIVERSAL HIGHER EDUCATION: COSTS AND BENEFITS, *American Council on Education, Washington, D.C., 1971.*

ACADEMIA AND POLITICS IN AMERICA, *by Seymour M. Lipset, reprinted from Thomas J. Nossiter (ed.),* IMAGINATION AND PRECISION IN THE SOCIAL SCIENCES, *pp. 211–289, Faber and Faber, London, 1972.*

POLITICS OF ACADEMIC NATURAL SCIENTISTS AND ENGINEERS, *by Everett C. Ladd, Jr., and Seymour M. Lipset, reprinted from* SCIENCE, *vol. 176, no. 4039, pp. 1091–1100, June 9, 1972.*

THE INTELLECTUAL AS CRITIC AND REBEL: WITH SPECIAL REFERENCE TO THE UNITED STATES AND THE SOVIET UNION, *by Seymour M. Lipset and Richard B. Dobson, reprinted from* DAEDALUS, *vol. 101, no. 3, pp. 137–198, Summer 1972.*

COMING OF MIDDLE AGE IN HIGHER EDUCATION, *by Earl F. Cheit, address delivered to American Association of State Colleges and Universities and National Association of State Universities and Land-Grant Colleges, Nov. 13, 1972.*

THE NATURE AND ORIGINS OF THE CARNEGIE COMMISSION ON HIGHER EDUCATION, *by Alan Pifer, reprinted by permission of The Carnegie Commission for the Advancement of Teaching, speech delivered Oct. 16, 1972.*

THE DISTRIBUTION OF ACADEMIC TENURE IN AMERICAN HIGHER EDUCATION, *by Martin Trow, reprinted from* THE TENURE DEBATE, *Bardwell Smith (ed.), Jossey-Bass, San Francisco, 1972.*

THE POLITICS OF AMERICAN SOCIOLOGISTS, *by Seymour M. Lipset and Everett C. Ladd, Jr., reprinted from* THE AMERICAN JOURNAL OF SOCIOLOGY, *vol. 78, no. 1, July 1972.*

MEASURING FACULTY UNIONISM: QUANTITY AND QUALITY, *by Bill Aussieker and J. W. Garbarino, reprinted from* INDUSTRIAL RELATIONS, *vol. 12, no. 2, May 1973.*

PROBLEMS IN THE TRANSITION FROM ELITE TO MASS HIGHER EDUCATION, *by Martin Trow, paper prepared for a conference on mass higher education sponsored by the Organization for Economic Co-operation and Development, June 1973.*

Escape from the Doll's House

WOMEN IN GRADUATE

AND PROFESSIONAL SCHOOL EDUCATION

by *Saul D. Feldman*

Department of Sociology
Case Western Reserve University

A Report Prepared for
The Carnegie Commission on Higher Education

MCGRAW-HILL BOOK COMPANY
*New York   St. Louis   San Francisco   Düsseldorf
London   Sydney   Toronto   Mexico   Panama
Johannesburg   Kuala Lumpur   Montreal
New Delhi   São Paulo   Singapore*

ESCAPE FROM THE DOLL'S HOUSE
Women in Graduate and Professional School Education

Copyright © 1974 by The Carnegie Foundation for
the Advancement of Teaching. All rights reserved.
Printed in the United States of America. No part of this publication
may be reproduced, stored in a retrieval system, or transmitted, in any
form or by any means, electronic, mechanical, photocopying, recording,
or otherwise, without the prior written permission of the publisher.

*This book was set in Vladimir by University Graphics, Inc.
It was printed on acid-free, long-life paper and bound by
The Maple Press Company. The designers were Elliot Epstein
and Edward Butler. The editors were Nancy Tressel and
Michael Hennelly for McGraw-Hill Book Company and Verne A.
Stadtman and Karen Seriguchi for the Carnegie Commission on
Higher Education. Milton Heiberg supervised the production.*

Library of Congress Cataloging in Publication Data

Feldman, Saul D
Escape from the doll's house.

A revision of the author's thesis, University of
Washington.
Bibliography: p.
1. Universities and colleges — United States —
Graduate work of women.   2.   Professional education of
women — United States.   I.   Carnegie Commission on
Higher Education.   II.   Title.   III.   Title: Women in
graduate and professional school education.

LC1756.F44 1973   376'.65   73-12829
ISBN 0–07–010069–1

123456789MAMM7987654

Contents

To G. M.

Ein Weiser prüft und achtet nicht,
Was der gemeine Pobel spricht.

TAMINO

Foreword

One of the strongest forces in American social history has been the belief that the more education one has, the better are one's chances for prestige and financial success. As a result of this belief and the rising ability of the middle class to pay for higher education, the number of college graduates and holders of advanced degrees has increased dramatically. The majority of these highly educated men and women will enter professional fields. For women, graduate education may provide an "escape from the doll's house," not only for the housewife, but also for those in such low-paying, sexually stereotyped occupations as clerical and secretarial work. Just as women are sexually segregated in the American occupational structure, however, so are they segregated in certain "female" academic fields. As the Carnegie Commission discusses in its report *Opportunities for Women in Higher Education*, most women graduate students enter the fields of education, the social sciences, and library science, although more women than in the past have recently begun to obtain advanced degrees in traditionally male-dominated fields.

This study by sociologist Saul Feldman focuses on the training and experiences of women in graduate and professional schools, particularly on how they are regarded by faculty and fellow graduate students, and on their self-images and career expectations. It makes extensive use of the data collected in the Carnegie Commission's National Survey of Faculty and Student Opinion, conducted in 1969. Dr. Feldman first gives a vivid history of the struggle of women to attain higher education. Then, using the methodology of social science, he gauges the extent of some of the prejudices that women currently face in graduate education and the effect of these prejudices upon women's academic performance and career choice.

The recent women's movement has brought to light the sexual stereotypes that can constrict the lives of both men and women, but it is also a subject of heated, sometimes fruitless, discussion. We welcome any attempt to identify, both clearly and factually, the effects of these stereotypes. In this thorough study of the sex-based inequalities in graduate education, Dr. Feldman has succeeded in doing so.

Clark Kerr

Chairman
Carnegie Commission
on Higher Education

January 1974

Acknowledgments

This book is a revision of my dissertation from the Department of Sociology, University of Washington. The research was conducted while I was at the Survey Research Center at the University of California, Berkeley. Individuals in Berkeley, Seattle, and Cleveland aided in the creation of this book: Martin Trow, as project director of the massive Carnegie study, created an atmosphere unusual in research projects. He directed a project that was unique in scope, in range of subject matter, and in the encouragement of individual autonomy in his professional staff.

The massive data gathering meant massive data processing problems. Judy Roizen, Don Trumell, and Harvey Weinstein wrote programs that made the data easy to manipulate and a pleasure to work with. Margaret Baker's and Abdul Singh's data processing links with the 360 and the 6400 created the numerous sample tapes, indexes, tables, and correlation matrixes that made data analysis a much simpler process.

I received much-needed statistical and sampling advice from Francis Many and Bill Nicholls. Bloody arguments with Lynn Flame-Jones clarified my early conceptualizations. Oliver Fulton, Karen Paige, Gertrude Selznick, and Steve Steinberg offered many helpful suggestions for the data analysis. Alison Hooson, librarian of the Survey Research Center, kept me informed of new and relevant material.

Technical assistance was provided by Mary Renner, Eva Sinacore, and Richard Scheffer. Barbara Penney, Anna Lu, and Gwen Rosenthal took my illegible typing and created a readable first draft.

Edward Gross was my dissertation chairman until his sabbatical, and Herbert Costner willingly served as his replacement. I thank them both for their guidance.

Dissertations and books are not the same. Verne Stadtman of the Carnegie Commission and Linda Noelker made many helpful suggestions for revision. Karen Seriguchi was a thoughtful and sensitive editor.

Finally, a special thanks to Travis Hirschi, who invited me to serve as his research assistant on the Carnegie project. By his example and approach to survey research, my two years in Berkeley became an invaluable learning experience.

Epigraph

I hadn't really wanted to marry at all. I wanted to make something of myself, not just give it away. But I knew if I didn't marry I would be sorry. Only freaks didn't. I knew I had to do it quickly, too, while there was still a decent selection of men to choose from. Dr. Watson might be right about personality not hardening until thirty, but old maids started forming at twenty-one. I was twenty. The heavy pressure was on. In years I was still safe, but in distance I was borderline. I had finished college and started graduate school. The best catches were being picked off while I was educating myself right out of the running.

I had altered my ambitions once for love; I didn't dare do it again. My first love, philosophy, still claimed me. Now I had to choose a mate who would share me with it. That ruled out Prince Charming.

After a lot of careful thought I chose Frank. Not that he was perfect—no one is. But I was fond of him, none of his parts were missing, and unlike all the other eligibles I knew, he seemed willing and able to make a little room in his future for mine.

Franklin Raybel was in the History Department at Columbia, studying Modern European History. He had a perfect name for a title page and a graduate fellowship, which meant he probably had a good future. It was an important point for me, because if we were both going to be teaching, my husband would have to be able to get a job at a university large enough to accommodate me, too.

Like me, Frank was a Midwesterner sufficiently threatened by New York to need fortification. From Gary, Indiana, and twenty-seven, he had come farther and further than I. I would have preferred someone from the Philosophy Department, but my Columbia classmates all treated me either as an interloper or an anomaly.

"So you're the dish I heard about; I was hoping I'd get into a class with you," they said. In my seminars no one ever listened to a single word I said without grinning, and then as soon as I had finished they'd all return to their heated disputes as though I had never spoken. They treated me a little better than they treated the older women in the department, at least acknowledging (after class) that I existed. But it was still a terrible comedown after Baxter College, where my classmates had listened to what I had to say and Alport had encouraged me.

Those Columbia classes were all the more disheartening because in them were held the headiest discussions I had ever been privileged to sit in on. Theses and antitheses, arguments and counter-arguments, premises and conclusions ricocheted off the walls and exploded midair above the mahogany conference table in brilliant illuminations. After only a couple of weeks of classes, however, I felt so intimidated, and then stupid, that I didn't dare participate. I just did my reading and tried to look as though I considered all that disputation beneath me. I chose obscure minor figures to write my papers on, hoping no one in the seminars would know enough about my subjects to ridicule me. And on weekends when the philosophers invited me to their parties, instead of sitting dumb and pretty through their snappy talk, I helped their girlfriends from other departments (English, Teacher's College, Barnard) serve the food and coffee that kept them going at each other till two A.M.

"How come *you're* studying philosophy?" my colleagues would ask me over beer with bemused smiles. "Do you really want to get a Ph.D.? Do you really expect to teach?" The way they asked their questions, I knew better than to answer yes. I quickly learned that there was only a handful of teaching jobs in philosophy in the country—all coveted, all for them.

"I just like philosophy, that's all," I'd answer. "I don't know what I'll do with my Ph.D. Maybe I can work for a philosophical journal. Maybe I can teach in a finishing school."

ACKNOWLEDGMENT: From *Memoirs of an Ex-Prom Queen,* by Alix Kates Schulman. Copyright © 1969, 1971, 1972 by Alix Kates Schulman. Reprinted by permission of Alfred A. Knopf, Inc.

1. Introduction: The Escape from the Doll's House

NORA: What do you consider my most sacred duties?
HELMER: Do I need to tell you that? Are they not your duties to your husband and your children?
NORA: I have other duties just as sacred.
HELMER: That you have not. What duties could those be?
NORA: Duties to myself.
HELMER: Before all else, you are a wife and a mother.
NORA: I don't believe that any longer. I believe that before all else I am a reasonable human being, just as you are—or, at all events, that I must try and become one. I know quite well, Torvald, that most people would think you right, and that views of that kind are to be found in books; but I can no longer content myself with what most people say, or with what is found in books. I must think over things for myself and get to understand them.[1]

With these words, Nora Helmer stated her reasons for leaving her husband, Torvald, in a play that created quite a controversy when it was first published in 1879. When Nora told her husband, "I have existed merely to perform tricks for you, Torvald," she was describing the position of many middle-class Victorian women. A few years later, an American feminist stated her perceptions of women's duties: " . . . the preparation of food and the removal of dirt, the nutritive and excretive process of the family are feminine functions" (Stetson, 1898, p. 225).

Nora's slamming the door on Torvald may be considered symbolic of her contemporaries' attempts to change the status and roles of women. Feminism became a social movement, dealing with such social issues as suffrage, temperance (Gusfield, 1963), and property

[1] From Henrik Ibsen, *A Doll's House, The Wild Duck, The Lady from the Sea,* trans. R. Farquharson Sharp and Eleanor Marx-Aveling, Everyman's Library edition, 1958, p. 68, published by E. P. Dutton & Co., Inc., and used with their permission.

rights for women (Rossi, 1964, p. 609). Women in increasing numbers began to enter the labor force; whereas in 1900 there were
4.5 men per 1 woman in the labor force, there are today 1.8 (Gross,
1968, p. 198).

Yet despite the increased representation of women in the labor
force, there is strong evidence to suggest that women are not entering male-dominated fields and that sexual segregation in the
American occupational structure is as strong today as it was in
1900 (Gross, 1968). Furthermore, despite the increased representation of women in the labor force, the percentage of women in
managerial and professional positions has remained constant
(Knudsen, 1969).

Many have seen the status of women in American society as
similar to that of a minority group. In his classic study, *An American Dilemma,* Gunnar Myrdal called the position of women in
American society "a parallel to the Negro problem" (1944, pp. 1073
–1078). Helen Hacker (1951, p. 65) compared the "caste-like
status of women and Negroes," and Roger Barker (1948, p. 33)
used the analogy of physical disability to describe the problems of
women in male-dominated fields:

Uncertainty of status for the disabled person obtains over a wide range of
social interactions in addition to that of employment. The blind, the ill, the
deaf, the crippled can never be sure of what the attitude of a new acquaintance will be, whether it will be one of rejection or acceptance, until the new
contact has been made. This is exactly the position of the adolescent, the
light-skinned Negro, the second generation immigrant, the socially mobile
person, and the woman who has entered a predominantly masculine
occupation.

Although many have decried the exclusion of women from male-
dominated fields, one noted social critic felt that their nonparticipation was in fact an indication of the superiority of women:

What men, in their egoism, constantly mistake for a deficiency of intelligence in women is merely an incapacity for mastering that mass of small
intellectual tricks, that complex of petty knowledges, that collection of
cerebral rubberstamps, which constitutes the chief mental equipment of
the average male. A man thinks that he is more intelligent than his wife
because he can add up a column of figures more accurately and because he
can understand the imbecile jargon of the stock market, and because he is
able to distinguish between the ideas of rival politicians, and because he is
privy to the minutiae of some sordid and degrading business or profession,

say soap-selling or the law. But these empty talents, of course, are not really signs of a profound intelligence; they are, in fact, merely superficial accomplishments, and their acquirement puts little more strain on the mental powers than a chimpanzee suffers in learning how to catch a penny or scratch a match. The whole bag of tricks of the average business man, or even of the average professional man, is inordinately childish. It takes no more actual sagacity to carry on the everyday hawking and haggling of the world, or to ladle out its normal doses of bad medicine and worse law, than it takes to operate a taxi-cab or fry a pan of fish.[2]

Despite H. L. Mencken's views of the advantages of being a woman, women labor force participants are subject to sex-specific factors impeding their careers. Caplow (1954, pp. 234–236) noted five such factors:

1 Women generally have discontinuous occupational careers, interrupted by marriage, childbirth, child-care problems, etc.

2 Women are generally secondary wage earners, supplementing rather than generating family income. This has led to the view that women should therefore be paid less than men.

3 Women tend to be less spatially mobile. Women are thus more limited in accepting employment or moving than are men.

4 The reserve labor force of women is greater than the reserve labor force of men. Since some qualified women are more likely to be out of the labor force because of the discontinuity of their career lines, employers have less difficulty in hiring women. The supply may be greater than the demand, resulting in increased competition for jobs.

5 Women are controlled by sex-specific employment laws. Although these laws may exist under the guise of protecting women, Caplow maintains that they are also used to reduce the effectiveness of women as competitors for men's jobs.

Although Caplow was dealing mainly with occupations other than the professions, we note similar inequalities when we compare professional men and women. Perrucci (1970, p. 252) compared men and women at similar stages in scientific and engineering careers. On the average, men's annual salaries exceeded women's annual salaries by $1,400 in engineering and $600 in science (see also Rossi, 1965). Linn (1971) found that married women dentists were less likely to practice full time than married male dentists, and Lopate (1968) noted that women physicians are more limited than men in where they can find employment.[3]

A college education obviously does not exempt women from the problems facing less educated women. An early guide (Bennett, 1917, pp. 269–270) for college-educated women reminded them of their obligations:

Just as long as laboring women are employed for hours that are unduly long, just that long will there be demands upon educated women. Just as long as there are underpaid factory girls, there will be underpaid doctors of philosophy. For selfish reasons, if for no others, the college girl must recognize her place in the world of women. But chiefly because she is high-minded, unselfish, and looking with a glorified vision toward a day of realized democracy, must she understand fully her relation to this great group of which she is a unit, and her obligations to its betterment.

The problems of differential treatment do not begin when women enter the working world. Women face differential treatment in academia both as students and as staff members. William Harper, president of the University of Chicago, stated in 1906:

In colleges and universities for men only, women may not find a place upon the faculty. In a certain great state university, in which there are as many women students as men students, women are represented in the faculty by a single individual, and she has been appointed within the last three years. In some of the women's colleges, women find a place. In others, second rate and third rate men are preferred to women of first rate ability (in Woody, 1929*b*, p. 327).

One of the earliest studies of academic women (1,025 women who received their Ph.D.'s between 1877 and 1924) was published in 1930. About 60 percent of the respondents were engaged in college teaching, and most stressed the importance of the doctorate for their position. Like their male counterparts, these early academic women reported that they received a substantial increase in salary once they obtained the doctorate, although many felt that there was discrimination against them with regard to obtaining appointments, promotions, and salary increases. A doctorate per se was not enough to ensure equality (Hutchinson, 1930).

---

[3] The limiting of professional women to certain loci of employment is not a recent phenomenon. A 1922 guide encouraging women to enter chemistry warned of "the tradition that industrial work (i.e., industrial chemistry) is not a woman's sphere" (Bureau of Vocational Information, 1922, p. 47).

Hutchinson asked female Ph.D.'s to give advice to women who were thinking of pursuing a doctorate. A Ph.D. in English stated:

I advise no one to take the Ph.D. degree. It leads only to college teaching positions; and at present our higher education is so hopelessly in the grip of mediocrity (as embodied in boards of trustees, administration, etc.) that no serious, intelligent and creative woman can long be content in that profession. The salaries are small. The same brains and energy applied elsewhere earn far more. The social life is uninteresting. College faculties are now filled almost entirely with stupid nonentities, old maids of both sexes. If one is enthusiastic, teaching draws one's vitality so that there is none left for creative work or creative living. Idealism is impossible in that atmosphere of timidity and compromise (Hutchinson, 1930, p. 111).

Hutchinson found that about 80 percent of the women doctorates were not married. A Ph.D. in astronomy warned:

I would *not* advise a Ph.D. as preparation for housekeeping and child rearing, most especially not a Ph.D. in astro-physics, nor in physics, nor in mathematics. If a woman has the slightest expectation of marriage, yet wishes to advance professionally and engage in scientific work, she had better take an M.D. or an R.N. or a Ph.D. in Home Economics.

Even apart from the above consideration I would advise a woman against taking a Ph.D. unless she plans to *teach* the subject. Most of the *research* is done at big observatories, which, without exception, relegate or tend to relegate women to positions as computers. These computers do most of the work for a man who gets the credit. There is good reason for this; the night work and handling of large telescopes is very exhausting physically. Even strong men complain of it. A vigorous woman can do it, and a few have done so, but after a few years the strain tells on them much more proportionately than on the men. Then, too, the *conventions* are a great handicap. People *will* talk. *For this very reason* the Mt. Wilson observatory (largest and richest in the world) allows no woman at the mountain station where the telescope work is done; even visiting scientists fall under this rule (Hutchinson, 1930, pp. 117–118).

Over time the percentage of doctorates issued to women has remained constant. Doctorates issued to women in 1900 numbered 9 percent, compared to 13.3 percent in 1970. Furthermore, the higher the academic degree, the less likely women are to receive it. In 1970, women received 43.2 percent of the bachelor's degrees, 34.8 percent of the master's degrees, and only 5.4 percent of the first-professional degrees issued by American colleges and universities (Hooper, 1972). Table 1 indicates the great expansion in post-

	Master's	Doctorate	Ratio—percentage of master's/ percentage of doctorates
1957	33.3 (61,955)	10.7 (8,756)	3.112
1960	31.6 (74,497)	10.4 (9,829)	3.038
1963	31.1 (91,418)	10.7 (12,822)	2.907
1966	33.9 (140,772)	11.6 (18,239)	2.922
1967	34.7 (157,892)	11.9 (20,621)	2.916
1968	35.8 (177,150)	12.6 (23,091)	2.841
1969	37.3 (194,414)	13.1 (26,189)	2.847
1970	39.8 (209,387)	13.3 (29,872)	2.984

TABLE 1 *Percentage of female master's and doctoral degree recipients, selected years, 1957–1970 (absolute numbers in parentheses)*

SOURCE: Based on U.S. Office of Education data. For further details see Lerner (1970, p. 132).

graduate education in a period of 13 years. Yet, although the number of master's degrees and doctorates issued in the United States has tripled since 1957, the representation of women has remained relatively constant. Over time, there appears a very slight decrease in the ratio of women receiving master's degrees to women receiving doctorates, but the underrepresentation at the doctoral level is still very evident.

Table 2 documents the same pattern of unequal representation more specifically. Of the 33 fields listed in this table, women received the majority of bachelor's degrees in 15, yet, in no field did women receive the bulk of the doctorates, and in only 9 did they receive the bulk of the master's degrees. To examine field differentials, we computed two attrition ratios. The first was computed by dividing the percentage of women receiving a bachelor's degree in a field by the percentage receiving a doctorate. Certain fields have especially high female attrition ratios. Women are at least four times as likely to receive a bachelor's degree in mathematics, computer science, and business as they are to receive a doctorate in these fields.

Attrition does not occur only from the bachelor's to the doctorate

TABLE 2 *Percentage of female degree recipients for selected fields, 1970–71 (absolute numbers in parentheses)*

	Bachelor's	Master's	Doctorate	Ratio— percentage of female bachelor's/ percentage of female doctorates	Ratio— percentage of female master's/ percentage of female doctorates
Library science	92.0 (1,013)	81.2 (7,028)	28.2 (39)	3.26	2.88
Elementary education	90.9 (90,960)	81.7 (17,079)	47.0 (219)	1.93	1.74
Speech pathology and audiology	87.7 (1,427)	81.7 (845)	31.4 (70)	2.80	2.60
French	84.4 (7,325)	77.0 (1,437)	46.4 (192)	1.82	1.66
Social work	75.4 (4,690)	60.3 (6,148)	31.0 (126)	2.43	1.95
Spanish	75.1 (7,537)	63.5 (1,480)	41.7 (168)	1.80	1.52
Linguistics	67.3 (254)	50.9 (352)	24.7 (150)	2.72	2.06
English	67.0 (51,649)	62.1 (7,521)	29.8 (1,008)	2.25	2.08
Art	65.7 (12,402)	46.1 (1,956)	37.1 (52)	1.77	1.24
Russian	61.3 (715)	53.6 (110)	0 (14)	*	*
Sociology	59.3 (33,662)	37.4 (1,809)	20.7 (574)	2.85	1.81
Secondary education	57.6 (3,718)	45.9 (5,425)	19.8 (212)	2.91	2.32
Anthropology	55.5 (4,386)	44.0 (766)	26.1 (241)	2.13	1.69
Music	55.0 (6,069)	47.6 (2,435)	16.3 (326)	3.37	2.92
Dramatic arts	54.8 (3,685)	47.2 (1,039)	18.0 (122)	3.04	2.62
Psychology	44.6 (37,493)	36.1 (3,234)	23.8 (1,443)	1.87	1.52
Bacteriology	40.5 (353)	36.5 (74)	19.0 (42)	2.13	1.92
Physical education	38.6 (24,773)	31.2 (4,410)	24.4 (283)	1.58	1.28

TABLE 2 *(continued)*

	Bachelor's	Master's	Doctorate	Ratio— percentage of female bachelor's/ percentage of female doctorates	Ratio— percentage of female master's/ percentage of female doctorates
Mathematics	38.4 (24,366)	30.5 (4,509)	8.3 (971)	4.63	3.67
Botany	36.0 (547)	32.1 (312)	12.6 (223)	2.86	2.55
History	35.1 (44,931)	32.8 (5,169)	12.1 (991)	2.90	2.71
Biochemistry	24.3 (568)	39.4 (251)	15.7 (517)	1.55	2.51
Geography	20.9 (4,167)	18.6 (649)	10.4 (164)	2.00	1.79
Philosophy	20.1 (5,790)	24.8 (602)	9.1 (394)	2.21	2.73
Political science	20.1 (27,636)	20.7 (2,318)	12.1 (700)	1.66	1.71
Zoology	20.0 (5,414)	34.8 (692)	17.2 (418)	1.16	2.02
Chemistry	18.7 (11,157)	21.2 (2,206)	7.9 (1,953)	2.37	2.69
Computer science	14.5 (1,624)	12.6 (1,131)	2.7 (110)	5.37	4.67
Economics	12.0 (15,958)	13.1 (1,997)	7.3 (721)	1.64	1.79
Geology	11.1 (2,360)	10.2 (606)	3.4 (289)	3.26	3.00
Business	10.0 (30,672)	4.4 (8,721)	1.1 (190)	9.09	4.00
Physics	6.7 (5,051)	6.8 (2,180)	2.9 (1,449)	2.31	2.34
Engineering	0.8 (50,357)	1.1 (16,457)	0.6 (3,638)	1.33	1.83

*Too few cases for calculation of ratios.
SOURCE: Hooper (1973).

level, however. We computed a second ratio by dividing the percentage of women receiving a master's degree in a field by the percentage of women receiving a doctorate. Every field showed female attrition from the master's to the doctoral level, with the highest attrition ratios in computer science and business. There is little relationship between the percentage of women receiving a bachelor's degree in a field and the master's-doctorate attrition ratio.

Among students *enrolled* in doctoral degree programs, sex has been found to be a strong predictor of attainment of this degree. Stark (1967) studied the career patterns of graduate students enrolled in four academic disciplines at the University of California at Berkeley. Women admitted to Ph.D. programs were much less likely than their male counterparts eventually to obtain the doctorate. Mooney (1968) examined a group of Woodrow Wilson Fellows and attempted to predict who would obtain a doctorate (after a maximum of 8 years). Woodrow Wilson Fellows are select students who receive financial aid with the expectation that they will obtain the Ph.D.; yet even among this group, sex is the most powerful predictor of success in graduate school (see also Wegner, 1969).

With the revival of the feminist movement, more attention is being paid to the status of women in academia. For example, the academic senates at the University of California at Berkeley (Colson, Scott, et al., 1970) and the University of Chicago (Bradburn et al., 1970) have sponsored studies on the status of women on their campuses. At Ohio State University (Schoen et al., 1971) the board of trustees established such a study, while at other schools, for example, the University of Michigan (McGuinan, 1970) and the University of Wisconsin (Women's Research Group, 1970), autonomous women's groups have examined the problems of women on their respective campuses. The status of women within academic disciplines, for example, anthropology (Fischer & Golde, 1968), sociology (Rossi, 1970), and political science (Schuck, 1970) has become a focal point of investigation. Some researchers have reported their findings in general academic publications (Graham, 1970; Harris, 1970; and Scully, 1970) and in the mass media (Alexander, 1970; Koch, 1971; and Woodring, 1970).

The main thrust of these reports is the general underrepresentation of women at the graduate and faculty levels, but there are more specific charges as well, for example, greater difficulty in receiving financial aid among students and unequal treatment with regard to duties, salary, and promotion among faculty. A recurring theme is that many of the difficulties that academic women face may be largely the result of a tradition of antifemale discriminatory behavior within academia.

Antifemale attitudes are evident in subtle as well as in unsubtle ways. In the mid-1960s the panic that the United States was not producing enough Ph.D.'s was still present; thus, one author (Beach, 1965, p. 127) democratically made a plea for more women:

The shortage of Ph.D.s for college and university teaching posts may be met in part by two groups of students whose potential usefulness has not fully been explored. Foreign-born and women teachers may well be able to step in where they would have been less welcome a generation ago.

More recently, Jencks and Riesman (1968, pp. 298–299) praised academia for being less prejudiced against women than the rest of society, despite their intimation that most women do little with their education:

Most graduate schools expect women who apply to graduate schools of law, medicine, or even the arts and sciences to stop working when they have children and not to return to a professionally respected role. Since this expectation is often realistic, it is hard to argue against the professional schools' misogynistic prejudices.

Jencks and Riesman sound much like Mencken when they describe female graduate students:

Yet even the woman who drops out and does nothing tangible with her education often makes an intangible contribution, both to society and to the graduate school in which she is briefly enrolled. The presence of women in graduate courses seems to us to have a small but significant effect on the attitudes of the professors and the male students, and it is almost invariably a benign effect. Women seem less easily caught up in the gamesmanship of the academic profession and less easily inducted into its ritualistic excesses. Just as very few girls collect stamps, play chess, become science-fiction afficionados, or take up other hobbies, so, too, relatively few women become entranced with the apparatus of scholarship that serves so many men as a substitute for thought. This indifference to academic games for their own sake can combine with passivity in the face of adult authority to produce rote learning and mechanical imitation as answers to external pressure. Yet it still seems to us that women are somewhat more likely than men to fuse their human and academic concerns, and that this makes the admission of women in more than token numbers an asset in a graduate school. Yet this may be precisely why many scholars want to keep women out (Jencks & Riesman, 1968, pp. 299–300).[4]

---

[4] Copyright © 1968 by Doubleday & Company, Inc. From *The Academic Revolution* by Christopher Jencks and David Riesman.

Discriminatory attitudes may be much less subtle than those exemplified by Beach or Jencks and Riesman. Jessie Bernard quotes a department chairman's attitude toward female graduate students:

My own practice is to appoint women to about 50 percent of our graduate assistantships and to about 30 percent of our instructorships. My fear that this is too large a proportion of women appointees arises from the considerations: (1) that women are less likely to complete the degree programs upon which they embark; (2) that even if they do, marriage is very likely to intervene and to prevent or considerably delay their entry into the teaching profession; (3) that even when they do become full-time teachers (at whatever level, including the university), their primary sense of responsibility is to their homes, so that they become professional only to a limited degree; (4) that they are far less likely than are men to achieve positions of leadership in their profession, either through research and publication or through activity in academic organizations (Bernard, 1964, p. 48).[5]

Caplow and McGee maintained (1965, p. 194) that "women scholars are not taken seriously," and evidence of their assertion may be seen in the advice given to women in academia. Women at Berkeley have reported that they were discouraged from entering certain fields or from continuing in graduate education; some were told that scholarship is unfeminine; others noted that men rather than women received the benefits of informal training; and others stated that they were advised not to train for academic positions (Colson, Scott, et al., 1970, pp. 69–71). In her correspondence to a research project on higher education, one female graduate student wrote, "Somehow at the University of _____ there is a stigma attached to graduate women."

What are the bases of this discriminatory behavior? Are women not completing their graduate education because they are less able or because they are discriminated against? If women are less able, some academians may perceive their prejudice as having a valid base.[6] But academic reports do not generally compare men and women of equal talent. We would be better able to document discrimination, for example, if we could demonstrate that equally

---

[5] Copyright © 1964 by the Pennsylvania State University. From *Academic Women* by Jessie Bernard. Reprinted by permission of the Pennsylvania State University Press.

[6] See, for example, George Lundberg's classic justification (1958, p. 293) of prejudicial behavior: " . . . the mores *require* us to discriminate against the disreputable and the disapproved."

talented women receive fewer of the rewards than men and are held back for no other apparent reason than their sex.

Even if they are equal in ability, women may fail to obtain the rewards that men obtain simply because they lack the same dedication. If women are for some reason *perceived* as less dedicated, however, and therefore are treated as such, they may well lower their academic commitment. Assuming a lower level of commitment, faculty members may pay less attention to their female students, who then become less successful. The prophecy becomes self-fulfilling.

An academic vice-president (and professor of psychology) at Iowa State University stated his perception of the commitment of graduate women:

Too many young women are casually enrolling in graduate schools across the country without having seriously considered the obligation which they are assuming by requesting that such expenditures be made for them. And they are not alone to blame. Equally at fault are two groups of faculty— undergraduate instructors who encourage their female students to apply to graduate school without also helping them consider the commitment that such an act implies, and graduate admissions counselors who blithely admit girls with impressive academic records into the graduate programs without looking for other evidence that the applicant has made a sincere commitment to graduate study (Scully, 1970, p. 4).

Views of women in academia divide into two schools of thought: (1) Women are essentially no different from men in their academic abilities but are victims of a sex-based discriminatory system. (2) Women are different physiologically and temperamentally and are socialized differentially than men. These differences handicap women when they attempt to compete with men.

The emphasis upon anatomical differences has lessened over the years. A psychologist has stated, "Except for their genitals, I don't know what immutable differences exist between men and women" (Weisstein, 1969, p. 58). But some believe that these genital differences create *other* immutable differences. "Anatomy is destiny" is one view, and since men cannot have babies, they are forced to "give birth" to work. Karen Horney wrote, "Is not the tremendous strength in men of the impulse to create work in every field precisely due to their feeling of playing a relatively small part in the creation of human beings?"[7] Erik Erikson's statement, "The modalities of a woman's commitment and involvement, for better *and* for worse, also reflect the ground plan of her body" (Erikson, 1964, p. 600)[8] is also illustrative of this argument. Biology creates a "feminine core" in a woman's identity that will result in a "harmonious balance of passivity, masochism, and narcissism" (Deutsch, 1945). In this view, women are so different anatomically (and, as a result, psychologically) that their lack of success in higher education is expected, because they are really out of the "female element."

A second view minimizes the biological differences but emphasizes that women are socialized differently than men. Thus, women may be idealistic rather than pragmatic (Bezdek & Strodtbeck, 1970) and men may be exploitative rather than accommodative (Uesugi & Vinacke, 1963) because of differential socialization. Roger Brown stereotypes the end product of this differential socialization:

In the United States, a *real* boy climbs trees, disdains girls, dirties his knees, plays with soldiers, and takes blue for his favorite color. A *real* girl dresses dolls, jumps rope, plays hopscotch, and takes pink for her favorite color. When they go to school, real girls like English and music and auditorium; real boys prefer manual training, gym, and arithmetic. In college the boys smoke pipes, drink beer, and major in engineering or physics; the girls chew Juicy Fruit gum, drink cherry Cokes, and major in the fine arts. The real boy matures into a man's man who plays poker, goes hunting, and drinks brandy, and dies in the war; the real girl becomes a "feminine" woman who loves children, embroiders handkerchiefs, drinks weak tea and "succumbs" to consumption.[9]

Komarovsky (1953, pp. 53–59) feels that girls are socialized to be neater, more restrained, gentler, more emotionally demonstrative, more dependent, and more family-oriented than boys.[10] Maccoby (1970) believes women are socialized to be less analytic in their thinking than men; Turner (1964) states that women are socialized to be less ambitious than men; and Auvenen (1970)

[7] In Bierstedt (1963, p. 330). See also Ashley-Montagu (1953) for a similar view.
[8] See Millett's (1970, pp. 210–220) rejoinder.
[9] Copyright © 1965 by The Free Press. From *Social Psychology* by Robert Brown, p. 161.
[10] For general reviews of sex differentials in socialization, see Hudson (1968); Leland & Lozoff (1969); E. Maccoby (1966); and Seward & Williamson (1970).

maintains that women are socialized to be more aware of their traditional sex role than men. [11]

In Eleanor Maccoby's view, some women, despite their differential socialization, may enter "masculine" fields. They do so for a price.

Suppose a girl does succeed in maintaining throughout her childhood years, the qualities of dominance, independence, and a striving that appear to be requisites for good analytic thinking. In so doing, she is defying the conventions concerning what is appropriate behavior for her sex. She may do this successfully in many ways but I suggest that it is the rare intellectual woman who will not have paid a price for it; a price in anxiety. And this anxiety can do more than affect a woman's emotional life and personality; it can also have repercussions on her intellectual activity (E. Maccoby, 1970, p. 26).

THE STATUS OF WOMEN IN GRADUATE EDUCATION It is beyond the scope of this book to offer a crucial test of either the discrimination model or the differential physiology or differential socialization model. We are, however, in an excellent position to examine the current status of women in graduate education. The data that we have utilized are from probably the most comprehensive survey of American higher education ever undertaken. These data were gathered during the spring of 1969, under the sponsorship of the Carnegie Commission on Higher Education and the U.S. Office of Education and with the cooperation of the Office of Research of the American Council on Education.

The data consist of 32,963 completed comprehensive mail questionnaires from graduate students in 158 colleges and universities and 60,028 completed questionnaires from faculty in 303 institutions. Additional data (not utilized in this volume) were gathered from over 70,000 undergraduates as well as from a sample of full-time academic researchers and academic deans. [12]

Enrollment statistics tell us a great deal about the current status of women in graduate education. Table 2 shows us that women

---

[11] Recent research at the Psychohormonal Research Unit of Johns Hopkins Medical School enhances the argument of the importance of socialization over physiological differences. Ten young females, who had been accidentally masculinized in utero, were studied over a period of time. What shaped gender identity among these hermaphrodites was not physiology but the way they were socialized. Those socialized as male assumed male traits, while those socialized as female assumed female traits (see Scarf, 1972).

[12] Full details on data-gathering procedures may be found in Appendix A.

are concentrated in certain fields that are extensions of the traditional feminine role (e.g., elementary education, nursing) or fields that have been viewed as proper extensions of femininity (although not necessarily direct expressions of the feminine role), such as French or art. Few women are found in technical or mathematical fields, such as physics or chemistry, or in fields that have an implied relationship to expressions of power (e.g., business, political science, or economics).

When we examine overall enrollment in graduate education (Table 3), we can see that women constitute a minority of graduate students in all types of institutions, whether colleges or universities.[13] They are more likely to be found, however, in medium- or low-quality colleges than in universities or in high-quality colleges. Graduate education at medium- or low-quality colleges is often oriented toward a master's degree in education, and we would thus expect higher female enrollment at such institutions. There is no relationship between the quality of a *university* and female representation. Women constitute about a quarter of the enrollment at high-, medium-, and low-quality universities.

At all institutions (Table 4), women are less likely to be full-

[13] We have used independent objective measurements to determine institutional quality. See Appendix A for complete details. We have used the U.S. Office of Education (OE) classification scheme to distinguish between *colleges* and *universities.* The OE defines universities as "institutions which give considerable stress to graduate instruction, which confer advanced degrees as well as bachelor's degrees in a variety of liberal arts fields, and which have at least two professional schools that are not exclusively technological" (Chandler, 1969, p. 3). *Four-year colleges* is an "all other" or residual category.

TABLE 3 *Sex distribution of graduate* students by institutional type, fall 1969*	*Percentage male*	*Percentage female*	*Projected total†*
High-quality universities	74.1	25.9	172,306
Medium-quality universities	71.1	28.9	258,236
Low-quality universities	74.7	25.3	222,089
High-quality colleges	73.8	26.2	60,757
Medium-quality colleges	56.7	43.3	120,682
Low-quality colleges	58.7	41.3	171,764
TOTAL	68.8	31.2	1,005,834

* Includes graduate and professional-school students.

† Weighted data based on entire sample (N = 32,963). See Appendix A for further details. All survey data presented in this volume are weighted.

	Males	Females	Gamma of sex differences
TABLE 4 Percentage of graduate students attending full time, by sex and institutional type (weighted totals in parentheses)			
High-quality universities	85.0 (127,089)	78.5 (44,458)	.216
Medium-quality universities	67.1 (183,087)	53.1 (74,370)	.286
Low-quality universities	57.0 (165,147)	46.4 (55,918)	.209
High-quality colleges	61.1 (44,542)	47.8 (15,784)	.263
Medium-quality colleges	32.6 (67,547)	26.3 (51,581)	.151
Low-quality colleges	23.8 (99,974)	13.7 (70,195)	.325

NOTE: Gamma is a measurement of the strength of a relationship between variables. The higher the gamma, the stronger the relationship. Gamma in these tables will always range from .00 (no relationship) to a maximum of 1.00 (absolute relationship). See Mueller et al. (1970, pp. 279–292).

time graduate students than men. Enrollment status is strongly affected by institutional quality. At high-quality universities, 79 percent of all women are full-time students, as compared to 46 percent at low-quality universities. At medium- and low-quality colleges, few students are enrolled full time, although, again, men are more likely to be full-time students than women.

Men and women differ only slightly with respect to citizenship and race. Among male graduate students, 8 percent are not United States citizens, compared to less than 4 percent of the females. This difference reflects the status of women in other nations; that is, men are more likely to be sent to another country for graduate study than women. Ninety-three percent of both men and women are Caucasian. Among nonwhite students, 26 percent of the men are black, compared to 47 percent of the women. On the other hand, 52 percent of the nonwhite males are Asian, compared to 32 percent of the women.

Men and women graduate students differ little in their social class origins (Table 5). The vast majority come from white-collar, professional, or semiprofessional homes; comparatively few sons or daughters of skilled or unskilled workers attain a graduate education. This does not mean a lack of educational mobility, however, for 67 percent of the men and 61 percent of the women in graduate school come from homes in which neither parent was a college graduate.

TABLE 5
Father's occupation, graduate students, by sex (in percentages)

	Males	Females
College or university teaching or administration	2.0	3.4
Elementary or secondary teaching or administration	2.9	3.1
Physician	3.0	2.7
Lawyer	2.2	2.1
Other professional	8.9	10.0
Total professional	19.0	21.3
Managerial, administrative, semiprofessional	17.5	13.8
Owner, large business	1.4	2.1
Owner, small business	17.7	17.0
Other white-collar	6.2	9.8
Total white-collar or semiprofessional	42.8	42.7
Skilled wage worker	6.3	6.8
Semi- or unskilled wage worker	18.4	14.4
Armed forces	7.5	6.1
Farm owner or manager	1.4	2.9
Other	4.7	5.7
TOTAL	100.1	99.9
Weighted totals	(178,932)	(213,244)

SOURCE: Data from special random subsample of 6,000 men and 6,000 women.

As Table 6 indicates, there are few differences between graduate men and women in religious background. Most were raised within one of the three major religions, although 24 percent of the men and 19 percent of the women state that their current religion is "none" (not indicated in table).

TABLE 6
Religion raised in, graduate students, by sex (in percentages)

	Males	Females
Jewish	10.2	10.4
Liberal Protestant	18.5	19.2
Moderate Protestant	24.6	26.4
Conservative Protestant	13.5	11.3
Roman Catholic	24.6	22.3
None	3.4	3.9
Other	5.1	6.4
TOTAL	99.9	99.9
Weighted totals	(178,932)	(213,244)

TABLE 7 *Undergraduate GPA of graduate students, by sex (in percentages)**

	A+/A	A−	B+	B	B−	C+	C or below	Total	Weighted totals
Males	6.5	11.3	18.7	17.7	20.3	20.9	4.5	99.9	(178,932)
Females	6.7	18.1	26.7	18.6	17.1	11.3	1.6	100.1	(213,244)

* Gamma = .236.

Taking undergraduate grade-point average as one indicator of student ability, Table 7 shows that graduate women were "better" undergraduates than the men. Undergraduate GPAs of B+ or better were achieved by 37 percent of the men, compared to 52 percent of the women. Thus, the greater proportion of men are entering graduate school with lower undergraduate averages than their (fewer in number) female counterparts.

Although most graduate students do not come from fraternities or sororities, men are more likely than women to have been "Greeks," as undergraduates. Among the men, 35 percent claim fraternity membership, and 28 percent of the women claim sorority membership. Among both men and women "Greeks" less than one-third were members for all four undergraduate years.

As Table 8 indicates, the differences in political identification between men and women are slight, although women are more likely to view themselves as middle-of-the-road or liberal than are men.

Probably one of the strongest differences between men and women is in marital status. Graduate women are much more likely to remain single or to have been divorced than their male counterparts. We shall discuss the effects of differential marital status in Chapter 6.

As the data have shown, there are surprisingly few differences between men and women graduate students on many basic demographic variables. Although men and women have similar racial, religious, and class backgrounds, sex-related inequality in American graduate education is still evident. Tables 2 and 3 are empirical

TABLE 8
Self-rated political stance of graduate students, by sex, United States citizens only (in percentages)

	Left	Liberal	Middle-of-the-road	Moderately conservative	Strongly conservative	Total
Males	6.2	35.0	25.8	28.4	4.6	100.0
Females	4.2	39.1	29.2	25.0	2.4	99.9

	Single	Married	Divorced or separated	Total*	Weighted totals
Males	29.2	69.0	1.8	100.0	(687,387)
Females	38.9	55.6	5.6	100.1	(312,305)

TABLE 9
Marital status of graduate students, by sex (in percentages)

* Less than 1 percent are widowed.
NOTE: Weighted totals are based on the entire sample.

demonstrations of this inequality. Table 3 shows that whatever the quality of the institution, fewer women are enrolled as graduate students than men. In Table 2 we see that the higher the academic degree, the less likely women are to receive it. Although they represent slightly over half the United States population, women did not receive 50 percent of even the bachelor's degrees issued, let alone master's or doctorates. The situation of women in graduate education is underenrollment, greater attrition once enrolled (see, e.g., Bradburn et al., 1970; Schoen et al., 1971; and Stark, 1967), and lower probability of receiving a doctorate after obtaining a master's degree.

But enrollment figures alone do not tell the full story. This book will examine four aspects of inequality in graduate education: academic disciplines, career choice, effects of marital status, and statements of discrimination. Although this book is about women, we can document patterns of sex-based inequality only by comparing the status of women with the status of men. The problems of women have suddenly come to the forefront as an important social problem. It is an issue that is bound in rhetoric and emotion from both men and women. In this book we hope to allow the data to speak.

2. Women in American Higher Education: A Historical Perspective

Higher education in the United States began in 1636 with the founding of Harvard College. Yet it was not until 1837, when Oberlin College admitted four women, that higher education became available for American women. One of the major reasons for the slow development of women's education was the rash of objections surrounding the idea. Although these objections differed in substance, the underlying theme in almost all the arguments against the education of women was that it would somehow defeminize them. Some thought, for example, that women could not physiologically stand the pressures of education. A book published in the 1880s stated that "the identical education of the two sexes is a crime before God and humanity that physiology protests against, and that experience weeps over" (Earnest, 1953, p. 196). Speaking before an international conference on women, a participant stated:

A girl cannot be given the same education as a boy for she is physiologically different. Besides, it must be remembered that the reproductive function forms a more important part in her organization than in his, so that if her training is to be beneficial it must be made subservient to that which is essential for the healthy development of all her powers.

A girl's physique is slow in maturing, and is of such delicacy that any part may be easily overstrained, and this may have the effect of impairing its powers for life.

For example, if a girl's brain, which is quick and active, is worked to its *full* power while she is maturing, it will be cultivated to the detriment of other parts of the body. The practical result of this is shown in one of two ways; either the whole economy is exhausted by the strain that is put upon the brain, and a girl in course of time becomes utterly shattered and anaemic, or the blood is utilized too exclusively to feed the brain and other organs, being deprived of their due nourishment, act imperfectly, and may even become stunted in their growth (Hawtrey, 1900, p. 170).

Others extended this argument. If women had weaker bodies than men, did it not also follow that they had weaker minds? Reacting to those who took this tack, a feminist wrote:

And the clearness and strength of the brain of the woman prove continually the injustice of clamorous contempt long poured upon what was scornfully called "the female mind." There is no female mind. . . . As well speak of a female liver (Stetson, 1898, p. 149).

Even if one denied the existence of physiological or mental barriers, one encountered other objections. Many felt women should only receive an education for the purpose of better being able to perform their womanly tasks. Benjamin Rush, an early advocate of women's education, wrote in 1787 that although of first importance were duties of the house, women should have knowledge of history, biography, English grammar, chemistry, music, religion, and dancing (Woody, 1929a, p. 108). Similarly, John Burton, speaking at a school for "young ladies," stated:

To be obedient Daughters, faithful Wives, and prudent Mothers; to be useful in the affairs of a House, to be sensible Companions, and affectionate friends, are, without doubt, the principal objects of female duty. The accomplishments, therefore, which you should acquire, are those which will contribute to render you serviceable in domestic, and agreeable in social life (Burton, 1794, p. 96).

Many of the objections against women's education concerned the fate of educated women on the marriage market. A colonial poem described the desirability of an educated wife:

One did command to me a wife both fair and young
That had French, Spanish, and Italian tongue.
I thanked him kindly and told him I loved none such,
For I thought one tongue for a wife too much.
What! love ye not the learned?
Yes, as my life,
A learned scholar, but not a learned wife (Woody, 1929a, p. 108).

With the increasing education of women, a series of studies appeared, attempting to demonstrate the lower marriage rate among college-educated women.[1] To many, especially to those who be-

[1] For a review of this controversy, see Goodsell (1923).

lieved in eugenics, this lower marriage rate was cause for alarm, quite possibly signaling the end of the human race. A sociologist wrote, "To speak plainly, children have become, to many women, a nuisance, or at least unwelcome beings of an alien domestic world which years of intellectual training have unfitted the college women to like or understand" (Wells, 1909, p. 737). If college women were less likely to marry and have children, those of a weaker biological strain would predominate, bringing about in due course "race suicide." As one forecaster of doom wrote:

Women college graduates are not greatly sought after as mates, to share in the work of getting a living and founding a family, because they are not prepared psychologically and technically for the jobs of cooking, sanitation, nursing and child rearing, and are not seeking that mode of life except under specially selected conditions. They have culture and intelligence and demand high standards in husbands and homes, but they are not prizes in the matter of efficiency in domestic life (Sprague, 1915, p. 162).

As this quotation illustrates, arguments against female education were based not only on physiological grounds but also on the belief that education was somehow not in keeping with what should be the proper socialization of women. Whether for physiological, psychological, or sociological reasons, however, the general feeling was that women were different from men in more than appearance. Beliefs in immutable differences between men and women were used to justify differential education. These arguments, voiced by many, including college faculty and administrators, were originally used to restrict initial entry. But the arguments did not cease once women were admitted.[2]

The first semblance of organized higher education for women did not appear until about 1821, with the creation of Troy Seminary— the first of many female "academies" or "seminaries." Troy Seminary's founder, Emma Willard, placed great emphasis on teaching women mathematical skills rather than more readily applied subjects such as stitchery. In 1836 Mary Lyon established Mount Holyoke Seminary (later Mount Holyoke College), stating: "It is no part of our design to teach young ladies domestic work. This branch

---

[2] The similarity between earlier pronouncements against the education of women and more recent arguments is striking. More recent arguments tend to have more of a sociological or psychoanalytic base, but the themes are remarkably alike (see Chapter 1).

of education is important, but a literary institution is not the place to gain it" (Woody, 1929*a*, p. 301). The early seminaries were really glorified high schools until about 1850. After this date, they were viewed more as competitors of colleges (Woody, 1929*a*, p. 363). The reasons for their founding varied. Milwaukee Female Seminary was founded by Catherine E. Beecher as a place "to take young misses from the primary schools and conduct them systematically onward to a thorough knowledge of the whole circle of sciences as taught in similar institutions" (Woody, 1929*a*, p. 377).[3] On the other hand, Monticello Seminary at Godfrey, Illinois, was founded in 1836 by wealthy sea captain Benjamin Godfrey as a place where women could learn to be better wives and mothers. Godfrey described his inspiration for this seminary:

One morning in 1830, while lying in my bed recovering from a severe sickness, my wife came into the room and made some remarks as she left. Our little daughter who had just begun to lisp a few words, caught the remarks, and, while playing by herself on the floor, repeated them over and over for some time. This led me to reflect on the powerful influence of the mother on the minds, manners, habits and character of her children, and I resolved to devote a large part of my possessions to the intellectual and moral improvement of women (in McClelland, 1944, pp. 17–18).

Thomas Woody (1929*a*, p. 563) examined the catalogs of 163 seminaries (in existence from 1742 to 1871) and found that the following numbers of schools taught these subjects: English grammar, 139; natural philosophy, 123; rhetoric, 121; geography, 113; chemistry, 112; plane geometry, 100; composition, 96; French, 89; drawing, 80; logic, 81; history, 76; German, 22; calisthenics, 22; embroidery, 20; surveying, 14; housework, 2; physics, 1; and basket making, 1. Over time the emphasis in the female seminaries became more academic and less geared toward "practical skills." For example, from 1749 to 1829, 42 percent of the 55 seminaries in existence offered plain needlework, while only 15 percent offered algebra and 2 percent offered geology. Of 107 schools in existence from 1830 to 1871, only 5 percent offered plain needlework, while 83 percent offered algebra and 60 percent geology. We assume that women were more likely to be literate in these later years and

---

[3] Milwaukee Female Seminary became in 1853 Milwaukee Female College. In 1895 it merged with Downer College, becoming Milwaukee-Downer College, and in 1964 it became part of Lawrence University at Appleton, Wisconsin.

thus greater emphasis was placed on subjects such as algebra, botany, and chemistry—fields that before had been almost exclusively male domains.

At the same time that female seminaries and academies were flourishing, a movement began to educate women to become teachers. A New York State Committee recommended that women be educated to become teachers because:

> . . . it is the *manner* and the very weakness of the teacher that constitutes her strength and assures her success. For that occupation she is endured with peculiar faculties. While man's nature is rough, stern, impatient, ambitious—hers is gentle, tender, enduring, unaspiring. One always wins; the other sometimes repels; the one is loved; the other sometimes feared (Woody, 1929*a*, p. 463).

The general feeling was that female seminaries offered women too general an education and one not specifically designed for teacher training. As a result, teachers seminaries or normal schools were created in Philadelphia in 1848, in Boston in 1852, and in New York City in 1867. By 1872 there existed 101 normal schools, and the percentage of women teachers rose from 57 percent in 1880 to 70 percent in 1900 and to 84 percent in 1918 (Woody, 1929*a*, pp. 471–497).

Despite the "beefing up" of their curricula, female seminaries and normal schools were still not the full equivalent of colleges. One of the first people to attempt to break the sex barrier in an American university was Lucinda Foote, who on December 22, 1783, at the age of 12, was examined in Latin and Greek. She was able to translate and understand passages from the *Aeneid,* the orations of Cicero, and the Greek Testament. She was found "fully qualified, except in regard to sex, to be received as a pupil of the Freshman class of Yale University" (Woody, 1929*b*, p. 137). Miss Foote was not admitted.

A major turning point occurred in 1836, when a governmental body, the Georgia State Legislature, endorsed the idea of a college for women. Georgia Female College, as this new institution was to be called, came into existence partially through the persuasive oratory of Daniel Chandler, who told the Georgia Legislature in 1835:

In our country there are 61 colleges, containing expensive philosophical and chemical apparatus, valuable cabinets of minerals, and libraries that embrace more than 300,000 volumes—and to the disgrace of the nation be it spoken, not one is dedicated to the cause of female education (Woody, 1929b, p. 140).

In the North, a group of clergymen and laymen decided to found "a real college for women," and in 1852 Auburn Female University was chartered, moving to Elmira in 1855 and changing its name to Elmira Female College.

Matthew Vassar was a poorly educated man who through hard work built up a large brewery in Poughkeepsie, New York. Seeking a worthy cause to which to donate his fortune, Vassar decided to build a large hospital. His niece, Lydia Booth, who was in charge of the Cottage Hill Seminary in Poughkeepsie, talked to Vassar in 1845 about the educational needs of women. After his niece's death in 1860, Vassar decided to further the cause of female higher education, giving more than $400,000 for that purpose. This new women's college was to have a curriculum including science ("with full apparatus"); economics; political science; aesthetics; domestic science; hygiene; "Moral Science, particularly bearing on the filial, conjugal, and parental relation"; the classics; and the Bible (Earnest, 1953, pp. 179–180). Vassar and other colleges for women that were being founded (Smith, 1871; Wellesley, 1875; Bryn Mawr, 1880; and Mills, 1885) were modeled after male colleges. Vassar and Wellesley instituted set schedules for their students similar to the enforced schedules of men's colleges of 30 years earlier (ibid., pp. 184–185).

Sophia Smith, another early benefactor of women's education, was a New England woman who came into a large inheritance. Seeking a worthy cause for her newly found fortune, Smith sought the counsel of Rev. John M. Greene, who persuaded her to use the money to found a new college for women. The first board of trustees at Smith College was all male, and it set forth the policy that "the requirements for admission will be substantially the same as at Harvard, Yale, Brown, Amherst, and other New England colleges" (ibid., pp. 140–141). Smith College was built on four principles: the education would be equal to that of men (with special emphasis on the classics); biblical study would be prominent; there would be a cottage system for residence rather than massive buildings; and men would have a part in governance and instruction, "for it is a misfortune for young women or young men to be wholly educated by their own kind" (Thwing, 1906, p. 345).

Early women's colleges admitted all who were qualified. Although they attempted to follow a male model of education, this was not always possible. Women did not receive equivalent secondary education, and, as a result, almost all women's colleges had a "preparatory department" that gave their students remedial education in subjects they needed for college. (It was not underprivileged backgrounds that caused this educational handicap. All but 6 of the first 139 Vassar students came from professional or business backgrounds.) Most women's colleges maintained their preparatory programs until the beginning of the twentieth century (Newcomer, 1959, p. 131).

In their early history, women's colleges were not taken seriously. A tongue-in-cheek editorial appeared in the *New York Times:*

What do you think of the idea of a woman's college? And why not? After Allopathic, Homeopathic, and patient pill colleges, universities, and all that sort of thing, why not let the girls have one (Earnest, 1953, p. 180).

Some viewed women's colleges as creating an "unhealthy" situation for their students. One critic wrote:

The college education may have excellencies for men in its *frottement,* its preparation for the world, its rough destruction of personal concept, but for women it can only be hardening and deforming. . . . The perpetual contact of men with other men may be good for them, but the perpetual contact of women with other women is very far from good. The publicity of a college must be odious to a very young girl of refined and delicate feeling (Ouida, 1894, pp. 614–615).

What then must college women have been like? Martha Thomas, a former president of Bryn Mawr College, wrote:

Before I myself went to college, I had never seen but one college woman. I had heard that such a woman was staying at the house of an acquaintance. I went to see her with fear. For even if she appeared in hoofs and horns, I was determined to go to college all the same. But it was a relief to find this Vassar graduate tall and handsome and dressed like other women (Thomas, 1908, p. 65).

The education of women also created semantic problems. How could a first-year woman student be called a fresh*man?* Elmira solved the problem by using "protomathian," while Ingham University and Rutgers Female used "novian." Vassar began with the term "first-year student" but by its third year used "freshman," as the president pointed out that *man* is part of *human* and even *woman* (Newcomer, 1959, p. 20). Also, how could a woman college graduate be a *bachelor?* Baylor solved this problem by issuing the degrees Maid of Arts and Maid of Philosophy (Aiken, 1957, p. 103). And, when women became physicians, how could one use a male term such as *doctor?* If female emperors are *empresses,* why can there not be *doctresses* (Thompson, 1947, p. 122)?

Even at the time of the founding of women's colleges, some women were obtaining their college degrees in a coeducational setting. Coeducation can mean one of three things: education for men and women in the same college (but not necessarily with the same curriculum); identical education for men and women; or education in coordinate colleges such as Harvard and Radcliffe (Woody, 1929*b*, p. 224). Oberlin College was the first coeducational college in the United States. (Of the first four women to graduate, in 1841, two married classmates, one married a professor, and one married the president of the college [McClelland, 1944, p. 14].) Antioch College began as a coeducational institution in 1852. State universities and colleges were quicker to become coeducational than private ones: Iowa was coeducational from the date of its founding in 1856, the University of Wisconsin became coeducational in 1860, and the University of Washington in 1862. By the 1890s the coeducational movement spread to private schools such as Brown (1890), Yale Graduate School (1890), and Tufts (1892).

One major reason for the rise of coeducation was economy. It appeared that the education of women was no passing fancy, but the creation of separate facilities would cost too much money. In addition, some schools, such as Cornell, Johns Hopkins, and Rochester, were promised special endowments if they admitted women. The fact that the education at women's colleges was believed to be inferior to that at other institutions of higher education provided further incentive. Two critics wrote:

The graduates of Vassar . . . are not prepared to take charge of even our high schools. They cannot fit young men for college.

Coeducation is at present a necessity for young ladies who desire to be accredited with thorough scholarship. A diploma from Michigan University is of much more value to a lady than one from any college for women (Woody, 1929*b*, p. 263).

Others felt that coeducation was more in accord with "nature"—men and women were not meant to be separated. Furthermore, coeducation was believed to have a refining influence on both men and women and to work as a stimulus to study (Woody, 1929*b*, p. 264). President James H. Fairchild of Oberlin said that coeducation makes "men of boys and gentlemen of rowdies" (Woody, 1929*b*, p. 236), while a professor at the same institution denied rumors of romantic liaisons by stating, "Nothing acts as a better antidote for romance than young men and women doing geometry together at eight o'clock every morning" (Earnest, 1953, p. 195). At the University of Michigan, janitors noted that the men no longer pushed one another up and down stairs or held boxing matches in the lobbies.

Still, all were not in favor of coeducation. Psychologist G. Stanley Hall wrote:

Coeducation in the middle teens tends to sexual precocity. This is very bad; it is one of the subtlest dangers that can befall civilization (Earnest, 1953, p. 197).

Hall's objection was amplified by William C. Russell, vice-president of Cornell:

When I have heard a lady student calling one young man into the room, shutting the door, kissing him, it has embittered months of existence (Rudolph, 1962, p. 327).

And an editorial in the *San Francisco Examiner* admonished, "When the little winged god comes in the window, study flies out" (Rudolph, 1962, p. 327).

The aims of a college education for women at the turn of the century, whether in a coordinate college, a coeducational setting, or a women's college, were enunciated by Charles Thwing (1894, pp. 25–26), president of the College for Women at Western Reserve University:

(1) She should have a healthy body.

(2) She should be able to observe closely.

(3) She should be able to reason soundly.

(4) She should know something in many fields of knowledge.

(5) She should know much in one field of knowledge.

(6) She should be able to speak and to write English correctly.

(7) She should have a moral nature, clean and fine.

(8) She should have a will, well trained, obedient to the conscience.

(9) She should be impressed with a sense of the value of work.

(10) She should have the bearing of a true lady.

Jessie Bernard (1964, pp. 30–37) divided the history of women's higher education in the United States into four periods: (1) on trial in the eyes of the world (late nineteenth century), (2) reform in the elitist colleges—service in the land-grant colleges (1900–1920), (3) surging flood of disillusion (1920–1930), and (4) the great withdrawal (1930–1960).

The second period of women's higher education was marked by expansion. Women's colleges became centers of antiwar activity and social service and were characterized by Calvin Coolidge as "hotbeds of radicalism" (Bernard, 1964, p. 33). During this period women's colleges formed schools of social work, and public institutions began to emphasize public service careers for women by expanding teacher education and placing a strong emphasis on home economics.

By the twenties, the idea of higher education for women was firmly established. Early battles had been fought and won, and the great interest in the problems of women's education declined. The greatest expansion has been completed, but even in the present, women are underrepresented within American higher education. In 1929, women received 40 percent of the bachelor's degrees conferred in the United States, but by the academic year 1967–68, this figure had risen to only 44 percent.[4]

The status of women in American higher education has gone from no representation to a current state of underrepresentation. Despite opposition, women in increasing numbers received bachelor's degrees and began to apply for graduate education. If we assume that possession of a baccalaureate degree is an indication of academic competence, then the success of women in acquiring

[4] The growth previous to 1929 was quite marked. Women received 15 percent of the bachelor's degrees issued in 1870 and 17 percent of those issued in 1890. By 1910, the figure reached 23 percent and by 1920, 34 percent.

graduate education should be an important test of the presence and possible effects of antifemale attitudes. Table 2 demonstrated that the higher the academic degree, no matter what the field, the less likely women are to receive it. This underrepresentation stems from two factors: women are less likely than men to be admitted to graduate school, and, once admitted, they are less likely to complete the degree requirements.

To the arguments against educating women, another was added at the graduate level: women should not receive intensive graduate or professional education because it is wasted. Their first interest, "naturally," is in being wives and mothers. Why spend years educating them, if they will retire to a husband and children? Although this argument was directed chiefly at women at the more intensive graduate and professional levels, it was even used against educating women to become teachers:

After your college girl has graduated, she may, possibly, spend three years in teaching. By that time she is tolerably certain to get married. And *then* what becomes of her higher education (Kingsley, 1924, p. 161)?

GRADUATE AND PROFESSIONAL EDUCATION Although Harvard was founded in 1636 and Yale in 1701, it was not until 1861 that a Ph.D. was issued by an American institution of higher education. Graduate education in the United States really began in 1876 with the founding of Johns Hopkins University. Before that time, American college graduates could receive a master's degree 3 years after they graduated from college, provided they had stayed out of trouble and had paid a fee of five dollars. College graduates who sought a more rigorous graduate education left the United States to study in Germany and obtained doctorates at such centers of learning as Göttingen, Berlin, Leipzig, and Heidelberg.[5]

The real move for graduate education in the United States began with the founding of three institutions dedicated almost exclusively to the further education of college graduates and to the encouragement and generation of research among students and faculty. These institutions—Johns Hopkins University, Clark University, and the University of Chicago—became the models that established universities such as Yale, Harvard, and Columbia emulated in the creation of their graduate schools. By 1900, the university system,

[5] For historical accounts of early graduate education, see Ryan (1939), Storr (1953), and Veysey (1965).

with its emphasis on graduate education, had become a fully institutionalized part of American higher education.[6]

A woman could receive a graduate education somewhat more easily than an undergraduate education. Perhaps it was thought that the woman with the A.B. was already "lost," or perhaps the expanding graduate schools accepted women more readily because they needed all the qualified students they could find. At any rate, the first University of Pennsylvania graduate catalog (1885) stated that "Women are admitted to any course for the Ph.D. degree on the same conditions as men." When Columbia, Yale, Harvard, and Brown opened their graduate schools, they, too, admitted women on the same basis as men. One of the last holdouts was Johns Hopkins University, which finally yielded in 1907. Although Johns Hopkins had no intention of admitting women to its undergraduate program, the stated university policy became, "Women who have taken the baccalaureate degree at institutions of good standing are to be admitted to graduate courses . . . provided there is no objection on the part of the instructor concerned" (Woody, 1929*b*, p. 337).

In 1885, Bryn Mawr became one of the first women's colleges to offer postgraduate degrees (to women only), admitting only students who "presented a diploma from some college of acknowledged standing" (Woody, 1929*b*, p. 334). The Bryn Mawr program consisted of 3 years beyond the A.B., during which the candidate had to write a dissertation and acquire a knowledge of Latin, French, German, and Greek. By 1900 Bryn Mawr had issued 44 master's and 18 doctoral degrees.

In American higher education as a whole, women received 9 percent of the doctorates issued in 1900, 11 percent in 1910, and peaked to 18 percent in 1920. More recently, women received only 11 percent of the doctorates issued in 1957 and 13 percent of those issued in 1969.

During the period of early expansion of graduate education and women's education, the Association for Collegiate Alumnae, now the American Association of University Women (AAUW), was formed. This organization deemed itself the sole accrediting body for women's undergraduate educational programs. Whenever a woman wanted to enter into a graduate program, she was to first

[6] This date was established as a turning point by Berelson (1960, p. 14). By this time, many American scholarly journals and learned societies had been established, and in 1900 the Association of American Universities was founded.

present her undergraduate degree program for approval by a three-fourths vote of the AAUW board and members at large. Only after approval was she deemed eligible for admission into a graduate program in the United States or abroad. This sanction, however, was recognized by nobody but the AAUW. An authorized history of the AAUW expressed their concern:

The numbers of young women entering college increased with unexpected and unparalleled rapidity in the years immediately following the panic of 1893. To the novelty of college education was now added the lure of graduate study abroad under conditions which made a great appeal to young women unfamiliar with life outside their own country. As a result, a good many untrained young women, with no real urge for advanced scholarship, began to seek admission to foreign universities, even where such admission had been but a few years ago so hardly won. It was feared by many thoughtful women that courtesies extended to women whose training was not sufficient to give them admission to the colleges of the Association might result in experiences which would prove damaging to the chances of well-trained and earnest women of all nations who might later apply for the same courtesies (Talbot & Rosenberry, 1931, p. 149).

The AAUW, as a self-proclaimed representative of an emerging minority group, tried a power play by sending the following petition to major European universities:

To The Governing Bodies of European Universities the Association of Collegiate Alumnae Respectfully Submits the Following Memorial and Petition:

1. The privileges courteously granted to American women by the European universities are frequently claimed by women who are untrained or insufficiently trained, and who thus abuse the privileges of the universities and cast discredit upon the scholarship of American women.

2. The variable value of the Bachelor of Arts degree in the United States makes the presentation of a college diploma no guarantee of sufficient preparation for advanced study.

3. It is difficult for Academic Faculties to gain the information which will enable them to discriminate between worthy and unworthy applicants for admission to the privileges of the universities.

4. Therefore, the Association of Collegiate Alumnae respectfully petitions the governing bodies of the European universities to receive its official certificate, signed by its President and by the Chairman of its Council to Accredit Women for Study at Foreign Universities, as a guarantee of the

sufficient training, good character, and serious purpose of any woman presenting said certificate.

5. The Association also respectfully petitions the same governing bodies to grant to all women presenting said certificate any and all privileges which may at that time be open to any woman.

6. In return for this courtesy the Association pledges itself to recommend only such women as a thorough investigation shows to be worthy of such privileges.

The Association also pledges itself to investigate the record of any woman who may apply for its certificate, thereby making it possible for every properly qualified American woman to produce the same.

7. The Association respectfully urges a favorable consideration of this memorial and petition by the governing boards of the European universities, in the hope that it will advance the interests of well-trained American women at these universities, and provide a safeguard to the professors against imposition upon their courtesy (Talbot & Rosenberry, 1931, pp. 150–151).

The AAUW issued certificates of approval to those individuals it felt it could certify as suitable for graduate education; however, the European universities never recognized the AAUW or its certificates, and by 1902 the AAUW abandoned this strategy.[7]

An important figure in the history of higher education for women in the United States is Elizabeth Blackwell, who in 1844 became the first woman to receive an American medical degree. Dr. Blackwell originally ran a boarding school for girls, and became involved in feminist activities. When she found that no woman in the United States had been admitted to medical practice, she decided to become a physician. Miss Blackwell took governess jobs in the houses of physicians so that she could read medical books, and by '1847 had saved enough money to apply to medical school. School after school turned her down, although some suggested she might attend if she wore men's clothing. Miss Blackwell rejected this idea, stating that she was on a "moral crusade . . . a course of justice and common sense, and it must be pursued in the light of day" (Fancourt, 1965, p. 27).

Miss Blackwell was finally accepted in 1847 by Geneva Medical

---

[7] This strategy reflects attitudes quite similar to E. Franklin Frazier's (1957) description of the attitudes of the rising black middle class in the mid-fifties. They were most concerned that lower-class blacks would give all blacks a "bad name" and thus retard chances for upward mobility.

School (now Hobart College). "The circumstances of her admission were strange: the faculty, not wanting to take responsibility for her rejection, had turned the matter over to the students, who—in an uproarious general assembly—voted a unanimous 'yes' as a joke" (Lopate, 1968, p. 4).

Similar circumstances surrounded the admission of Harriet Hunt to Harvard Medical School. Miss Hunt applied originally in 1847, but her application was refused. She was accepted in 1850 but was then asked to withdraw her application. Harvard had admitted blacks that year, and the combination of black students and a female student was more than the Harvard Medical School felt it could handle (Woody, 1929*b*, p. 352).

Medical education for women was encouraged by Dr. Samuel Gregory, who felt that women, not men, should practice obstetrics. In public lectures on midwifery, Dr. Gregory stated that "Male-midwifery trespassed upon female delicacy, and was a great temptation to immorality, tending to lead women down the paths of prostitution, and inducing young men to go into medicine because of their curiosity about women" (Lopate, 1968, p. 71). As a result of Gregory's efforts, a Female Medical Education Society was created in 1848 in Boston, dedicated to midwifery and the diseases of women and children. This school became, in 1852, the Boston Female Medical College. This new institution had high standards for its students, with a 3-year course of study (4 months per year) leading to a medical degree. Boston Female Medical College later merged with Boston University, on the stipulation that women be admitted on the same basis as men. In 1850, the Women's Medical College of Pennsylvania (which only became coeducational in 1969) was founded in Philadelphia.

Between 1850 and 1895, 19 women's medical colleges were established, but by 1900 only 8 survived. More and more medical schools were admitting women. The University of Michigan began admitting them in 1870, as did medical schools in Switzerland. In the 1890s, Cornell and Johns Hopkins established their medical schools as coeducational institutions (although Hopkins did so only because it was offered half a million dollars if it admitted women). After objections from members since 1868, the American Medical Association decided in 1915 to admit women. Medical education for women became an accepted fact, although even by 1969 women constituted slightly less than 8 percent of medical school graduates.

At no stage in its history has higher education for women been without controversy and opposition. Each step to eliminate sex-based inequality was met with resistance—a resistance which continues today. Until recently, women in higher education have been rather docile, accepting underrepresentation and lower status. The history of women's education indicates that the problems of women in higher education are not new—they have simply suffered from a lack of publicity. It is only recently that more people have shown their concern over the status of academic women.

History reveals a tradition of discrimination against women, but history tells us little about the characteristics of women within the system. It may be that women are less competent than men and, hence, rather than overt "sexism," prejudicial attitudes toward women are reactions against less competent students. The hard data are spotty, however. In no way can the historical approach control for ability. If we see instances where women who are equally as qualified as men receive fewer rewards, then we move from the level of allegation to the level of hard evidence. The history of women's education in the United States suggests that the differences between men and women are largely created by a discriminatory system. Social science may allow us to examine these allegations in a more systematic manner.

3. Masculine and Feminine Academic Disciplines: Their Characteristics

In his classic essay "Class Status and Party," Max Weber (1946, pp. 180–195) distinguished among three dimensions of social inequality—economic wealth (privilege), authority (power), and status honor (prestige). When we examine the occupations that have been modally adopted by women in American society, we find that they generally have relatively low amounts of power (Caplow, 1954, pp. 230–246),[1] privilege (Oppenheimer, 1968), and prestige (Epstein, 1970, pp. 151–166).

Much has been written on sex-typing of occupations. Sociologist Robert Merton stated that "Occupations can be described as sex-typed when a large majority of those in them are of one sex and when there is an associated normative expectation that this is as it should be" (in Epstein, 1970, p. 152). Certain occupations, such as key punch operator, have been defined as female from the start (Gross, 1968, p. 202), but others, such as elementary school teaching, have evolved from male-dominated to almost exclusively female occupations.

What is defined as a male field or a female field varies even within Western society. In the United States, medicine is defined as a male field, while in the Soviet Union it is female; and in the United States almost all dentists are men, while in Denmark the majority are women. In the United States, women enter professions such as nursing and teaching, where they can best apply the "feminine" characteristics of "expressiveness and people-orientation," and they do not enter professions such as law or engineering, which require "masculine" characteristics such as "coolness, detachment, analytic objectivity, or object orientation" (Epstein, 1970, p. 155).

---

[1] A popularized presentation of characteristics of women's occupations may be found in Bird (1968, pp. 76–103).

Furthermore, because of the discontinuous nature of female employment patterns, female professions are more likely to be those in which long or set career lines are not essential (Oppenheimer, 1968, pp. 227–231) or those with little tradition of professionalization (Vollmer & Mills, 1966, p. 340).

We thus see an occupational sorting pattern that is strongly sex-related. This is true not only in the occupational system but within higher education as well (see Table 2). Obviously, the two are related, but there has been little systematic or empirical study of the characteristics of "masculine" or "feminine" academic disciplines. The education of women in America has been marked by a tradition that certain disciplines are more proper for women than others. In the early seminaries, women studied enough to give them a little education in spelling, history, and religion—enough education, perhaps, to become a prized wife but not enough to become independent. By the 1850s, elementary education was deemed a proper female field. After the establishment of formal training in social work, that, too, became a proper academic discipline for women. But no matter what women studied, there were some educators who urged that higher education prepare women, above all, for their role as wives. The president of Mills College urged that college women be taught "the theory and preparation of a Basque paella, of a well-marinated shish-kebob, lamb kidneys sauteed in sherry, an authoritative curry; the use of herbs; even such simple sophistications as serving cold artichokes with cold milk" (White, 1950, p. 49).[2]

Some academicians are becoming more aware of sex-based sorting into academic disciplines and are recruiting more women into male fields ranging from dentistry (Talbot, 1961) to physics. In the fall of 1971, the physics department of the University of Oklahoma instituted Project New Avenues to encourage women to enter physics. Offering undergraduate women scholarships and employment, this project has, as an integral part of its program, remedial education in mathematics and physics. A recruiting leaflet (*Career Opportunities . . . ,* n.d., pp. 2–3) describes the program:

[2] He also urged that women's college education should include emphasis on family and textiles as well as food. "A girl majoring in history or chemistry could well find time for one such course which, we may be sure, would do much to enliven her own life and that of her family and friends in later years. It is rumored that the divorce rate of home economics majors is greatly below that of college women as a whole" (White, 1950, p. 78).

The department of Physics at the University of Oklahoma has initiated a program to offer to women a real opportunity to go into physics. This program is designed to better women's needs as well as recognize and work with their particular strengths and their primarily culturally determined difficulties. In order to effectively close the competitive gap between men and women students, women students will be taught separately in their physics courses for most of the first two years. The first year course (5 semester hours each semester) will be a combined lecture-laboratory course. Since it is expected that many of the students entering this program will not have had a strong pre-college interest in physical phenomena, one of the main functions of the first-year program will be to stimulate interest and give the students some appreciation of the history and philosophy of physics. The laboratory portion of the first year course is designed to help the girls acquire mechanical skills with tools that boys have been developing in their earlier years as well as learning basic laboratory techniques.

In this chapter we shall examine which academic disciplines are viewed as masculine or feminine and the characteristics associated with these fields. Previous attempts to examine characteristics of academic fields have not been systematic. For example, Jessie Bernard (1964, p. 125) maintained that women are sorted into disciplines that have a fixed and noncontroversial body of knowledge (because "the opinions of women often do not carry much weight"). David Riesman (1964, p. xx) felt that "a field such as political science, which emphasizes power, attracts or fosters relatively few women, whereas anthropology, at least where it emphasizes kinship more than kingship, finds much more place for women."

To determine if (and how) academic disciplines are viewed in terms of masculinity and femininity, we conducted a small study involving the masculine-feminine image of 45 fields. Respondents were 352 undergraduates in sociology courses at San Francisco State College; the University of California, Berkeley; the University of Arizona; Southern Methodist University; and the University of Wisconsin.[3] (Although we would have preferred a random sample of students, we were more concerned with using undergraduates rather than graduate students. It is in the four undergraduate years that students have the most contact with courses, faculty, and students from a wide variety of disciplines.) Respondents were

[3] I would like to thank Elizabeth Rooney, Richard Hawkins, Ted Smith, and Gerald Thielbar for their cooperation in allowing the questionnaire to be administered to their students.

presented 45 academic disciplines listed at random and were asked to rate each field on a seven-point semantic differential rating scale on the polar type "masculine-feminine."[4]

The semantic differential has been used previously as a way of measuring stereotyped imagery of ethnic groups (Prothro & Keehn, 1957; Snider, 1962; Feldman & Kohout, 1967) and occupational incumbents (O'Dowd & Beardslee, 1960; Thielbar & Feldman, 1969). The use of a seven-point scale allows respondents the option of not stereotyping—in this case seeing some or all fields as equally masculine or feminine by placing responses in the neutral category; however, as Table 10 indicates, this was not the typical response. Fields were scored from 1 to 7, with 1 given to the line closest to "masculine" and 7 given to the line closest to "feminine." For descriptive purposes, we have deemed all fields with a mean score of 1 to 3 masculine, those with a mean of between 3 and 4 neutral, and those with a mean of 4 to 7 feminine.

[4] The semantic differential is a device used to learn how people perceive selected subjects. Respondents are presented with a series of opposite adjectives (e.g., sweet-sour, hot-cold, masculine-feminine) and a stimulus word that they are to describe through the use of these polar opposites. Generally, a pair of polar-opposite adjectives are arranged on a straight line and separated by a series of equally spaced marks (in this case, short lines). The respondents check the mark closest to what they feel describes the stimulus word. The semantic differential used in this study is included in Appendix C. For general discussions of the semantic differential, see Osgood et al. (1967) and Kerlinger (1964, pp. 546–580).

TABLE 10 *Stereotyped imagery of the masculinity-femininity of selected academic disciplines*

	Mean	Standard deviation
Masculine		
Electrical engineering	1.58	0.843
Mechanical engineering	1.59	0.842
Civil engineering	1.62	0.861
Chemical engineering	1.72	0.905
Agriculture/forestry	1.93	0.858
Law	1.94	0.946
Physics	2.00	0.965
Dentistry	2.03	1.012
Business	2.10	1.047
Architecture	2.18	1.054
Geology	2.34	1.010
Chemistry	2.36	1.046

	Mean	Standard deviation
Medicine	2.50	1.050
Mathematics	2.61	1.105
Biochemistry	2.69	1.137
Economics	2.72	1.111
Political science	2.90	0.958
Educational administration	2.99	1.259
Neutral		
Bacteriology	3.05	1.138
Physiology	3.17	1.087
Zoology	3.18	0.985
Philosophy	3.23	1.021
History	3.34	1.046
Botany	3.39	1.005
Geography	3.44	1.026
Psychology	3.57	1.061
Journalism	3.61	1.095
Anthropology	3.63	0.896
Physical and health education	3.66	1.155
German	3.71	1.126
Sociology	3.80	0.924
Feminine		
Educational psychology	4.10	1.171
Speech	4.19	0.916
Spanish	4.29	0.858
Art	4.31	0.881
Dramatics	4.36	0.831
Music	4.39	0.985
Secondary education	4.59	1.287
Social work	4.71	1.003
English	4.83	1.136
French	4.98	1.003
Library science	5.50	1.114
Elementary education	6.01	1.073
Nursing	6.47	0.818
Home economics	6.51	0.815

As we might expect, engineering is viewed as the most masculine discipline, while home economics and nursing are viewed as the most feminine disciplines (Table 10). When we separated discipline perceptions by sex of respondents, we found that women tended to view all disciplines as more feminine than men scored them; however, the overall Pearson product-moment correlation between the perceptions of men and women was $+.99$.[5] Perceptions of masculinity and femininity do not cluster by broad types of disciplines. For example, within the old professions, law is viewed as more masculine than medicine; in the pure physical sciences, physics is viewed as more masculine than chemistry; sociology is viewed as the most feminine social science and is far removed from political science; and within the languages, German (the language of science) is viewed as the most masculine, followed by Spanish and then French (the language of the arts).

What remains problematic is how the perception of masculinity or femininity of a discipline is related to its actual male or female enrollment. Table 11 lists the percentages of female graduate students, bachelor's degree recipients, and faculty in the order of the perceived masculinity of each discipline.

In Table 2 we found a large attrition for women from the receipt of a bachelor's degree to the receipt of the doctorate. The same trend is very much in evidence in Table 11. There are more female bachelor's degree recipients than female graduate students in almost every one of the listed disciplines. Furthermore, although women constitute the majority of bachelor's degree recipients in 15 fields (anthropology, German, sociology, speech and dramatic arts, Spanish, art, music, secondary education, social work, English, French, library science, elementary education, nursing,

---

[5] "Correlation reduces to mathematical terms the degree of inherent association which exists between any two variables occurring simultaneously in the same universe" (Franzblau, 1958, p. 64). The Pearson product-moment correlation, like all such measures, may range from -1.00 to $+1.00$. A negative correlation shows an inverse relationship between variables (the higher the score of one variable, the lower the score of the other), and a positive correlation shows a direct relationship (the higher the score of one variable, the higher the score of the second, or the lower the score of one variable, the lower the score of the second). The closer the score is to $+1.00$ or -1.00, the stronger the relationship is. For example, we find that women tend to score all fields as more feminine than men; however, there is a correlation of $+.99$ between the perceptions of men and the perceptions of women. This means that, although the scores may be different, there is almost perfect agreement about which fields are masculine and which are feminine.

	Graduate students, 1968–69[a]	Bachelor's degree recipients, 1968–69[b]	Faculty
Electrical engineering	0.6 (17,678)	0.4 (11,629)	0.6 (6,265)
Mechanical engineering	0.6 (8,772)	0.4 (9,474)	0.5 (5,780)
Civil engineering	0.9 (6,772)	0.5 (5,958)	0.1 (4,246)
Chemical engineering	1.0 (4,877)	0.9 (3,504)	0.9 (1,994)
Agriculture/forestry	5.6 (7,677)	3.1 (9,594)	0.9 (10,187)
Law	5.8 (64,220)	–	4.3 (3,228)
Physics	4.8 (14,503)	5.9 (5,535)	3.6 (10,944)
Dentistry	1.1 (15,542)	–	c
Business	4.0 (65,747)	8.2 (42,224)	16.3 (25,741)
Architecture	11.7 (1,424)	4.3 (3,188)	4.3 (3,666)
Geology	7.9 (3,543)	10.4 (1,974)	4.2 (4,864)
Chemistry	14.1 (17,492)	18.3 (11,795)	9.3 (15,529)
Medicine	8.8 (35,733)	–	7.7 (15,133)
Mathematics	23.2 (20,677)	37.6 (27,015)	13.6 (23,441)
Biochemistry	22.6 (3,393)	24.8 (347)	6.6 (2,291)
Economics	10.6 (10,585)	10.6 (16,907)	5.9 (9,133)
Political science	18.7 (10,591)	20.8 (23,920)	10.7 (9,518)
Educational administration	22.7 (22,707)	–	9.4 (2,073)
Bacteriology	30.8 (3,227)	47.2 (1,357)	16.6 (2,621)
Physiology	21.1 (1,785)	24.2 (73)	10.0 (3,089)
Zoology	23.9 (4,018)	21.9 (5,511)	7.3 (2,993)

TABLE 11 Female participation in academic disciplines (in percentages, weighted totals in parentheses)

	Graduate students, 1968–69[a]	Bachelor's degree recipients, 1968–69[b]	Faculty
TABLE 11 *(continued)*			
Philosophy	17.8 (4,931)	22.3 (4,659)	11.5 (5,896)
History	28.2 (20,247)	35.3 (41,079)	11.3 (15,965)
Botany	26.2 (2,156)	34.7 (577)	9.0 (1,445)
Geography	15.6 (2,836)	21.6 (3,338)	10.7 (3,108)
Psychology	33.8 (21,643)	43.1 (29,495)	18.5 (15,255)
Journalism	30.8 (1,853)	40.7 (5,197)	10.1 (2,221)
Anthropology	41.4 (3,678)	57.6 (2,990)	13.4 (2,234)
Physical and health education	34.3 (8,623)	40.8 (17,997)	40.9 (15,360)
German	51.6 (2,611)	59.4 (2,718)	27.7 (3,422)
Sociology	35.6 (8,682)	61.1 (26,555)	20.2 (8,507)
Educational psychology	47.0 (4,999)	35.0 (133)	21.4 (3,429)
Speech	49.5[d] (6,894)	58.5[e] (8,825)	23.4[f] (9,734)
Spanish	57.3 (4,734)	75.5 (7,243)	39.2 (2,794)
Art	51.0 (4,332)	67.9 (9,321)	20.7 (8,303)
Dramatic arts	42.8[d] (4,299)	58.5[e]	23.4[f]
Music	44.1 (7,145)	57.3 (5,021)	23.5 (12,967)
Secondary education	45.5 (17,650)	60.8 (2,366)	39.7[g] (8,112)
Social work	61.5 (12,829)	80.5 (3,388)	43.1 (3,117)
English	54.5 (30,443)	67.7 (54,359)	33.5 (34,338)
French	68.7 (4,889)	82.7 (7,910)	45.0 (4,024)
Library science	81.8 (10,982)	93.6 (1,000)	60.2 (3,400)

	Graduate students, 1968-69[a]	Bachelor's degree recipients, 1968-69[b]	Faculty
Elementary education	78.9 (42,781)	90.7 (81,251)	39.7[g]
Nursing	98.5 (2,916)	98.6 (10,380)	96.1 (6,892)
Home economics	90.6 (3,484)	97.3 (9,075)	89.2 (5,453)

[a] SOURCE: Chandler and Hooper, 1970.
[b] SOURCE: Hooper and Chandler, 1971.
[c] Dentistry not listed as separate department in faculty data.
[d] Speech and dramatic arts are not separated by the U.S. Office of Education. Estimates are from the Carnegie data.
[e] Speech and dramatic arts are not separated by the U.S. Office of Education. Speech percentage is used as best estimate of dramatic arts.
[f] Speech and dramatic arts not separated in faculty data. Speech percentage repeated as best estimate of dramatic arts.
[g] Elementary and secondary education are not separated.

and home economics), women are the majority of graduate students in only 10 fields (German, Spanish, art, social work, English, French, library science, elementary education, nursing, and home economics), and at the faculty level they are the majority in only 3 fields (library science, nursing, and home economics—all applied disciplines strongly associated with femininity).

The stereotyped imagery of the masculinity or femininity of a discipline is very strongly related to the percentage of female participants within the discipline. The best predictor is the percentage of female graduate students, with a Pearsonian correlation of $+.97$. The percentage of female faculty correlates $+.89$, and the percentage of female bachelor's degree recipients correlates $+.95$.

We cannot establish causal ordering of the relationship between perceptions and enrollment; that is, we cannot state that certain fields are viewed as feminine and then women are encouraged to enter them or that women for some reason enter fields that are *then* defined as feminine. At this point there is reciprocity; because fields are viewed as feminine, women enter them, and because women are in them, they are viewed as feminine.

What is most important is that fields *are* viewed as being masculine or feminine and that undergraduates are well aware of this distinction. In fact, these perceptions reflect reality and show great awareness of actual female enrollment patterns. The strongest

correlation (and therefore the greatest awareness of female enrollment patterns) is with graduate enrollment. There is a meaningful
distinction between undergraduate and graduate work in an
academic discipline, and the labeling of fields as "masculine" or
"feminine" corresponds very closely to male and female participation in these fields at the graduate level.

Differences between female participation at the graduate and
at the undergraduate level may be exemplified by examining
sociology. Many female sociology majors use this field as an entrée
into other fields, such as social work; thus, high female representation at the baccalaureate level (61 percent) is reduced to one-third
at the graduate level. People become identified and involved with a
field most intensively at the graduate level, and this is why we are
concerned about the characteristics of masculine and feminine
graduate fields.

Like female-dominated occupations, female-dominated academic
disciplines are low in prestige, low in economic rewards, and low
in power. Moreover, they have other characteristics that set them
apart from male-dominated fields. Female-dominated fields are
in the humanities, with great emphasis on teaching, while male-
dominated fields are more mathematical, with greater emphasis
on research.

PRESTIGE We could measure the prestige of academic disciplines in many
ways. One way is simply to ask incumbents of a discipline, directly
or indirectly, how prestigious their field is. Using the graduate
student questionnaire, we measured prestige through three items:
(1) "Exciting developments are taking place in my field," (2) "My
field is among the most respected academic disciplines," and (3)
"My field gets a good share of the best students." Table 12 lists
the percentages of graduate students who strongly agree with these
items.

Men and women differ little in the perceptions of their disciplines.
The disciplines perceived as having the most exciting developments
are medicine and biochemistry—over 90 percent of the students
strongly agree that exciting developments are taking place. Languages, including English, rank lowest. The scientific disciplines
in general are perceived as having exciting developments, and indeed it is in these disciplines that new developments are taking
place. Rapid change has never been a feature of the humanities, and
it is not surprising that they are viewed as having fewer exciting

TABLE 12 *Percentage of graduate students "strongly agreeing" to items of discipline prestige, by field and sex (weighted totals in parentheses)*

	Exciting developments			Most respected			Best students		
	Males	*Females*	*Total**	*Males*	*Females*	*Total*	*Males*	*Females*	*Total*
Electrical engineering	75.1	—	75.2	37.3	—	37.0	53.6 (30,307)	—	53.0 (30,802)
Mechanical engineering	53.8	—	53.9	25.8	—	25.8	30.7 (13,970)	—	30.7 (14,042)
Civil engineering	50.8	—	50.6	13.1	—	13.1	12.0 (9,082)	—	12.0 (9,104)
Chemical engineering	59.8	—	59.9	41.8	—	42.0	45.6 (9,123)	—	45.3 (9,219)
Agriculture/ forestry	63.6	74.9	65.6	12.9	24.0	13.4	12.7 (9,962)	27.4 (398)	13.3 (10,376)
Law	54.3	67.6	58.2	46.5	50.1	46.7	58.5 (42,173)	57.8 (3,297)	58.4 (45,571)
Physics	67.1	67.4	67.2	67.8	55.9	67.6	64.2 (18,641)	47.5 (582)	63.9 (19,310)
Dentistry	59.4	—	59.4	42.5	—	42.2	42.6 (11,547)	—	42.6 (11,685)
Business	45.3	53.5	45.6	11.8	5.8	11.5	17.3 (76,742)	16.5 (3,510)	17.3 (80,372)
Architecture	63.6	75.9	65.6	11.6	15.4	12.2	7.4 (2,462)	8.9 (501)	7.6 (2,976)
Geology	73.4	71.9	73.3	13.8	41.1	16.5	13.4 (6,572)	3.5 (681)	12.3 (7,263)
Chemistry	75.5	69.5	74.6	51.9	57.4	52.5	45.4 (19,031)	52.7 (3,069)	46.6 (22,228)
Medicine	92.8	92.9	92.8	71.9	58.1	71.0	70.7 (23,762)	57.0 (1,764)	69.0 (25,636)
Mathematics	55.1	51.3	54.2	53.2	64.2	56.8	52.3 (23,011)	56.8 (8,744)	53.4 (31,793)
Biochemistry	91.2	95.9	92.1	54.8	52.9	54.4	47.5 (3,920)	52.3 (850)	48.5 (4,770)
Economics	42.6	35.9	42.0	32.3	14.8	30.6	23.0 (9,978)	13.4 (1,275)	22.2 (11,265)
Political science	47.0	46.2	46.8	9.4	7.7	9.1	13.4 (14,628)	13.4 (3,067)	13.4 (17,730)

TABLE 12 *(continued)*

	Exciting developments			Most respected			Best students		
	Males	Females	Total*	Males	Females	Total	Males	Females	Total
Educational administration	54.5	56.2	54.9	13.3	7.9	12.4	9.9 (25,937)	5.7 (6,777)	9.1 (32,760)
Bacteriology	78.4	93.3	82.6	41.8	53.7	45.2	34.0 (4,530)	39.9 (1,841)	35.8 (6,382)
Physiology	76.3	75.8	76.2	44.7	47.9	45.3	40.7 (3,651)	30.4 (997)	38.6 (4,648)
Zoology	78.8	82.2	79.5	25.1	40.1	28.2	26.6 (4,562)	27.6 (1,243)	26.8 (5,805)
Philosophy	31.6	38.2	32.6	19.0	20.1	19.2	27.2 (4,324)	20.0 (833)	26.0 (5,157)
History	31.4	33.3	31.9	35.8	14.8	28.9	18.9 (21,682)	13.4 (9,393)	17.1 (32,207)
Botany	78.3	63.7	75.2	18.2	9.4	16.3	27.3 (2,370)	9.4 (695)	23.7 (3,084)
Geography	43.3	47.0	44.1	1.8	0.0	1.4	2.0 (2,767)	0.0 (787)	1.6 (3,554)
Psychology	73.4	65.0	69.9	22.4	9.2	17.2	24.3 (24,659)	26.4 (17,156)	25.2 (41,922)
Journalism	53.2	67.6	58.2	13.3	6.0	10.5	11.1 (1,481)	12.3 (1,013)	11.5 (2,494)
Anthropology	57.1	72.1	64.2	12.0	13.6	12.8	18.9 (2,136)	14.9 (2,108)	17.1 (4,245)
Physical education	50.0	63.9	55.5	0.9	0.0	0.5	4.0 (8,379)	6.8 (5,329)	5.2 (13,849)
German	5.7	4.5	5.0	7.5	4.5	5.8	10.4 (1,475)	9.0 (1,363)	9.5 (3,131)
Sociology	47.5	49.4	48.1	5.6	7.6	6.1	9.0 (6,319)	11.5 (2,703)	9.8 (9,022)
Educational psychology	50.7	63.2	57.8	7.7	12.7	10.5	9.6 (13,811)	11.7 (16,575)	10.8 (30,486)
Speech	57.2	76.6	65.8	2.0	8.6	5.0	1.5 (2,697)	6.8 (4,185)	3.9 (6,894)
Spanish	16.4	24.2	21.0	22.3	10.0	14.7	6.3 (1,440)	12.0 (3,023)	9.8 (4,463)
Art	72.5	55.5	63.9	20.4	5.9	13.1	18.3 (3,822)	9.3 (4,048)	13.8 (7,870)
Dramatic arts	59.0	63.5	61.1	0.6	0.0	0.3	5.4 (1,837)	3.8 (2,443)	4.7 (4,229)

	Exciting developments			Most respected			Best students		
	Males	Females	Total*	Males	Females	Total	Males	Females	Total
Music	28.5	45.1	35.6	11.7	9.3	10.7	22.4 (7,801)	19.3 (5,490)	21.1 (13,291)
Secondary education	51.5†	46.6	48.3	20.7	17.6	18.7	13.9 (28,992)	8.4 (54,642)	8.1 (83,843)
Social work	60.8	55.2	57.6	2.1	4.0	3.3	6.5 (8,328)	4.1 (10,401)	5.2 (18,780)
English	27.2	31.2	29.6	20.3	40.8	32.5	27.4 (18,221)	36.4 (26,575)	32.7 (44,841)
French	20.0	13.6	14.9	7.9	9.5	9.1	9.3 (1,284)	11.6 (5,866)	11.1 (7,163)
Library science	51.2	40.2	49.4	26.6	4.0	7.9	28.5 (1,748)	2.7 (8,678)	7.2 (10,444)
Elementary education	51.5†	46.6	48.3	20.7	17.6	18.7	13.9	8.4	8.1
Nursing	—	64.3	64.0	—	3.4	3.8	—	11.8 (3,197)	12.0 (3,252)
Home economics	—	60.7	61.2	—	4.8	4.8	—	7.8 (5,256)	7.7 (5,356)

* Total includes those who did not identify their sex.
† Elementary and secondary education not separated. Joint percentage used as best estimate of each field.

developments.[6] Exciting fields appear to be oriented toward science, not toward teaching. And, for their research and scientific efforts, incumbents of exciting fields are better paid than are persons in less exciting fields.

Our most direct measurement of a discipline's prestige is the item "My field is among the most respected academic disciplines." Men and women differ little in the perception of their field's standing. The fields viewed as most prestigious in this respect are

[6] The characteristics associated with discipline contexts are based on correlational analysis. The actual correlations between the percentages agreeing with various items will be found in Appendix B. Significance levels are presented both in this chapter and in Appendix B; for example, $p < .001$, or a significance level of .001, means that the likelihood of such a correlation occurring merely by chance is less than one in a thousand.

medicine, physics, and mathematics—all older, established disciplines. Whereas 71 percent of the medical students strongly agree that their field is among the most prestigious, less than 1 percent of students in physical education or dramatic arts agree. Like exciting fields, most respected fields are based in mathematics or science rather than in the humanities. They are also those fields in which there is less interest in teaching among students and faculty. Prestigious fields appear to be "where the action is," and that action is scientific research.

In a study of the relationship among the variables of power, privilege, and prestige in 10 functionally important occupations, a correlation of +.85 was found between the social standing of an occupation (prestige) and the perceived financial rewards accruing

TABLE 13
Correlation matrix: discipline prestige

	Feminine imagery: semantic differential	Percentage of female graduate students	Exciting developments		
			Males	Females	Total
Feminine imagery: semantic differential	1.000				
Percentage of female graduate students	.97*	1.000			
Exciting developments, males	−.37‡	−.38‡	1.000		
Exciting developments, females	−.36‡	−.35‡	.90*	1.000	
Exciting developments, total	−.29	−.30‡	.98*	−.96*	1.000
Most respected, males	−.44†	−.40†	.47†	.36‡	.44†
Most respected, females	−.52†	−.46†	.49†	.45†	.47†
Most respected, total	−.52†	−.49†	.47†	.38‡	.44†
Best students, males	−.49*	−.45†	.48†	.38‡	.46†
Best students, females	−.50*	−.44†	.40‡	.41†	.40†
Best students, total	−.55*	−.52*	.46†	.39‡	.43†

*$p < .001$
†$p < .01$
‡$p < .05$

to incumbents of the occupation (Feldman & Thielbar, 1972). We find a similar relationship between privilege and prestige in academic disciplines. Fields that rank high in academic prestige are fields that are well-paying.

The final prestige indicator is "My field gets a good share of the best students." The old professions of medicine and law have the highest percentages of students strongly agreeing with this item, while geography and speech are seen as least likely to attract the best students. There are strong differences even within broad categories of disciplines. Among graduate students in electrical engineering, 53 percent agree that their field attracts the best students, compared to only 12 percent of the students in civil engineering. Sociology is seen as the social science least likely to attract the

	Most respected			Best students		
	Males	Females	Total	Males	Females	Total
	1.000					
	.85*	1.000				
	.97*	.93*	1.000			
	.93*	.84*	.93*	1.000		
	.85*	.89*	.91*	.90*	1.000	
	.91*	.88*	.95*	.98*	.95*	1.000

best students. None of the three foreign languages (French, German, and Spanish) are perceived as attracting the best students. Fields with "best students" share the same characteristics as do our other prestige indicators. They are mathematically oriented, well paying, and low in teaching interest among students and faculty.

Prestigious fields, surprisingly, are not those in which incumbents rate themselves highly. It is the less prestigious disciplines whose incumbents are more likely to state that they are "among the best students in their department"—in other words, that they are better than their field. More prestigious disciplines tend to be more competitive, and because of an abundance of bright students, students in these fields seem less likely to call themselves "among the best."

Table 13 notes how the three measurements of prestige are interrelated and how they are related to masculine-feminine imagery and to the percentage of female graduate students. There are very strong correlations between men's and women's perceptions of prestige within all three items; furthermore, there is a positive correlation among all three measures of prestige. As can be seen, the prestigious disciplines are those that are predominantly male and those that are viewed as masculine. There is a $-.55$ correlation ($p < .001$) between the stereotyped feminine imagery of a field and the perception that a field attracts the best students. There is also a strong negative correlation ($-.52$, $p < .01$) between a field being viewed as "most respected" and the strength of the perceived femininity of that discipline. Feminine or female-dominated fields are viewed as less exciting, less respected, and less likely to attract the best students than male-dominated fields. This is true whether the male or the female incumbents of the field rate its prestige.

FINANCIAL REWARDS AND POWER

To examine financial rewards (privilege) and power, we turn to the faculty data. We have chosen two measures: (1) the percentage of faculty who have done paid consulting in the past year and (2) the percentage of faculty whose academic (institutional) salary is over $20,000 per year.

Consulting may be looked upon not only as a source of added income but also as an indirect measure of the "power" of a discipline, that is, as a chance to exert the influence and knowledge of a discipline outside the academic setting. The old adage states that

"Knowledge is power," but not all disciplines are equal in producing consultants who are dispensers of knowledge to paying clients. Table 14 shows the percentages, by sex and field, of faculty who have done paid consulting in the past year.

In almost every field, women are less likely to serve as consultants than men. We suspect that, given the choice, individuals seek the counsel of men rather than women; even in home economics, a greater percentage of male faculty than of women have done paid consulting. The less theoretical fields have produced more faculty consultants than the more theoretical. For example, 80 percent of the men and 67 percent of the women in educational administration have done paid consulting in the past year. High rates of consulting are also found in engineering, architecture, psychology, and elementary and secondary education. As we might expect, the languages have the least representation among paid consultants, although men are more likely to have done paid consulting than women.

According to our data, approximately 8 percent of all faculty within American higher education earn $20,000 a year or more as their basic institutional salary, but the percentage earning this

TABLE 14
Faculty financial rewards, by field and sex *(weighted totals in parentheses)*

	Percentage engaged in paid consulting			Percentage with institutional income of $20,000+		
	Male	*Female*	*Total*	*Male*	*Female*	*Total*
Electrical engineering	56.4	—	56.6	8.6 (6,123)	—	8.6 (6,265)
Mechanical engineering	61.3	—	61.0	8.6 (5,645)	—	8.5 (5,780)
Civil engineering	75.8	—	75.8	10.1 (4,179)	—	10.0 (4,246)
Chemical engineering	70.4	—	69.9	18.0 (1,959)	—	18.3 (1,994)
Agriculture/ forestry	35.4	17.8	35.5	9.2 (10,557)	4.4 (95)	9.2 (10,817)
Law	57.0	44.2	56.8	37.3 (3,023)	5.8 (137)	35.8 (3,228)
Physics	37.5	10.6	36.5	8.8 (10,398)	3.4 (393)	8.0 (10,994)

TABLE 14 (continued)	Percentage engaged in paid consulting			Percentage with institutional income of $20,000+		
	Male	Female	Total*	Male	Female	Total
Business	57.3	13.5	50.3	7.4 (20,924)	0.7 (4,067)	6.3 (25,741)
Architecture	71.1	37.3	69.9	4.7 (3,405)	0.0 (155)	4.6 (3,666)
Geology	54.0	6.7	52.0	10.6 (4,612)	1.3 (201)	10.2 (4,864)
Chemistry	32.9	11.6	30.9	10.0 (13,789)	0.0 (1,412)	9.7 (15,529)
Medicine	56.9	38.4	55.5	46.3 (13,625)	17.1 (1,142)	44.0 (15,133)
Mathematics	25.8	11.6	23.7	1.9 (19,937)	0.7 (3,136)	1.4 (23,441)
Biochemistry	38.9	4.9	36.6	28.1 (2,123)	3.6 (150)	26.3 (2,291)
Economics	48.1	37.9	47.6	13.0 (8,414)	0.8 (531)	12.2 (9,133)
Political science	39.4	13.7	36.4	7.7 (7,490)	0.6 (900)	6.9 (8,518)
Educational administration	80.0	67.4	78.9	15.1 (1,806)	0.0 (187)	13.8 (2,073)
Bacteriology	37.8	22.6	35.3	22.9 (2,155)	18.0 (428)	22.0 (2,621)
Physiology	38.6	17.2	36.2	20.5 (2,699)	3.2 (300)	18.6 (3,089)
Zoology	27.2	6.4	25.8	8.3 (2,750)	0.0 (218)	7.6 (2,993)
Philosophy	15.7	0.5	13.9	5.9 (5,187)	0.0 (675)	5.3 (5,896)
History	22.0	9.9	20.7	5.6 (13,924)	2.2 (1,771)	5.2 (15,965)
Botany	32.1	17.6	31.2	9.8 (1,297)	0.0 (129)	8.9 (1,445)
Geography	32.7	16.7	31.0	3.0 (2,727)	0.4 (326)	2.4 (3,108)
Psychology	56.6	43.1	54.1	8.8 (12,190)	3.4 (2,770)	8.0 (15,255)
Journalism	44.5	36.7	43.5	4.3 (1,958)	0.0 (219)	4.1 (2,221)
Anthropology	48.1	52.3	48.0	11.9 (1,863)	8.9 (288)	11.6 (2,234)

	Percentage engaged in paid consulting			Percentage with institutional income of $20,000+		
	Male	*Female*	*Total**	*Male*	*Female*	*Total*
Physical education	25.0	16.8	21.4	1.9 (8,853)	0.7 (6,133)	1.4 (15,360)
German	18.2	5.1	14.9	8.2 (2,424)	1.4 (931)	6.5 (3,422)
Sociology	50.1	25.0	44.9	7.6 (6,568)	0.9 (1,689)	6.2 (8,507)
Educational psychology	64.1	50.4	61.5	4.1 (2,609)	0.9 (709)	3.5 (3,429)
Speech	39.8†	33.4	38.4	3.2 (7,379)	0.6 (2,250)	2.6 (9,734)
Spanish	18.2	8.8	14.4	5.3 (1,662)	0.0 (1,069)	3.3 (9,734)
Art	34.7	26.6	33.0	2.1 (6,381)	0.4 (1,667)	1.7 (8,303)
Dramatic arts	39.8†	33.4	38.4	3.2	0.6	2.6
Music	42.2	24.1	38.6	3.0 (9,698)	0.4 (2,973)	2.4 (12,967)
Secondary education	69.5‡	45.5	59.7	4.4 (4,766)	0.9 (3,133)	3.0 (8,112)
Social work	74.8	49.2	64.0	8.0 (1,726)	1.7 (1,309)	5.2 (3,117)
English	21.4	13.2	18.7	4.7 (22,297)	0.4 (11,225)	3.3 (34,338)
French	16.8	9.4	13.3	5.8 (2,180)	0.0 (1,780)	3.2 (4,024)
Library science	29.7	15.5	21.3	3.7 (1,329)	0.0 (2,008)	1.5 (3,400)
Elementary education	69.5‡	45.5	59.7	4.4	0.9	3.0
Nursing	17.9	22.5	22.3	2.1 (262)	1.2 (6,450)	1.2 (6,892)
Home economics	39.4	28.6	29.4	2.9 (569)	1.5 (4,689)	1.6 (5,453)

* Weighted total includes those not answering, "What is your sex?"

† Faculty questionnaire did not separate speech and dramatic arts. Same percentages used for both.

‡ Secondary education and elementary education not separated. Same percentages used for both.

amount varies by sex and academic discipline (Table 14). Without exception, women faculty in all fields are less likely to earn $20,000 than are men. The fields that pay their faculties the most are law and medicine. In both of these fields most faculty could easily earn an equal salary by being practitioners. Other fields, however, also have a high percentage of faculty making over $20,000. Biochemistry has 26 percent, although 28 percent of the men earn that much, compared to less that 4 percent of the women. In sociology, about 8 percent of the male faculty earn over $20,000, compared to less than 1 percent of the women. Of all the fields stereotyped as feminine (educational psychology to home economics), there is not one in which even 8 percent (the national average) of the incumbents earn over $20,000.

Fields that are high in paid consultants tend to emphasize graduate education and offer their students alternatives other than college or university teaching. They are research-oriented disciplines with little emphasis on the humanities. In other words, these fields are less theoretical and are apt to have an impact on the world outside academia.

As we stated before, the well-paying fields are also high in prestige. In addition, they are likely to stress research rather than

TABLE 15 *Correlation matrix: financial rewards*

	Feminine imagery: semantic differential	Percentage of female graduate students	Paid consultants			$20,000+ incomes		
			Male	Female	Total	Male	Female	Total
Feminine imagery: semantic differential	1.000							
Percentage of female graduate students	.97*	1.000						
Male consultants	—.29	—.30‡	1.000					
Female consultants	.15	.13	.80*	1.000				
Total consultants	—.38‡	.39†	.99*	.81*	1.000			
Male $20,000+	—.44	—.42†	.26	.15	.30	1.000		
Female $20,000+	—.26	—.21	.13	.17	.17	.73*	1.000	
Total $20,000+	—.48†	—.47†	.27	.16	.32	.99*	.74*	1.000

*$p < .001$
†$p < .01$
‡$p < .05$

teaching and to have a high rate of research output among their faculty.[7] As the matrix in Table 15 demonstrates, the high-paying fields are also masculine fields.

Although there is a strong correlation between female participation in a field and the percentage of incumbents consulting or earning over $20,000 a year, consulting and high institutional salary are not strongly related to each other. Fields in which people earn $20,000 or more are not necessarily those in which many faculty are engaged in paid consulting. This is true by sex as well. Fields in which men or women rank high on one measurement are not necessarily those in which they will rank high on the other.

What is clear is that female-dominated or feminine fields have lower salaries than male-dominated fields; furthermore, they are less likely to be fields where knowledge may be used for paid consulting. Female fields are characterized by economic inequality, and their knowledge is less likely to be marketed outside academic settings.

TEACHING ORIENTATION In the history of women's education in America, the teaching of the young gradually came to be accepted as a proper activity for college-educated women. Women (as a minority) also joined the teaching staffs of some colleges and universities. It was our hypothesis that the disciplines in which women study and which they staff are those that have a greater emphasis on teaching. We asked all faculty and those graduate students who planned to enter college or university teaching whether their interests were primarily in teaching or research. Table 16 presents the percentages, by field and sex, of those whose interests lie heavily in teaching.

Women graduate students and faculty are more strongly teaching-oriented than their male counterparts. For example, among sociology faculty, 28 percent of the men express strong teaching orientation, compared to 50 percent of the women. Similar differences exist in such diverse fields as zoology (men, 19 percent; women, 60 percent), anthropology (men, 4 percent; women, 16 percent), and mathematics (men, 48 percent; women, 75 percent).

In addition to differences by status (whether student or faculty

[7] We are well aware of the danger inherent in this type of analysis of falling victim to the ecological fallacy (Robinson, 1950). Thus we do not assert that faculty who are strongly teaching-oriented are not as well paid as others. We are stating that *disciplines* in which the faculty are strongly teaching-oriented tend to have less well-paid faculty.

TABLE 16 Percentages of faculty and graduate students with a strong teaching orientation, by field and sex (weighted totals in parentheses)	Faculty			Graduate students*		
	Males	*Females*	*Total†*	*Males*	*Females*	*Total†*
Electrical engineering	29.2	—	29.2	6.0 (5,158)	—	6.6 (5,208)
Mechanical engineering	35.2	—	35.4	21.6 (2,765)	—	21.6 (2,765)
Civil engineering	28.4	—	28.5	28.6 (1,748)	—	28.6 (1,748)
Chemical engineering	9.2	—	9.0	14.2 (1,886)	—	14.0 (1,906)
Agriculture/ forestry	25.7	13.8	25.7	5.6 (3,707)	—	5.4 (3,898)
Law	25.1	28.3	25.3	28.0 (2,158)	—	28.9 (2,210)
Physics	23.4	49.4	24.3	7.1 (7,351)	36.7 (198)	7.9 (7,549)
Dentistry	—	—	—	33.1 (898)	—	32.2 (923)
Business	53.5	78.4	57.8	36.7 (9,660)	46.9 (931)	37.5 (10,618)
Architecture	38.3	16.6	37.4	10.0 (566)	—	12.7 (668)
Geology	17.2	42.7	18.2	8.7 (2,837)	14.4 (149)	9.0 (2,996)
Chemistry	30.8	59.4	33.3	10.0 (7,660)	10.0 (1,628)	10.0 (9,009)
Medicine	23.4	30.1	23.7	11.1 (2,315)	29.0 (137)	12.1 (2,451)
Mathematics	47.8	75.2	51.7	17.2 (9,927)	40.4 (1,993)	34.4 (11,943)
Biochemistry	3.1	6.5	3.4	1.6 (1,980)	18.7 (308)	3.9 (2,287)
Economics	26.0	47.5	27.2	15.9 (5,134)	29.2 (442)	16.9 (5,576)
Political science	28.7	52.3	31.1	20.9 (7,080)	17.5 (1,487)	20.3 (8,567)
Educational administration	35.0	25.6	33.7	32.4 (4,433)	16.1 (752)	29.8 (5,185)
Bacteriology	7.1	22.7	9.6	1.9 (2,336)	14.4 (726)	4.7 (3,073)

	Faculty			Graduate students*		
	Males	*Females*	*Total†*	*Males*	*Females*	*Total†*
Physiology	11.7	23.2	12.7	3.4 (1,875)	26.2 (570)	8.6 (2,445)
Zoology	19.2	60.1	22.2	0.7 (2,776)	6.7 (533)	1.7 (3,309)
Philosophy	30.3	47.4	32.3	31.0 (3,354)	34.5 (676)	31.6 (4,030)
History	31.0	55.1	33.5	27.7 (12,144)	25.5 (2,429)	27.3 (14,611)
Botany	10.8	41.2	13.5	6.6 (1,489)	12.8 (338)	7.8 (1,827)
Geography	39.1	44.3	39.5	13.0 (1,369)	6.4 (421)	11.5 (1,789)
Psychology	27.0	44.8	30.2	16.2 (10,984)	38.4 (3,847)	22.0 (14,831)
Journalism	56.8	76.8	58.9	57.6 (98)	8.8 (175)	26.3 (273)
Anthropology	4.4	15.8	5.7	7.0 (1,576)	10.7 (1,352)	8.7 (2,928)
Physical education	71.1	80.0	74.8	43.1 (4,205)	72.1 (2,157)	53.1 (6,503)
German	37.6	54.6	42.4	28.9 (1,009)	41.1 (857)	34.4 (1,866)
Sociology	27.9	50.4	32.4	16.2 (3,653)	6.7 (1,251)	13.8 (4,904)
Educational psychology	38.4	50.5	40.8	20.4 (2,592)	51.2 (2,147)	34.2 (4,757)
Speech	57.1	59.2	57.6‡	17.1 (1,602)	40.2 (668)	23.9 (2,270)
Spanish	36.7	55.7	43.7	37.7 (872)	28.4 (1,085)	32.4 (1,957)
Art	24.1	47.8	29.8	39.3 (2,178)	29.1 (1,833)	34.6 (4,010)
Dramatic arts	57.1	59.2	57.6‡	58.4 (1,158)	63.5 (980)	60.8 (2,138)
Music	56.6	64.0	58.5	59.3 (4,672)	53.2 (2,336)	57.4 (7,008)
Secondary education	47.4	66.2	55.0	54.7 (6,241)	41.1 (3,150)	50.2§ (9,407)
Social work	43.4	64.0	52.2	30.4 (924)	57.0 (237)	36.1 (1,161)

TABLE 16 *(continued)*	Faculty			Graduate students*		
	Males	*Females*	*Total†*	*Males*	*Females*	*Total†*
English	48.6	63.3	53.7	31.0 (12,492)	27.4 (9,958)	29.4 (22,450)
French	43.5	54.0	48.4	27.7 (657)	51.6 (1,900)	45.5 (2,557)
Library science	40.7	51.6	47.0	45.3 (210)	23.9 (914)	29.0 (1,124)
Elementary education	47.4	66.2	55.0	54.7	41.1	50.2§
Nursing	62.3	63.4	63.5	—	50.1 (1,044)	50.8 (1,057)
Home economics	51.4	62.9	61.3	—	41.1 (1,967)	41.1 (1,967)

* Asked only of those planning to enter college or university teaching.
† Totals include respondents who did not state sex.
‡ Faculty questionnaire did not separate speech and dramatic arts. Same percentage used for both.
§ Secondary education and elementary education not separated. Same percentage used for both.

member) and by sex, there are strong differences by academic discipline. Of the biochemistry faculty, 3 percent are strongly teaching-oriented, compared to almost 75 percent of the faculty in physical education. The biological sciences tend to have the lowest faculty interest in teaching—even less than the physical sciences. Similar patterns are found among the graduate students: 2 percent of those in zoology, compared to 57 percent of those in music, express strong teaching interests.

We previously observed that fields with a strong teaching orientation offer less prestige, power, and privilege than research-oriented fields. And, as we have also indicated, teaching-oriented fields are in the humanities. These fields not only offer less power, privilege, and prestige, but they also offer less in terms of self-image. Faculty and students in these fields are less likely to consider themselves intellectuals, and students are less likely to view themselves as scholars or scientists. These correlates bear out the popular impression that teaching is beneficial neither monetarily nor in terms of self-image. The benefits are more likely to be intrinsic—teaching is its own reward.

Most academic disciplines offer other careers than teaching to their graduate students. For example, according to our data, 38 percent of the graduate students in chemistry plan to enter industrial research, and 25 percent of those in political science plan to enter government administrative positions. Humanities fields, however, usually offer as their chief occupational choice college or university teaching. In dentistry, 9 percent of the students plan teaching as their future career, in social work, 7 percent, and in journalism, 13 percent, compared to 74 percent in German, 76 percent in anthropology, and 88 percent in philosophy. There is, however, only a slight correlation between the percentage of graduate students planning college or university teaching careers and the percentage of graduate students strongly teaching-oriented. Fields in which the bulk of students become teachers rather than practitioners do not necessarily produce the most committed teachers. The committed teacher stands out among his or her colleagues in any field.

Table 17 shows how our measures of teaching orientation are related to one another and to the percentage of female graduate students. Fields that contain a high percentage of faculty committed to teaching also contain a high percentage of graduate students (future college or university teachers) who are highly teaching-

TABLE 17 *Correlation matrix: strong teaching orientation*

	Feminine imagery: semantic differential	Percentage of female graduate students	Faculty			Graduate students		
			Male	Female	Total	Male	Female	Total
Feminine imagery: semantic differential	1.000							
Percentage of female graduate students	.97*	1.000						
Male faculty	.51*	.47†	1.000					
Female faculty	.43†	.38‡	.77*	1.000				
Total faculty	.58*	.55*	.99*	.77*	1.000			
Male graduate students	.57*	.51*	.73*	.62*	.76*	1.000		
Female graduate students	.39‡	.40‡	.66*	.49†	.67*	.51*	1.000	
Total graduate students	.61*	.58*	.79*	.64*	.81*	.90*	.81*	1.000

*p < .001
†p < .01
‡p < .05

oriented. Despite the tendency for women to be more teaching-oriented than men, the correlations between male and female graduate students and between male and female faculty are high (+.51 for graduate students and +.77 for faculty). Therefore, teaching orientation is an excellent predictor of the masculinity-femininity image of a field and of the rate of female participation. The more likely the incumbents are to be strongly teaching-oriented, the more likely the discipline is to be female.

RESEARCH ACTIVITIES Table 18 shows the percentages of male and female faculty who are not engaged in research or publication.[8] Research activity, like strong teaching orientation, is not equally distributed among all academic disciplines. Certain fields, such as biochemistry, physiology, and anthropology, show high involvement in research activity by practically all their faculty. On the other hand, over 60 percent of the faculty in physical education, library science, or nursing are not involved in research. As in the case of teaching orientation there are strong research-activity differences by sex, with women showing less research involvement than men. For example, in sociology, 18 percent of the men score 0 on this index, compared to 42 percent of the women. Strong differences are also found in such diverse disciplines as medicine (men, 9 percent; women, 22 percent), business (men, 41 percent; women, 80 percent), botany

[8] We have constructed an Index of Research Activity to summarize involvement in research. A score of 0 on this index means that a faculty member is not currently engaged in research and has had no publications in the past 2 years.

TABLE 18 Percentage of faculty scoring 0 on index of research activity, by field and sex	Males	Females	Total*
Electrical engineering	25.9	—	25.6
Mechanical engineering	29.5	—	29.2
Civil engineering	20.8	—	20.8
Chemical engineering	3.8	—	4.0
Agriculture/forestry	16.3	13.8	16.4
Law	12.2	20.3	12.4
Physics	20.5	56.8	21.7
Business	41.2	79.8	47.6
Geology	8.6	47.9	10.0
Chemistry	20.1	42.5	23.1
Medicine	9.1	22.2	10.0

	Males	Females	Total*
Mathematics	43.1	76.6	47.7
Biochemistry	1.3	18.9	2.5
Economics	17.6	23.6	18.0
Political science	20.5	36.5	22.2
Educational administration	22.9	22.8	22.8
Bacteriology	6.7	38.7	11.6
Physiology	8.0	8.4	7.9
Zoology	10.4	53.7	13.5
Philosophy	18.4	32.1	19.9
History	17.2	40.7	19.7
Botany	5.7	39.2	8.6
Geography	21.4	57.9	24.5
Psychology	18.6	34.0	21.4
Journalism	31.0	33.4	31.1
Anthropology	4.0	5.8	4.1
Physical and health education	55.7	69.6	61.6
German	29.5	51.8	35.6
Sociology	17.9	41.5	22.6
Educational psychology	17.9	37.9	21.9
Speech	36.1	38.2	36.4†
Spanish	32.4	43.1	36.1
Art	41.1	43.9	41.3
Dramatic arts	36.1	38.2	36.4†
Music	41.5	65.3	46.8
Secondary education	27.9	48.0	35.4‡
Social work	32.0	55.1	41.5
English	25.9	54.2	35.6
French	30.3	57.3	42.8
Library science	43.0	74.9	62.0
Elementary education	27.9	48.0	35.4‡
Nursing	41.2	65.2	64.2
Home economics	29.9	62.4	58.9

* Totals include respondents who did not state sex.
† Faculty questionnaire did not separate speech and dramatic arts. Same percentage used for both.
‡ Secondary education and elementary education not separated. Same percentage used for both.

(men, 6 percent; women, 39 percent), and home economics (men, 30 percent; women, 62 percent).

As we see in Table 19, the more likely a field is to be low in research activity, the more likely it is to be female-dominated or viewed as feminine.

HUMANITIES AND MATHEMATICS ORIENTATIONS We asked graduate students how important they felt an undergraduate background in mathematics and an undergraduate background in humanities were for their fields. Since women are supposedly socialized to be oriented toward the humanities rather than mathematics, we assumed female disciplines to be oriented toward the humanities rather than mathematics. As a second measurement of active interest in the humanities, we examined the percentage of graduate students in each discipline who strongly agree with "I enjoy reading poetry."

The students in those fields that have traditionally been categorized as the humanities are those who deem an undergraduate background in humanities most important (Table 20). Thus, 80 percent of the graduate students in French and 77 percent of those in German strongly agree that humanities are most important compared to 6 percent in both geology and mechanical engineering. Differences by sex are not large. The differences by sex in the enjoy-

TABLE 19
Correlation matrix: faculty research activity

	Feminine imagery: semantic differential	Percentage of female graduate students	Faculty scoring 0 on index		
			Male	Female	Total
Feminine imagery: semantic differential	1.000				
Percentage of female graduate students	.97*	1.000			
Male faculty 0 research	.40†	.43†	1.000		
Female faculty 0 research	.33‡	.34‡	.74*	1.000	
Total faculty 0 research	.61*	.64*	.94*	.80*	1.000

* $p < .001$
† $p < .01$
‡ $p < .05$

TABLE 20 *Humanities and mathematics orientation of graduate students, by sex and field (in percentages)*

	Humanities very important			Strongly enjoy poetry			Mathematics very important		
	Males	Females	Total*	Males	Females	Total*	Males	Females	Total*
Electrical engineering	8.9	—	8.9	7.0	—	7.3	94.8	—	94.7
Mechanical engineering	5.7	—	5.7	7.9	—	7.9	94.0	—	94.0
Civil engineering	7.3	—	7.3	11.0	—	11.3	86.1	—	85.9
Chemical engineering	9.4	—	9.4	10.4	—	10.3	92.8	—	92.9
Agriculture/ forestry	5.6	13.3	5.9	8.6	40.4	9.9	49.5	32.5	48.9
Law	36.2	43.5	36.7	16.9	51.6	19.4	6.1	4.5	6.0
Physics	8.9	2.2	8.7	14.4	28.2	14.8	94.0	85.2	93.6
Dentistry	13.4	—	13.2	8.7	—	9.0	11.3	11.9	11.7
Business	15.4	20.1	15.7	6.3	30.9	7.4	52.1	44.7	51.7
Architecture	35.6	55.6	38.7	27.3	51.9	31.6	20.0	10.9	18.4
Geology	5.9	6.7	6.0	14.6	21.0	15.2	70.0	39.8	67.2
Chemistry	7.5	12.7	8.1	15.5	34.3	18.4	78.0	85.7	79.1
Medicine	23.8	32.0	24.5	20.8	38.5	22.1	21.8	24.3	22.1
Mathematics	7.6	10.9	8.6	11.6	19.4	13.8	88.6	86.6	88.1
Biochemistry	7.3	11.6	8.1	16.6	56.8	23.9	57.5	54.2	56.9
Economics	21.0	26.7	21.6	13.5	33.8	15.7	67.9	68.1	67.9
Political science	41.0	46.1	41.8	15.1	46.7	20.8	17.0	21.7	18.9
Educational administration	37.0	58.1	41.4	12.5	40.1	18.2	18.4	31.5	21.2
Bacteriology	7.0	15.7	9.5	15.0	43.0	23.1	50.5	67.0	55.4
Physiology	9.9	10.4	10.0	13.5	32.6	17.5	52.6	55.9	53.3
Zoology	9.2	15.6	10.6	13.3	35.1	18.0	42.3	29.2	39.5
Philosophy	59.1	68.7	60.7	38.3	44.6	39.3	19.1	19.3	10.1
History	76.8	71.3	75.0	19.7	38.4	24.9	2.7	12.0	5.4
Botany	14.1	10.1	13.2	12.0	34.7	17.0	54.4	39.2	51.2
Geography	18.0	18.8	18.2	14.3	66.0	25.7	34.1	33.5	34.0
Psychology	36.9	38.9	37.7	14.5	32.8	22.0	24.0	16.5	20.9
Journalism	51.9	79.9	63.2	24.3	66.8	41.6	3.6	9.7	6.1
Anthropology	39.7	37.9	34.2	19.8	35.7	27.7	23.0	9.1	16.1
Physical and health education	14.5	17.7	15.7	6.4	31.1	16.2	8.3	12.1	9.9

TABLE 20   *(continued)*

	Humanities very important			Strongly enjoy poetry			Mathematics very important		
	Males	*Females*	*Total**	*Males*	*Females*	*Total**	*Males*	*Females*	*Total**
German	73.3	79.9	77.0	52.1	56.3	54.6	5.1	6.2	5.6
Sociology	49.0	52.6	50.4	17.8	31.6	22.0	30.6	22.7	28.2
Educational psychology	35.2	53.2	44.7	17.9	37.7	28.5	16.8	12.8	14.9
Speech	64.7	44.6	52.4	30.4	28.6	29.3	4.7	2.3	3.2
Spanish	73.0	78.4	76.6	53.0	34.6	40.7	6.2	3.5	4.4
Art	77.7	65.5	71.5	57.7	45.0	51.2	9.4	5.3	7.3
Dramatic art	85.1	96.0	91.3	56.1	75.9	67.6	4.3	1.1	2.4
Music	58.7	75.2	65.4	19.8	46.3	30.5	5.6	6.5	6.0
Secondary education	32.8	40.6	38.0	10.5	36.2	27.7	24.2	27.2	26.3†
Social work	53.8	50.1	51.9	29.9	40.4	35.9	7.0	3.0	4.8
English	77.3	69.3	72.5	63.5	82.1	74.4	10.0	7.5	8.5
French	77.9	81.1	80.4	46.6	54.5	53.0	10.2	6.2	6.9
Library science	27.5	63.4	57.4	25.4	44.5	41.2	12.9	4.4	5.8
Elementary education	32.8	40.6	38.0	10.5	36.2	27.7	24.2	27.2	26.3†
Nursing	—	42.6	42.3	—	35.3	35.7	—	15.0	15.1
Home economics	—	32.9	32.3	—	22.1	22.4	—	12.1	12.0

* Totals include respondents who did not state sex.
† Secondary education and elementary education not separated. Same percentage used for both.

ment of poetry, however, are very large. Reading poetry is a "feminine" activity, and in all disciplines women are much more likely to enjoy poetry than men. In geography, 66 percent of the women strongly enjoy poetry, compared to 14 percent of the men, and even in fields such as English, where poetry is often a part of the curriculum, 64 percent of the men strongly enjoy it, compared to 82 percent of the women.

Fields that show high orientation toward humanities do not show a high orientation toward mathematics. In French, 7 percent of the students see a mathematics background as very important and in German, 6 percent, compared to 95 percent of those in electrical engineering and 94 percent of those in physics. Within fields, men and women tend to agree on the importance of mathematics.

As we might expect, humanities and mathematical fields differ sharply in many respects. For example, those in mathematically oriented fields have a faith in science; those in humanities do not. Humanities are teaching-oriented and low-paying, while mathematical fields are research-oriented and high-paying. Humanities also tend to have incumbents who are politically left or liberal. In mathematical fields, where scientific inquiry is part of the orientation of a subject, students are more likely to reject a student image and consider themselves scholars or scientists. This is not the case in humanities.

Table 21 shows how our humanities and mathematics measures are correlated. As in the semantic differential test, male and female responses show a strong positive correlation. There is also a strong negative association between mathematical and humanities orientations.

Although the percentage of men and the percentage of total students who enjoy poetry are strongly related, no relationship exists between the percentage of female students who enjoy poetry and the femininity of a field. We speculate that men entering female fields are more likely to assume stereotyped female characteristics. That is, men in female fields are more likely to admit that they enjoy the activity of reading poetry. Similarly, in the previous matrix we saw that, although both were good predictors, the percentage of males who are teaching-oriented was a better predictor of discipline femininity than the percentage of teaching-oriented females. Fields in which men choose the feminine response are likely to be female-dominated fields.[9]

ATTITUDES TOWARD WOMEN Attitudes toward female graduate students were measured through the use of two items: "The female graduate students in my department are not as dedicated as the males" (asked of both students and faculty) and "Professors in my department don't really take the female graduate students seriously" (asked of graduate students). While the first item may be considered by some an objective statement, it may also be construed as a measurement of antifemale feeling. We hypothesized that a stronger impression of a lack of female dedication or of antifemale feelings would be found in masculine than in feminine fields because these sentiments might

[9] Some say (e.g., Winick, 1968) that the adoption of the behavioral patterns of the opposite sex is a phenomenon that is rampant in all aspects of our society.

TABLE 21
Correlation matrix: humanities and mathematics orientation

	Feminine imagery: semantic differential	Percentage of female graduate students	Humanities important		
			Males	Females	Total
Feminine imagery: semantic differential	1.000				
Percentage of female graduate students	.97*	1.000			
Humanities important, males	.63*	.62*	1.000		
Humanities important, females	.45†	.45†	.92*	1.000	
Humanities important, total	.60*	.59*	.98*	.98*	1.000
Enjoy poetry, males	.52*	.55*	.84*	.73*	.81*
Enjoy poetry, females	.09	.05	.49†	.55*	.51*
Enjoy poetry, total	.61*	.61*	.83*	.79*	.85*
Mathematics important, males	—.66*	—.62*	—.76*	—.82*	—.78*
Mathematics important, females	—.52*	—.51*	—.73*	—.74*	—.75*
Mathematics important, total	—.64*	—.61*	—.76*	—.80*	—.78*

*$p < .001$
†$p < .01$
‡$p < .05$

have contributed to the small percentage of women in these fields in the first place.

Table 22 shows the percentages of respondents who agree, either strongly or with reservations, with these two items. Among both students and faculty, women are less likely to agree that females are not as dedicated. For example, among graduate students, 20 percent of the men in library science agree, compared to only 3 percent of the women; 31 percent of the men in music agree, compared to 7 percent of the women; and 29 percent of the male law students agree, compared to 13 percent of the women. Similarly, among faculty, 25 percent of the men in sociology agree, compared to 4 percent of the women; in medicine, 24 percent of the men, compared to 5 percent of the women, agree; and in home econom-

	Enjoy poetry			*Mathematics important*	
Males	*Females*	*Total*	*Males*	*Females*	*Total*

1.000					
.58*	1.000				
.93*	.72*	1.000			
—.53*	—.48†	—.63*	1.000		
—.52*	—.52*	—.38‡	.58*	1.000	
—.55*	—.42‡	—.64*	.99*	.95*	1.000

ics, 30 percent of the male faculty agree, compared to 10 percent of the women. When we compare the total percentages, faculty and student patterns are similar. The biological and physical sciences contain the highest percentages of those agreeing, with especially high agreement in chemistry.

Being more sensitive to professors' attitudes toward them, women graduate students are more likely than men to state that professors do not take female students seriously. For example, approximately 50 percent of the women in political science and sociology agree with this item, compared to about 20 percent of the men. In these two fields no more than a third of all the students perceive that professors do not take women seriously. As we find in Table 23, fields that are male-dominated are those whose pro-

TABLE 22 *Attitudes toward female graduate students, by sex and field*

	Percentage of graduate students who agree: females are not as dedicated			Percentage of faculty who agree: females are not as dedicated			Percentage of graduate students who agree: faculty does not take female students seriously		
	Males	*Females*	*Total**	*Males*	*Females*	*Total**	*Males*	*Females*	*Total**
Electrical engineering	20.1	—	19.9	21.7	—	21.2	18.7	—	18.7
Mechanical engineering	19.4	—	19.2	20.4	—	19.8	19.6	—	19.5
Civil engineering	26.1	—	26.1	22.4	—	22.2	22.8	—	22.7
Chemical engineering	29.0	—	29.1	32.8	—	32.1	31.8	—	31.4
Agriculture/forestry	22.8	12.5	22.3	23.7	7.5	23.6	24.1	31.7	24.5
Law	28.7	13.4	27.7	13.9	5.5	14.5	30.3	46.8	31.5
Physics	24.6	21.8	24.5	25.5	3.7	25.2	23.5	16.7	23.1
Dentistry	18.2	—	18.0	—	—	—	28.9	—	29.0
Business	28.1	14.1	27.4	19.2	6.9	18.2	24.3	29.3	24.5
Architecture	34.7	22.2	32.4	25.4	7.9	25.2	25.6	44.5	28.5
Geology	22.8	4.1	20.9	22.1	19.1	22.2	24.4	23.5	24.2
Chemistry	37.2	24.7	35.5	39.9	19.8	39.7	25.4	32.1	26.3
Medicine	21.4	22.3	21.3	23.5	5.0	22.3	19.0	20.9	19.0
Mathematics	24.5	19.9	23.4	29.3	16.4	28.0	15.0	16.3	15.3
Biochemistry	27.5	24.8	27.0	43.8	8.6	41.7	17.1	30.8	21.4
Economics	23.8	23.8	24.0	23.0	14.5	22.4	24.0	32.3	25.0
Political science	24.2	19.3	23.4	20.1	10.2	19.2	20.0	50.1	25.9
Educational administration	18.6	5.4	16.1	16.8	0.0	15.5	11.8	36.9	17.1
Bacteriology	34.4	31.4	33.5	35.2	15.2	32.3	14.0	27.7	17.8
Physiology	32.3	19.9	29.9	32.3	14.3	30.7	24.7	35.0	27.7
Zoology	33.8	18.3	30.5	32.9	24.4	32.5	32.2	31.7	31.4
Philosophy	25.0	6.6	22.0	18.9	2.4	18.2	25.5	61.2	31.3
History	21.4	28.7	23.9	19.6	10.5	19.0	16.5	49.5	26.7
Botany	39.0	21.2	35.2	35.6	21.5	34.7	30.9	38.4	32.3
Geography	23.9	11.8	21.1	32.6	7.5	33.9	18.5	60.8	28.1
Psychology	22.6	12.7	18.6	31.1	8.1	28.0	20.1	23.8	21.8
Journalism	27.6	47.2	35.3	20.4	27.4	20.9	15.7	50.7	29.8

	Percentage of graduate students who agree: females are not as dedicated			Percentage of faculty who agree: females are not as dedicated			Percentage of graduate students who agree: faculty does not take female students seriously		
	Males	Females	Total*	Males	Females	Total*	Males	Females	Total*
Anthropology	28.4	14.8	21.9	21.1	13.6	19.7	28.9	38.3	33.6
Physical and health education	16.1	7.6	12.6	17.0	4.8	12.1	8.3	13.0	10.1
German	37.2	14.6	24.7	21.9	13.2	20.0	20.3	27.3	23.9
Sociology	23.3	24.0	23.5	25.0	3.6	22.7	21.8	50.5	30.4
Educational psychology	18.4	7.2	12.0	22.1	14.9	20.3	6.2	17.8	12.7
Speech	32.3	17.0	25.2	19.4	12.1	17.4†	16.1	9.3	11.9
Spanish	38.4	20.7	27.4	18.9	16.4	17.9	8.0	12.0	10.7
Art	32.2	18.8	25.5	36.2	17.1	33.2	17.8	30.4	29.3
Dramatic arts	12.0	14.1	13.0	19.4	12.1	17.4†	12.3	24.9	19.4
Music	31.4	7.3	20.7	15.4	4.6	13.3	19.5	15.6	18.0
Secondary education	12.6	13.9	13.6	20.2	4.6	14.7	9.4	13.8	12.3‡
Social work	9.3	5.1	6.9	13.1	7.2	13.3	8.6	4.8	6.4
English	21.1	19.2	20.0	21.4	14.1	19.2	15.8	24.4	20.9
French	34.3	21.3	24.0	26.8	11.5	22.2	11.0	15.2	14.4
Library science	20.1	3.3	6.4	13.0	6.7	8.5	11.3	8.4	9.1
Elementary education	12.6	13.9	13.6	20.2	4.6	14.7	9.4	13.8	12.3‡
Nursing	—	1.8	1.8	18.0	8.3	8.4	—	8.5	8.4
Home economics	—	2.7	2.7	30.1	10.0	12.6	—	4.9	4.8

*Totals include respondents who did not state sex.
† Faculty questionnaire did not separate speech and dramatic arts. Same percentage used for both.
‡ Secondary education and elementary education not separated. Same percentage used for both.

fessors are viewed as taking women least seriously. That is true whether the respondents are men or women.

The overall percentage of those who agree that females are not as dedicated is a good predictor of the feminine enrollment in a field. In general, fields in which all incumbents view females as not as dedicated are male-dominated or have a masculine imagery. Where women are a minority, there is usually more prejudice against them.

TABLE 23
Correlation matrix: attitudes toward female graduate students

	Feminine imagery: semantic differential	Percentage of female graduate students	Graduate students who agree: females not as dedicated		
			Male	Female	Total
Feminine imagery: semantic differential	1.000				
Percentage of female graduate students	.97	1.000			
F not dedicated, male graduate students	—.17	—.01	1.000		
F not dedicated, female graduate students	—.36*	—.35‡	.40‡	1.000	
F not dedicated, total graduate students	—.60*	—.58*	—.83†	.75*	1.000
F not dedicated, male faculty	—.20	—.21	.49†	.39‡	.49*
F not dedicated, female faculty	—.07	—.04	.48†	.49†	.49*
F not dedicated, total faculty	—.47†	—.47†	.52*	.51*	.69*
Faculty does not take F seriously, male graduate students	—.63*	—.66*	.44†	.14	.58*
Faculty does not take F seriously, female graduate students	—.52*	—.60*	.22	.39‡	.55*
Faculty does not take F seriously, total graduate students	—.59*	—.64*	.42†	.45†	.70*

* $p < .001$
† $p < .01$
‡ $p < .05$

OTHER CORRELATES AND NON-CORRELATES Much has been written (e.g., Hubback, 1957; Arreger, 1966; and Poloma & Garland, 1970) about the conflicts between the spouse role and the occupational role, especially among professional women. Researchers have consistently found that whenever women feel conflicts between the two roles, the spouse role will take precedence, although some women avoid or alleviate this conflict by remaining single or by obtaining a divorce. Because such conflict is probably more severe for women in male fields, where they

Faculty who agree: females not dedicated			Graduate students who agree: faculty does not take female graduates seriously		
Male	Female	Total	Male	Female	Total
1.000					
.41†	1.000				
.92*	.45†	1.000			
.33‡	.21	.44†	1.000		
.18	.07	.38‡	.55*	1.000	
.35†	.28	.55*	.86*	.85*	1.000

may have to "prove" themselves, we hypothesized that the percentage of married female graduate students would be lower in those fields. This is indeed the case. There is a +.32 correlation ($p < .05$) between the percentage of married female students and the feminine imagery of a field. No significant correlation exists between the total percentage of married students or the percentage of married men and feminine imagery.

Because women experience more conflict than men in maintaining the student role, we further hypothesized that disciplines that have a higher percentage of part-time students would be more likely to be female-dominated fields. We found a $+.40$ correlation ($p <$ .05) between the percentage of women enrolled part time and feminine imagery. No significant correlation exists between the percentage of men or the total percentage of students enrolled part time and the imagery of a field. Thus, we cannot predict the femininity of a field from the number of men enrolled part time, but we can do so from the number of part-time women.

We speculated that, because admitting women into graduate study is still not an accepted practice in all fields, female-dominated fields would be more likely to be those whose incumbents are politically left or liberal. We found, however, no relationship between the percentage of faculty or graduate students who are left or liberal [faculty $r = +.09$ (n.s.) and graduate $r = +.06$ (n.s.)] and the percentage of graduate women within a discipline.

We also speculated that, because the academic division of labor appears to assign teaching to women and research to men, female fields would be more likely to be antiresearch. We measured this attitude by strong agreement to "My field is too research-oriented." Men, surprisingly, tended to agree with this item more than women (49 percent of the men in sociology, compared to 38 percent of the women; 47 percent of the men in German, compared to 36 percent of the women; and 27 percent of the men in geology, compared to 10 percent of the women). We found no relationship between agreement with this item and the feminine imagery of a field.

In general, the data suggest that although attitudes vary by sex, women and men within a given academic discipline are quite similar. Women in chemistry resemble their male colleagues more than they resemble women in French. Likewise, men and women in English are similar to one another and are little like men or women in more male fields. The overall pattern is that both men and women tend to cluster in disciplines that are associated with their traditional sex roles and that male or female minority members tend to take the characteristics associated with their discipline rather than those associated with their sex.

The scope of our data does not allow us to answer an important question: are women placed in certain disciplines because these disciplines rank low in power, privilege, and prestige, or do these disciplines rank low in power, privilege, and prestige because they are dominated by women? We feel that there is a reciprocal effect and that, at this point, both may be true. Historical evidence seems to indicate that in some instances women were placed in a field because it did not pay well (e.g., teaching), while in other instances they were invited into a discipline because it was compatible with their sex role (e.g., nursing). Today both processes work upon each other to create inequality, and as this chapter has demonstrated, sex-based inequality goes far beyond underrepresentation.

4. The Ascent to the Ivory Tower: Men's and Women's Plans for Academic Careers

One of the possible outcomes of total automation is the creation of machines that will be used just to create other machines. Some have viewed graduate education as a similar, although somewhat less automated, machine. Out of our sample of 32,963 graduate students, 11,821 (or 36 percent) plan to enter a career within academia, and many of these will probably teach graduate students who will then teach other graduate students. This chapter focuses on the choices graduate students make among three academic careers.[1] We used as a sample all 11,821 students (8,616 men and 3,205 women) who stated that they planned to enter college or university teaching, full-time research in a university, or junior college teaching. Table 24 examines the academic career aspirations of men and women by sex and field context.[2]

Several patterns are clear. In all field contexts, women are more apt to plan junior college teaching than men. About 16 percent of the women in both female-minority and equalitarian fields plan this career, compared to 6 percent of the men in female-minority fields and 12 percent in equalitarian fields. Whatever the female participation rate of a field, about 85 percent of the men plan to enter college or university teaching; women, however, are less likely to enter college or university teaching even in fields in which they are the majority of graduate students. As we saw in the previ-

---

[1] Excellent articles dealing with factors associated with student choice of academic careers include Currie et al. (1966) and Trow (1961).

[2] We have labeled as *female-minority* fields those in which women comprise less than 30 percent of the graduate students, according to U.S. Office of Education statistics. (Because women make up about 30 percent of all graduate students, this percentage was used as a base line.) *Equalitarian* fields are those in which women comprise 30 to 50 percent of graduate students, and *female-majority* fields are those in which women comprise over 50 percent of the students.

TABLE 24
Academic career plans, by sex and field context (in percentages; weighted totals in parentheses)

	College or university teaching	Full-time research	Junior college teaching	Total
Female minority				
Males	85.1	9.0	5.9	100.0 (130,552)
Females	71.4	12.5	16.1	100.0 (21,175)
Total	82.4	9.5	8.1	100.0 (151,727)
Equalitarian				
Males	86.4	1.9	11.7	100.0 (40,508)
Females	80.8	3.6	15.6	100.0 (15,226)
Total	84.9	2.3	12.8	100.0 (55,734)
Female majority				
Males	85.2	1.6	13.2	100.0 (49,624)
Females	69.4	2.0	28.6	100.0 (48,704)
Total	77.4	1.8	20.8	100.0 (98,328)

ous chapter, female-dominated fields are teaching- rather than research-oriented disciplines. This is confirmed by the finding that almost 10 percent of all students in female-minority fields plan to enter full-time academic research positions, compared to about 2 percent in equalitarian or female-majority fields.

According to estimates based on our sample of 60,000 faculty, women constitute 13 percent of American university faculty (9 percent in high-quality universities), 25 percent of college faculty, and 26 percent of junior college faculty. The patterns of career plans indicated in Table 24 are much like actual female faculty participation.

According to the National Opinion Research Center study (Hodge et al., 1964) of occupational prestige, the occupation of college professor ranks below only United States Supreme Court Justice, physician, nuclear physicist, scientist, state governor, and federal Cabinet member (and is tied with chemist and member of House of Representatives). Hodge did not differentiate among university, college, and junior college faculty but rather chose the generic term "college professor." Within academia, college or university teaching would seem to be more desirable, offering more rewards (including power, privilege, or prestige) than junior college teaching.[3]

We shall examine some of the reasons why a student chooses to teach in a junior college rather than in a university. If women exhibit the behavioral patterns usually associated with a university teacher yet still feel they will eventually teach at the junior college level, then we have possible evidence of injustice in the system. The alternative interpretation is that "water seeks its own level"— that women are more likely to opt for junior college teaching because they are not as qualified for university teaching as are men.

Career choice is not a random process. There are significant differences between individuals choosing a career in junior college teaching and those choosing college or university teaching. In general, those opting for a junior college career are less research-oriented, have a less positive self-image, and are less involved with their disciplines, their professors, and their fellow graduate students than those opting for careers within universities or colleges.

What is most dramatic are the strong differences by sex. The variables mentioned above affect both men and women, but they affect women much more strongly. In order for a woman to aspire to a more prestigious career, she must have those qualities associated with that career choice. If she does not, she is much less apt to choose a prestigious career than her male counterpart.

A term in common parlance is "super nigger"—a black who, to attain what the white man has attained, has to be twice as good as the white man. We see the same phenomenon revealed by our data—women who aspire toward university careers are more qualified than their male counterparts. Those who are not plan to end up in junior colleges. On the other hand, men opt for university academic careers whatever their qualifications.

We have previously demonstrated that male-dominated fields are the most likely to appear antifemale. Logic might dictate that women would be best off in fields that they numerically dominate. This proves not to be the case. In female-majority fields, men have higher aspirations than women and are less affected by career

---

[3] Maccoby (1963) asked junior college faculty to rate the comparative prestige of four teaching positions. His results indicated that the ordering of prestige went from university teaching (highest) to four-year-college teaching to junior college teaching to high school teaching (lowest).

choice factors. In female-dominated fields, the men, not the women, are the most visible. And since tradition accords the better jobs to men, they can aspire toward and end up in the better positions.

Equalitarian fields are truly that—fields in which there are relatively few differences between men and women. Both men and women are equally affected by career choice factors. Neither men nor women tend to be visible and, since tradition seems to dictate that neither one sex nor the other predominates, standards are more universalistic than in the other types of fields.

HIGHEST DEGREE EXPECTED Because less than 4 percent of junior college faculty hold a Ph.D., it would stand to reason that graduate students who expect to obtain a Ph.D. would be less likely to anticipate entering a junior college than those who plan to obtain a lower degree. Table 25 looks at academic career aspirations by highest degree expected, and we see that this is indeed the case.

Whether or not they expect a Ph.D., at all levels of representation women are more likely to plan to enter junior college teaching than men. This pattern is most evident in female-majority fields. About 4 percent of the men who expect to obtain the doctorate plan to enter junior college teaching, compared to 12 percent of the women. Even more interesting is the pattern among those who are less "qualified" for college or university teaching. Of the men who never expect to obtain a doctorate, 72 percent plan to enter college or university teaching, compared to 53 percent of the women. Differential career plans are not wholly the result of differential degree plans.

INTEREST IN ACADEMIC CAREER Although all the graduate students in our subsample plan to enter a career within academia, not all are equally interested in an academic career. We hypothesized that those who expressed the strongest interest in an academic career would be more likely to enter university teaching. Differential career plans may thus be explained in part by differential interest in an academic career.

Academic career interest was measured by, "Are you interested in an academic career?" The possible responses were "very interested," "fairly interested," "fairly uninterested," and "very uninterested." Because almost all respondents chose one of the first two categories, we collapsed the "uninterested" responses into one category.

TABLE 25 Academic career plans, by sex, field context, and highest degree expected (in percentages)	College or university teaching	Full-time research	Junior college teaching	Total
Female minority				
Males—Ph.D.	87.1	9.3	3.5	88,108
Females—Ph.D.	78.6	13.5	7.9	13,435
				Gamma = .293
Males—no Ph.D.	71.2	4.2	24.6	18,871
Females—no Ph.D.	53.2	5.6	41.2	4,503
				Gamma = .354
Equalitarian				
Males—Ph.D.	93.7	1.9	4.4	25,825
Females—Ph.D.	87.6	3.9	8.5	8,359
				Gamma = .349
Males—no Ph.D.	75.6	0.5	23.9	9,068
Females—no Ph.D.	71.9	3.2	24.9	4,781
				Gamma = .077
Female majority				
Males—Ph.D.	95.1	1.2	3.7	24,674
Females—Ph.D.	86.1	1.7	12.2	21,923
				Gamma = .512
Males—no Ph.D.	71.6	1.5	27.0	17,427
Females—no Ph.D.	53.1	2.2	44.6	17,279
				Gamma = .370

Interest in an academic career is a stronger predictor of career plans among women than among men (Table 26). Women who express strong interest in academic careers are much more likely to plan to enter college or university teaching than women who express little interest; however, men who express little interest in an academic career are more likely to plan entrance into college or university teaching than women of the same disposition.

An interesting pattern develops among women expressing little interest in academic careers. In male fields, the "uninterested" women are more likely to seek careers as full-time researchers; in less research-oriented (female) fields, they plan to enter junior college teaching. Alternative academic career choice appears to be a matter of what types of jobs other than university teaching are available.

	College or university teaching	Full-time research	Junior college teaching	Total
TABLE 26 Academic career plans by sex, field context, and interest in an academic career (in percentages)				
Female minority				
Males—strong interest	87.7	8.1	4.2	88,442
Females—strong interest	76.3	9.7	14.0	14,554
				Gamma = .382
Males—fair interest	82.4	10.0	7.6	35,329
Females—fair interest	63.8	16.8	19.3	5,592
				Gamma = .434
Males—not interested	44.8	12.7	42.5	5,595
Females—not interested	36.6	32.1	31.3	761
				Gamma = .202
Equalitarian				
Males—strong interest	87.4	1.6	11.0	32,991
Females—strong interest	84.0	3.2	12.8	10,449
				Gamma = .130
Males—fair interest	80.9	3.6	15.5	5,713
Females—fair interest	76.5	3.7	19.8	4,139
				Gamma = .130
Males—not interested	81.0	1.3	17.7	1,098
Females—not interested	48.8	12.0	39.2	500
				Gamma = .574
Female majority				
Males—strong interest	89.7	1.6	8.6	34,362
Females—strong interest	72.7	1.8	25.5	33,494
				Gamma = .532
Males—fair interest	76.5	1.2	22.3	13,646
Females—fair interest	62.9	2.0	35.1	13,120
				Gamma = .310
Males—not interested	75.5	3.3	21.2	990
Females—not interested	51.9	5.9	42.1	1,786
				Gamma = .460

SPECIALIZATION

The curriculum at most junior colleges is quite general. In sociology, for example, most departments at the junior college level offer courses in introductory sociology or social problems, but few offer more specialized courses such as Sociology of Religion or Mass Communications. We would expect that students who do not plan an academic specialty (generalists) would be more likely candidates for a junior college teaching position than those who do plan a specialty. Table 27 compares those who stated that they do not intend to specialize with those who stated that they definitely have chosen or definitely plan to choose a specialty.

	College or university teaching	Full-time research	Junior college teaching	Total
Female minority				
Males—not specializing	64.6	7.7	24.8	5,933
Females—not specializing	28.0	5.7	66.3	1,177
				Gamma = .673
Males—definitely specializing	84.8	9.3	5.9	54,337
Females—definitely specializing	77.1	13.2	9.7	8,886
				Gamma = .237
Equalitarian				
Males—not specializing	61.6	0.4	38.0	2,848
Females—not specializing	62.2	0.0	37.8	528
				Gamma = .009
Males—definitely specializing	87.0	2.0	11.0	16,046
Females—definitely specializing	80.3	5.9	13.8	6,495
				Gamma = .220
Female majority				
Males—not specializing	71.2	0.0	28.8	2,161
Females—not specializing	35.7	0.0	64.3	2,747
				Gamma = .295
Males—definitely specializing	89.5	2.0	8.5	16,316
Females—definitely specializing	81.3	2.7	16.0	16,806
				Gamma = .321

TABLE 27
Academic career plans by sex, field context, and plans for specialization (in percentages)

Those who plan to specialize are indeed more likely to plan a college or university teaching or a research career than those who do not. Note that men and women are similar in equalitarian fields, but that in those fields in which either sex has a strong majority, women who do not plan to specialize are much more likely than men in the same category to plan to enter junior college teaching. Among those students who do have specialization plans, women are still less likely than men to plan a college or university teaching career. Having a definite specialty is strongly associated with women planning university teaching. Not specializing greatly decreases a woman's likelihood of entering college or university teaching but has a much smaller effect on men.

PROFESSIONAL ACTIVITIES For students planning careers as college or university teachers, many graduate school activities can be looked upon as aspects of anticipatory socialization. We would expect that graduate students who are actively involved in professional activities would be more likely to plan careers in college or university teaching. We shall examine tables dealing with three aspects of graduate school professional activity (meeting attendance, engagement in scholarly work, and article publication)—each requiring increasing involvement on the part of the student.

Table 28 compares career plans of students who have and those who have not attended professional meetings. Meeting participation is a somewhat passive activity, generally involving little output on the part of the student; still, those who attend meetings should be more involved in their fields than those who have never attended.

Table 29 gives the percentages of students who state yes or no to, "Are you currently engaged in any scholarly or research work that you expect to lead to publication under your own name?" Since teaching loads are generally heavy in junior colleges and teaching is the primary function of these colleges, we expected that individuals who are not engaged in scholarly or research work would be more likely to plan a junior college teaching career.

Table 30 compares graduate students who have published an article with those who have not. Students who have published not only have been engaged in scholarly work but have had their work presented to members of the profession. They should be much more likely to plan university teaching or research careers than nonpublishers.

Following our general model, we expected that if there were not

	College or university teaching	Full-time research	Junior college teaching	Total
Female minority				
Males—attended	84.0	9.5	6.5	98,419
Females—attended	74.0	12.4	13.5	15,288
				Gamma = .291
Males—never attended	85.1	7.2	7.2	31,755
Females—never attended	64.6	12.2	23.2	5,780
				Gamma = .502
Equalitarian				
Males—attended	83.4	2.3	14.3	28,534
Females—attended	81.8	3.8	14.4	12,029
				Gamma = .046
Males—never attended	94.0	0.6	5.3	11,874
Females—never attended	76.9	2.8	20.3	3,178
				Gamma = .644
Female majority				
Males—attended	86.4	1.8	11.8	38,617
Females—attended	67.5	1.6	30.9	35,163
				Gamma = .506
Males—never attended	81.0	0.9	18.2	10,939
Females—never attended	74.3	3.2	22.5	13,406
				Gamma = .176

TABLE 28 Academic career plans by sex, field context, and meeting attendance (in percentages)

particularistic criteria, the actively involved of either sex would be more likely to plan a college or university teaching career than those not actively involved. Although engagement in professional activities reflects the career plans of both men and women, it has a much stronger relationship with those of women. In the cases of both men and women, students who are professionally involved are less likely to plan junior college teaching careers. We note that, for instance, few men or women who engage in scholarly work in male-dominated fields plan to enter junior colleges; however, among those not engaged in scholarly work, 14 percent of the men, compared

TABLE 29 Academic career plans by sex, field context, and engagement in scholarly work (in percentages)	College or university teaching	Full-time research	Junior college teaching	Total
Female minority				
Males— scholarly work	85.3	11.7	3.0	84,401
Females— scholarly work	77.2	16.8	6.0	10,794
				Gamma = .261
Males—no scholarly work	82.1	4.1	13.8	46,054
Females—no scholarly work	65.3	8.2	26.5	10,230
				Gamma = .396
Equalitarian				
Males— scholarly work	91.7	2.9	5.4	20,608
Females— scholarly work	88.6	5.5	5.9	6,609
				Gamma = .163
Males—no scholarly work	81.1	0.7	18.3	19,777
Females—no scholarly work	74.8	2.1	23.1	8,602
				Gamma = .173
Female majority				
Males— scholarly work	93.4	3.4	3.3	21,194
Females— scholarly work	77.7	2.3	20.1	17,944
				Gamma = .609
Males—no scholarly work	79.0	0.3	20.7	28,327
Females—no scholarly work	64.2	1.9	33.9	30,341
				Gamma = .344

to 27 percent of the women, plan junior college teaching. Only in equalitarian fields are women who publish more likely to plan careers in university teaching or research than their male counterparts. Among the nonpublishers, the pattern reverts to men being more likely to enter the prestigious careers.

TABLE 30		College or university teaching	Full-time research	Junior college teaching	Total
Academic career plans by sex, field context, and article publication (in percentages)	*Female minority*				
	Males— published	82.5	16.2	1.3	32,173
	Females— published	73.8	23.2	3.0	4,039
					Gamma = .250
	Males—not published	84.9	6.7	8.4	96,094
	Females—not published	71.1	10.1	18.8	16,310
					Gamma = .382
	Equalitarian				
	Males— published	74.8	5.0	20.2	6,229
	Females— published	82.7	11.2	5.1	1,435
					Gamma = .306
	Males—not published	88.6	1.2	10.2	33,597
	Females—not published	81.0	2.8	16.2	13,235
					Gamma = .284
	Female majority				
	Males— published	89.0	6.4	4.6	6,085
	Females— published	82.7	4.0	13.4	32,000
					Gamma = .274
	Males—not published	84.5	1.0	14.6	41,604
	Females—not published	69.9	2.0	28.1	42,865
					Gamma = .393

The general pattern is as follows: for both men and women, engagement in professional activities increases the likelihood of entering college or university teaching or research; among those engaging in professional activities, however, women are more likely than men to plan to enter junior college teaching, and among those not engaging in professional activities, women are much more likely than men to do so.

RESEARCH ORIENTATION Interest in teaching versus research and planned entrance into college or university teaching produce a curvilinear relationship (Table 31). Students most heavily interested in research generally are most likely to plan to enter full-time research positions. Interest in a university teaching career increases among students who want a combination of teaching and research but declines among those who are heavily interested in teaching. The heavily teaching-oriented are most likely to reject college or university teaching in favor of junior college teaching.

Among the heavily research-oriented, women at all participation levels are more likely than men to plan to enter full-time research positions. The actual pattern seems to be that women become research associates[4]—lower level research positions than the faculty-equivalent appointments usually granted to men. Thus, the heavily research-oriented men are more likely to opt for university teaching positions than are women.

As we might suspect, among students with heavy teaching interests, women plan to apply their interests in junior colleges, and men are more likely to plan a college or university setting. Almost nobody with heavy teaching interests plans to become a researcher. Teaching-oriented women are more likely to plan junior college teaching careers if they are in fields in which they are either a numerical minority or a majority.

Closely allied to research orientation is the desire to advance the

[4] For an amplification of the "research associate" position among women, see Bradburn et al. (1970) and Bernard (1964). A letter addressed to the Carnegie project from a female research assistant in microbiology at a high-quality university stated in part:

I work for a woman in the Medical School. She is quiet and for the most part has swallowed a lot of pride and has calmly accepted the fourth class treatment handed or rather thrown at her. She is not alone. She is not a faculty member. She is as high as a woman can get in our department, which is the title of Research Associate. This title, of course, does not have a tenure clause attached so that should she not be able to obtain outside support from NIH [National Institutes of Health] they would have no proper recourse except to ask her to leave. Our department is considered lenient because it allows its Research Associates to write their own grant proposals. This does not entitle them to be principal investigators or publish as such despite the fact that they do the actual work themselves.

TABLE 31 *Academic career plans by sex, field context, and teaching-research orientation (in percentages)*

	College or university teaching	Full-time research	Junior college teaching	Total
Female minority				
"Very heavily in research"				
Males	50.2	49.5	0.3	6,699
Females	27.5	71.4	1.2	1,768
				Gamma = .453
"In both but leaning toward research"				
Males	80.9	17.7	1.4	39,498
Females	75.5	21.5	3.0	5,421
				Gamma = .162
"In both but leaning toward teaching"				
Males	91.0	1.6	7.5	60,099
Females	86.2	2.3	11.5	8,091
				Gamma = .229
"Very heavily in teaching"				
Males	82.5	0.6	16.9	19,970
Females	61.2	0.0	38.8	5,131
				Gamma = .501
Equalitarian				
"Very heavily in research"				
Males	64.9	13.6	21.5	1,111
Females	45.8	51.1	3.1	631
				Gamma = .136
"In both but leaning toward research"				
Males	91.2	5.7	3.2	6,899
Females	90.0	8.3	1.7	2,430
				Gamma = .057
"In both but leaning toward teaching"				
Males	92.0	0.8	7.1	16,769
Females	87.8	0.4	11.9	5,569
				Gamma = .237
"Very heavily in teaching"				
Males	84.4	0.4	15.3	13,779
Females	74.4	0.0	25.6	5,961
				Gamma = .302

TABLE 31 *(continued)*

	College or university teaching	Full-time research	Junior college teaching	Total
Female majority				
"Very heavily in research"				
Males	63.4	36.6	0.0	624
Females	44.6	55.4	0.0	543
				Gamma = .366
"In both but leaning toward research"				
Males	92.0	5.4	2.7	5,344
Females	72.8	6.9	20.3	5,885
				Gamma = .624
"In both but leaning toward teaching"				
Males	91.9	0.8	7.3	22,960
Females	75.6	0.9	23.4	20,455
				Gamma = .571
"Very heavily in teaching"				
Males	77.6	0.4	22.0	18,397
Females	63.0	0.3	36.7	19,533
				Gamma = .341

state of knowledge in a discipline. It would seem that students who agree with the item "I hope to make significant contributions to knowledge in my field" would be less likely to plan junior college teaching careers than those who disagree with this item. Table 32 compares career plans of those who strongly agree and those who strongly disagree with this item.

Unlike students with strong research orientations, those with strong interest in contributing to knowledge in their fields do not overwhelmingly plan to enter research positions, but they are less likely to plan to enter junior college teaching positions.

The greatest disparity appears between men and women in male-dominated fields. Whatever the level of interest in generating knowledge, about 83 percent of the men plan to enter college or university teaching. Among women, 79 percent of those with a strong interest in generating knowledge, but only 38 percent of those with no interest, plan to enter college or university teaching.

TABLE 32		College or university teaching	Full-time research	Junior college teaching	Total
Academic career plans by sex, field context, and interest in making significant contributions to knowledge (in percentages)	**Female minority**				
	Males—strong interest	83.5	13.6	3.0	57,667
	Females—strong interest	78.7	17.8	3.5	6,853
				Gamma = .148	
	Males—no interest	82.1	1.2	16.7	2,399
	Females—no interest	38.1	2.9	59.0	1,202
				Gamma = .752	
	Equalitarian				
	Males—strong interest	87.9	2.9	9.3	17,187
	Females—strong interest	91.4	3.8	4.8	4,684
				Gamma = .193	
	Males—no interest	81.6	0.0	18.4	724
	Females—no interest	64.5	0.0	35.5	389
				Gamma = .418	
	Female majority				
	Males—strong interest	92.6	3.1	4.3	15,272
	Females—strong interest	79.0	4.5	16.4	14,468
				Gamma = .537	
	Males—no interest	43.5	0.0	56.5	2,225
	Females—no interest	50.2	0.0	49.8	2,133
				Gamma = .134	

RELATIONS WITH PROFESSORS One of the functions of a graduate school is to instill in its students a professional self-image. Crucial to the creation of this self-image are a student's professors (Becker & Carper, 1956). We hypothesized that those students who have close relationships with their professors would be more apt to plan non-junior college careers. This may be true for several reasons. First, graduate students who have a professional self-image may find more satisfaction outside the junior college setting. Second, students who have a close relationship with a professor may receive his help in obtaining better jobs. Table 33 examines graduate students' career plans by the quality of their relationships with the professors closest to them.

This item works to a greater degree among women than among men. For example, in female-minority fields, 71 percent of the

	College or university teaching	Full-time research	Junior college teaching	Total
TABLE 33 Academic career plans by sex, field context, and relationship with closest professor (in percentages)				
Female minority				
"As a colleague"				
Males	84.2	12.5	3.4	35,382
Females	71.0	15.4	13.6	4,058
				Gamma = .378
"As an apprentice"				
Males	87.9	9.1	3.0	31,129
Females	81.1	9.3	9.7	4,830
				Gamma = .271
"As a student"				
Males	82.0	8.6	9.4	41,797
Females	68.6	14.9	16.5	8,665
				Gamma = .329
"No contact outside classroom"				
Males	82.2	3.8	14.1	16,536
Females	57.5	6.4	36.1	2,416
				Gamma = .529
Equalitarian				
"As a colleague"				
Males	91.1	2.3	6.6	12,515
Females	90.6	3.4	6.0	4,060
				Gamma = .024
"As an apprentice"				
Males	89.5	2.1	8.4	11,119
Females	79.1	3.4	17.5	3,314
				Gamma = .378
"As a student"				
Males	77.6	1.5	21.0	12,474
Females	81.0	3.2	15.8	5,349
				Gamma = .115
"No contact outside classroom"				
Males	91.6	1.2	7.2	3,593
Females	68.1	2.4	29.5	2,059
				Gamma = .670

	College or university teaching	Full-time research	Junior college teaching	Total
Female majority				
"As a colleague"				
Males	90.3	1.6	8.1	14,738
Females	75.5	2.8	21.3	13,316
				Gamma = .491
"As an apprentice"				
Males	91.1	1.6	7.2	10,993
Females	80.9	2.8	16.2	5,973
				Gamma = .410
"As a student"				
Males	84.7	1.7	13.6	15,143
Females	63.5	1.7	34.8	17,520
				Gamma = .519
"No contact outside classroom"				
Males	67.2	1.7	31.1	7,152
Females	63.6	1.4	35.0	11,010
				Gamma = .081

NOTE: A fifth choice, "an employee," had too few cases for stable percentaging. See question 29 of the graduate student questionnaire, Appendix C.

women with a collegial relationship with a professor plan to enter college or university teaching, compared to 58 percent of the women who have no contact with professors outside the classroom. Whatever their relationships with their closest professors, over 80 percent of the men in male-dominated fields plan to enter college or university teaching. Men with closer professorial relationships are, however, more likely to plan university research careers and less likely to plan junior college teaching careers than men who have no contact with professors outside the classroom.

In equalitarian fields, men appear less affected by their relationships with professors than are women. There is little difference between men and women with collegial relationships—about 91 percent plan to enter college or university teaching—but among students with no contact with professors, 92 percent of the men still plan a college or university teaching career, compared to 68 percent of the women.

In female-majority fields, differences are large at every level except "no contact." For example, among graduate students who have a collegial relationship, 8 percent of the men plan junior college teaching careers, compared to 21 percent of the women. "No contact" has a roughly equal effect on men and women. In equalitarian and female-minority fields, more research activities are available than in female-majority fields. Because they have few research opportunities, students in female-dominated fields depend more on professors for job opportunities and ego support than those in other fields; hence, those with no contact with professors are more likely to plan to enter junior colleges.

INFORMAL INTERACTION WITH FELLOW STUDENTS Socialization in graduate school does not take place only in formal classroom situations or with professors. One of the most powerful mechanisms of socialization is informal interaction among fellow students (Becker et al., 1961, and Becker & Carper, 1956). We hypothesized that students who engage in informal interaction with their fellow students are more likely to choose occupations that involve them more in their disciplines, that is, college or university teaching or research.

Table 34 compares the career plans of men and women who meet with their fellow students once a week or more and those of men and women isolates who meet informally with their fellow students once a year or less.

Students who meet informally with their fellow students are more likely to plan a college or university teaching career than those who do not. Isolates are probably less involved not only with their fellow students but also with departmental activity in general. Still, female isolates are more likely to choose junior college teaching than their male counterparts. In male-dominated fields, there are only minor differences in career plans between men and women who see their fellow students informally once a week or more; among the isolates, however, 82 percent of the men (the same percentage as those heavily involved in informal interaction), compared to 59 percent of the women, plan to enter college or university teaching.

There is little difference between men and women in equalitarian fields; they are similarly affected by informal interaction. In female-majority fields, men are affected less than women; even among students heavily involved in informal interaction, 7 percent of the men versus 14 percent of the women opt for junior college teaching careers.

	College or university teaching	Full-time research	Junior college teaching	Total
TABLE 34 *Academic career plans by sex, field context, and frequency of informal interaction with fellow students (in percentages)*				
Female minority				
"Once a week or more"				
Males	82.2	11.2	6.6	20,214
Females	80.1	9.8	10.1	2,604
				Gamma = .083
"Once a year or less"				
Males	82.3	7.9	9.8	11,667
Females	59.4	9.5	31.0	3,002
				Gamma = .515
Equalitarian				
"Once a week or more"				
Males	91.6	1.7	6.8	17,232
Females	88.2	2.9	8.9	6,322
				Gamma = .179
"Once a year or less"				
Males	62.0	3.0	35.1	2,938
Females	57.5	2.9	39.6	1,559
				Gamma = .092
Female majority				
"Once a week or more"				
Males	91.2	1.9	6.8	19,613
Females	84.0	2.4	13.7	16,829
				Gamma = .331
"Once a year or less"				
Males	66.6	0.7	32.7	5,617
Females	52.3	0.4	47.3	10,177
				Gamma = .292

SELF-IMAGE Earlier in this chapter we noted Maccoby's finding that academics themselves grant low esteem to junior college teachers. We hypothesized that graduate students with lower self-esteem would be more likely to enter fields with lower prestige—or, conversely, students with a positive self-image would be more likely to seek more prestigious academic positions. Overall, women are less likely to have a self-image as a top student than are their male colleagues.

For example, in the physical sciences 23 percent of the men and 13 percent of the women state that they are among the best students in their department. In the humanities 42 percent of the men versus 33 percent of the women state that they are among the best (Feldman, 1971*b,* p. 31). Women are also less likely to consider themselves intellectuals than male students. For example, 61 percent of the men in the physical sciences and 74 percent of the men in the humanities view themselves as intellectuals, compared to 48 per-

TABLE 35 Academic career plans by sex, field context, and self-rating of standing within department (in percentages)	College or university teaching	Full-time research	Junior college teaching	Total
Female minority				
"Among the best"				
Males	86.8	9.5	3.7	44,736
Females	83.6	12.4	4.1	5,228
				Gamma = .123
"About average"				
Males	79.8	9.1	11.1	30,206
Females	60.5	15.1	24.4	6,235
				Gamma = .416
Equalitarian				
"Among the best"				
Males	84.8	2.2	13.0	15,428
Females	86.7	3.3	10.0	4,671
				Gamma = .084
"About average"				
Males	87.2	1.1	11.7	6,975
Females	81.7	0.5	17.9	3,883
				Gamma = .214
Female majority				
"Among the best"				
Males	93.1	1.5	5.4	18,934
Females	76.7	2.1	21.2	18,055
				Gamma = .604
"About average"				
Males	74.4	0.4	25.2	12,467
Females	63.1	2.1	34.8	8,830
				Gamma = .246

cent of the women in the physical sciences and 66 percent of the women in the humanities (Feldman, 1971*b*, p. 32).

In their study of student interest in an academic career, Currie et al. (1966) found that those with an intellectual self-image were most likely to express an interest in an academic career. In the following two tables we compare career plans of graduate students with divergent self-images. In Table 35 those who state that they are among the best in their department are compared with those who state that they are about average.[5] Table 36 compares those who strongly agree that they are intellectuals with those who strongly disagree.

Similar patterns are found in Tables 35 and 36. Students with more positive self-images are more likely to reject junior college teaching careers. For example, among women in male-dominated fields, 84 percent of those who state they are among the best students in their department opt for college or university teaching, compared to 61 percent of those who see themselves as about average. The variations among men are not as wide as for women, but nevertheless they support the relationship between self-image and career plans.

The greatest difference between men and women is found among those in female-dominated fields who rate themselves among the best. In this category 93 percent of the men opt for college or university teaching, compared to 77 percent of the women. The superior male student in female-dominated fields stands out, and he may more easily obtain more prestigious academic positions. The superior female student in female-dominated fields is "just another woman," and there is probably no great push to place her as well as her male colleagues.

The effects of the self-image of intellectualism do not create a regular pattern. In general, students with a strong intellectual self-image are less apt to choose junior college teaching. In female-dominated fields, women follow a statistical pattern similar to the pattern usually associated with men. That is, whether they strongly agree or disagree that they are intellectuals, about 73 percent plan to enter college or university teaching. Among men in female-dominated fields, 94 percent of those with strong intellectual self-images plan to do so, compared to 81 percent who strongly disagree that

---

[5] The questionnaire contained the option "below average," but so few students chose this option that we do not have a stable percentage base.

TABLE 36 Academic career plans by sex, field context, and intellectual self-image (in percentages)	College or university teaching	Full-time research	Junior college teaching	Total
Female minority				
"Intellectual"				
Males	85.3	12.7	2.0	20,565
Females	83.0	10.5	6.5	3,271
				Gamma = .105
"Not intellectual"				
Males	71.5	7.7	20.8	10,115
Females	67.2	6.5	26.4	1,018
				Gamma = .110
Equalitarian				
"Intellectual"				
Males	93.2	4.0	2.8	5,513
Females	93.5	1.7	4.8	2,079
				Gamma = .009
"Not intellectual"				
Males	69.6	1.0	29.5	1,956
Females	66.2	2.0	31.8	979
				Gamma = .070
Female majority				
"Intellectual"				
Males	93.9	1.6	4.5	7,354
Females	72.2	2.5	25.3	7,191
				Gamma = .709
"Not intellectual"				
Males	81.3	0.0	18.7	3,304
Females	73.8	1.5	24.8	3,482
				Gamma = .204

they are intellectuals. Still, in either case, men are more likely to plan to enter college or university teaching than women.

In general, self-image is a good predictor of academic career plans, but the differences between the sexes are not as strong as those we found in other items.

INSTITU- TIONAL QUALITY In his study of graduate education, Bernard Berelson examined the effects of institutional quality on graduate education. He stated in part:

Certainly the better schools attract the better students (who then get to associate with a better group of students, for the stimulation and instruction that in itself provides) so their products should be better by that fact alone, even if their training were equivalent. At least this much can be said, I think: the better institutions get better students to start with, so that they are that far ahead in turning out a superior product (Berelson, 1960, p. 125).

Berelson then demonstrated that as institutional quality declines, the productivity of its Ph.D.'s declines. We may expand Berelson's argument. We hypothesized that students in high-quality universities would be less likely to plan junior college teaching careers than students in lower-quality universities.[6] Productive faculty may be role models for their students, encouraging them to seek a career in which they may carry out research. Since productive faculty are more often found in high-quality institutions and since higher-quality institutions probably do not view the training of junior college faculty as one of their functions, we would suspect that as institutional quality declines, the percentage of students planning junior college teaching careers increases.

In general, institutional quality has a much stronger effect on women than on men (Table 37). The percentage of men planning a college or university teaching career declines only slightly as the quality of the institution declines. On the other hand, 73 percent of the women from high-quality universities who are in male-dominated fields plan a college or university teaching career, compared to 62 percent in low-quality institutions. As quality declines, we also see a decrease in the percentage of women planning to be full-time university researchers. Women have to be bright to enter top-quality universities; even so, bright women are not so likely as less able men to plan to enter more prestigious academic positions.

What is most dramatic is the stability of the percentage of men who plan to enter junior college teaching in contrast with the large increase as the quality of the institution declines in the percentage of women who plan to do so. Thus, in equalitarian fields, 4 percent of the men in high-quality institutions versus 6 percent of the women plan junior college teaching careers. Within low-quality institutions, the percentage of men in these fields planning to enter junior colleges rises to only 8 percent, compared to 31 percent for women. We have no supporting data for the supposition, but it

[6] See Appendix A for a discussion of the criteria used in judging institutional quality.

	College or university teaching	Full-time research	Junior college teaching	Total
TABLE 37 *Academic career plans by sex, field context, and quality of current institution (in percentages)*				
Female minority				
High-quality university				
Males	87.3	10.8	1.9	33,586
Females	73.3	18.3	8.4	6,094
				Gamma = .427
Medium-quality university				
Males	86.7	9.8	3.5	38,963
Females	61.5	11.1	10.8	4,345
				Gamma = .363
Low-quality university				
Males	85.7	8.9	5.5	31,845
Females	61.5	11.1	27.5	4,345
				Gamma = .580
Equalitarian				
High-quality university				
Males	92.6	3.9	3.6	9,302
Females	91.0	3.4	5.6	4,390
				Gamma = .106
Medium-quality university				
Males	89.8	2.4	7.8	10,250
Females	91.0	3.3	10.7	4,424
				Gamma = .175
Low-quality university				
Males	88.7	2.9	8.4	5,067
Females	64.5	4.5	31.0	2,801
				Gamma = .617
Female majority				
High-quality university				
Males	93.2	2.3	4.6	8,282
Females	81.4	2.3	16.3	7,848
				Gamma = .515
Medium-quality university				
Males	89.9	1.1	8.9	14,275

	College or university teaching	Full-time research	Junior college teaching	Total
Female majority				
Medium-quality university				
Females	81.2	2.7	16.2	12,866
				Gamma = .340
Low-quality university				
Males	86.2	2.8	11.0	10,848
Females	72.2	3.1	24.8	9,200
				Gamma = .411

may be that low-quality institutions see their function to be training men for university careers and women for junior college teaching; at the higher-quality institutions, junior college teaching is not a prime objective for students, but these institutions may assume that more women than men will end up in such positions.

5. Dedication to Graduate Study: Beliefs and Behavior

Since the rebirth of the feminist movement, a new term has entered our vocabulary—*sexism:* prejudicial attitudes or behavior toward women simply on the basis of their sex.[1] Some women maintain that American graduate education is a sexist institution, containing many male faculty who believe that women are not equally as interested in their fields as men. We will take as a measure of prejudice within graduate education the response to the statement, "The female graduate students in my department are not as dedicated as the males."[2] When we examine the percentages of faculty and students who agree with the statement (Table 38), we find that they are the minority of both students and faculty. As we might expect, men are more likely to agree with this item than women, but the attitude toward women appears to be the same whether the individuals are students or faculty. Thus generational differences are not evident.

Even though only 20 to 25 percent of the faculty and graduate students in American higher education believe that women are not as dedicated as men, we cannot simply dismiss as meaningless the attitude of a small minority. Individuals with this attitude may have a key part in the careers of female students, and the belief that women lack dedication affects how they are educated (from the point of view of both faculty and peer interaction). As we will find, this view of women is not just another aspect of generalized prejudice or conservatism; rather, it is an independent phenomenon, and many who hold it are merely reporting what they actually see.

[1] Although it is not used in this manner, there is no reason why this term could not be applied to prejudicial behavior or attitudes toward men on the basis of their sex.

[2] All data dealing with correlates of agreement to this item are from a systematic sample. The smallest cell (female faculty in equalitarian fields) has 915 cases.

TABLE 38 *Faculty and student responses to "female graduates not as dedicated as males," by sex and field context (in percentages)*

	Strongly agree	Agree with reservations	Disagree with reservations	Strongly disagree	Total
	Faculty				
Female minority					
Males	6.0	19.4	33.4	41.2	11,014
Females	2.8	8.5	25.0	63.7	7,436
					Gamma = .394
Equalitarian					
Males	4.7	16.8	32.1	46.5	13,653
Females	2.7	4.5	19.9	72.9	6,605
					Gamma = .479
Female majority					
Males	6.6	14.6	31.4	47.4	12,317
Females	4.1	5.9	18.5	71.5	17,560
					Gamma = .418
	Graduate students				
Female minority					
Males	6.6	18.7	42.1	32.5	50,538
Females	3.1	15.4	28.2	53.2	50,632
					Gamma = .303
Equalitarian					
Males	5.2	22.3	34.3	38.2	61,377
Females	3.7	13.1	25.6	57.7	34,902
					Gamma = .323
Female majority					
Males	2.8	14.9	33.3	48.9	56,572
Females	2.6	7.3	26.1	64.0	96,639
					Gamma = .276

On the surface, women do not appear as dedicated. Given equal opportunities, however, they become as dedicated and productive as their male counterparts. The key is that many women appear to be denied the equal opportunities—even though many enter graduate school seemingly better qualified than men.

We will first demonstrate the independent nature of this view of women. Our dependent variable for the tables that follow is the questionnaire item "The female graduate students in my depart-

ment are not as dedicated as the males." The reader should be reminded that this questionnaire was administered in the spring of
1969—before the real birth of the recent feminist movement and
especially before the vast mass media coverage; thus, neither men
nor women were as sensitized to the issue as they would have been
even a year later.

One factor that we expected to be related to disagreement to
"females not as dedicated" was political radicalism. The radical

TABLE 39 Percentages of faculty and students who agree that females are not as dedicated as males, by approval of radical activism, sex, and field context (weighted totals in parentheses)	Students		Faculty	
	Males	*Females*	*Males*	*Females*
Female minority				
Unreservedly approve	23.7 (1,576)	13.3 (2,252)	17.3 (344)	13.7 (192)
Approve with reservations	24.6 (15,960)	18.5 (18,724)	23.8 (4,074)	10.1 (3,135)
Disapprove with reservations	23.7 (19,275)	20.2 (20,532)	25.2 (4,641)	11.6 (2,979)
Unreservedly disapprove	29.4 (13,305)	16.8 (8,430)	30.7 (1,890)	12.9 (1,098)
Gamma	−.073	−.016	−.107	−.070
Equalitarian				
Unreservedly approve	23.4 (3,049)	17.3 (1,548)	18.4 (544)	32.6 (115)
Approve with reservations	20.0 (24,836)	16.0 (14,513)	21.3 (6,561)	6.1 (2,589)
Disapprove with reservations	35.3 (20,782)	22.1 (12,435)	21.5 (4,846)	7.4 (2,964)
Unreservedly disapprove	30.4 (12,211)	9.2 (5,126)	22.8 (1,646)	6.8 (867)
Gamma	−.208	+.022	−.027	+.050
Female majority				
Unreservedly approve	20.1 (2,368)	8.9 (2,583)	18.7 (755)	7.9 (555)
Approve with reservations	19.2 (21,742)	15.3 (32,474)	22.1 (6,088)	12.0 (7,653)
Disapprove with reservations	19.2 (20,473)	8.7 (37,384)	19.1 (4,256)	8.9 (7,033)
Unreservedly disapprove	13.9 (9,965)	4.5 (23,545)	25.4 (1,168)	6.7 (2,234)
Gamma	+.084	+.360	+.001	+.164

movement has taken as an issue the position of many minorities in American society. Even though some women in the radical movement claim their job is to type and cook while the men become leaders, we would expect that those sympathetic to the movement would be more apt to see women as dedicated. Probably the best indicator of radicalism, according to an extensive study using Carnegie data (Hirschi & Zelan, 1971), is the item "What do you think of the recent rise of radical student activism?"

The data show no regular relationship between approval of radicalism and agreement that females are not as dedicated (Table 39). In certain instances the relationship is slightly positive, while in other cases it is slightly negative.

As an additional check of politics against attitudes toward women, we examined the relationship between self-designated political stance (left, liberal, middle-of-the-road, mildly conservative, strongly conservative) and agreement with "females not as dedicated." There was again no consistent relationship. It thus appears that the perception of women's performance is not a political item.

It may be, however, that women are viewed as another minority group and that those who disapprove of the advancement of other minorities would generally disapprove of the advancement of women.

Our best indicator of attitudes toward minorities in general is, "More minority undergraduates should be admitted here even if it means relaxing normal academic standards of admission." Table 40 examines the relationship between agreement with this statement and agreement with "females not as dedicated." As we see in this table, no consistent pattern emerges, and our hypothesis is again unsupported.

Several studies of intergroup relations (e.g., Eisenstadt, 1954, and Frazier, 1957) have discovered an interesting phenomenon. Often, those most prejudiced toward minority-group members are members of the same minority group who have attained some degree of success. In order to disavow any comparison between themselves and the less successful members of their group, the more successful members exhibit prejudicial attitudes toward the less successful. We hypothesized a similar phenomenon: academically successful women (that is, prolific publishers among faculty and graduate students who have published at least one article) will be more likely to agree that females are not as dedicated than unsuccessful women.

	Students		Faculty	
TABLE 40 Percentages of faculty and students who agree that females are not as dedicated as males, by approval to admit more minorities, sex, and field context (weighted totals in parentheses)	*Males*	*Females*	*Males*	*Females*
Female minority				
Strongly approve	25.2 (4,588)	16.7 (7,679)	20.3 (1,304)	6.5 (794)
Approve with reservations	22.0 (13,023)	20.2 (12,775)	24.0 (3,031)	13.8 (1,853)
Disapprove with reservations	29.1 (12,232)	19.5 (10,566)	27.1 (2,934)	10.2 (2,417)
Strongly disapprove	25.5 (20,543)	17.4 (19,077)	26.9 (3,665)	11.5 (2,291)
Gamma	−.010	+.019	−.080	−.020
Equalitarian				
Strongly approve	21.5 (8,324)	18.7 (4,443)	16.9 (2,074)	12.4 (579)
Approve with reservations	24.9 (16,692)	18.7 (9,884)	21.5 (3,962)	9.2 (1,824)
Disapprove with reservations	28.3 (13,511)	28.2 (7,336)	19.4 (3,574)	5.1 (1,850)
Strongly disapprove	31.0 (22,603)	8.4 (13,060)	26.2 (3,932)	5.4 (2,283)
Gamma	−.029	+.222	−.120	+.239
Female majority				
Strongly approve	26.6 (6,611)	19.0 (10,284)	21.4 (2,128)	9.2 (2,448)
Approve with reservations	16.7 (15,390)	8.7 (24,372)	19.3 (3,973)	11.3 (5,247)
Disapprove with reservations	10.6 (16,227)	9.3 (20,591)	21.3 (3,286)	8.6 (4,511)
Strongly disapprove	21.9 (18,038)	8.6 (40,811)	24.3 (2,836)	10.1 (5,232)
Gamma	+.159	+.098	−.059	+.015

Again, there is no clear relationship between the belief that females are not as dedicated as males and academic success (Table 41). In equalitarian fields, the more prolific faculty tend to agree with this item, but among graduates it is the less prolific who agree. A correlation that holds up strongly among graduate women in equalitarian fields disappears in masculine fields and runs in the other direction (slightly) in feminine fields. It therefore does not appear that having published has much of an effect on attitudes toward women—either among men or among women.

TABLE 41 Percentages of faculty and students who agree that females are not as dedicated as males, by article publication, sex, and field context (weighted totals in parentheses)

	Faculty			Students	
	Males	Females		Males	Female
Female minority					
None published	25.9 (1,698)	12.4 (2,670)			
1–2	29.4 (1,824)	11.7 (1,487)	Published	29.2 (8,719)	17.8 (6,425)
3–4	21.6 (1,502)	7.5 (951)	Not published	25.0 (40,030)	17.3 (40,569)
5–10	27.6 (1,771)	9.3 (841)			
11–20	25.8 (1,396)	10.2 (699)			
20+ published	22.2 (2,648)	16.1 (611)			
Gamma	+.054	+.028	Gamma	+.105	+.091
Equalitarian					
None published	16.9 (3,939)	6.9 (3,202)			
1–2	20.1 (3,091)	5.4 (1,456)			
3–4	21.8 (1,654)	9.1 (595)			
5–10	20.9 (1,884)	8.0 (727)	Published	28.4 (8,534)	24.6 (2,674)
11–20	27.8 (1,282)	13.8 (257)	Not published	27.5 (51,619)	16.6 (29,944)
20+ published	30.8 (1,572)	10.5 (121)			
Gamma	−.171	−.101	Gamma	+.022	+.241
Female majority					
None published	21.7 (4,039)	10.6 (8,971)			
1–2	17.1 (2,599)	8.9 (3,821)			
3–4	20.3 (1,706)	9.8 (1,626)	Published	18.1 (4,842)	7.6 (3,828)
5–10	24.8 (1,772)	9.9 (1,402)	Not published	17.8 (49,528)	10.3 (88,210)
11–20	31.5 (928)	13.5 (490)			
20+ published	14.7 (967)	7.9 (539)			
Gamma	−.028	+.038	Gamma	+.010	−.165

NOTE: The gamma among students is between "published" and "not published" within each sex.

108

In *Sexual Politics,* Kate Millett (1970, pp. 50–55) discussed the biblical base of many current attitudes toward women. Starting with the Garden of Eden, the Bible relates many accounts of woman as temptress. Another view of women is stated in 1 Cor.: "Let your women keep silence in the churches; for it is not permitted unto them to speak." Throughout the Bible, women are viewed as unequal to men, and this inequality is accepted by both men and women within the Bible. With few exceptions, the female role is clear-cut and stereotyped. We hypothesized that those who take a conservative religious stance would be more likely to accept biblical views of women and hence more convinced that women are not as dedicated as men. Religious conservatism was measured straightforwardly by, "I am basically conservative in my religious beliefs."[3]

Our hypothesis is again not substantiated by the data (Table 42). Although it does hold up slightly in male-dominated fields,

[3] This item was listed in the faculty questionnaire with a simple choice of yes or no, while the graduate-student questionnaire listed four levels of agreement and disagreement. For consistency, we collapsed the graduate student responses into yes and no.

TABLE 42
Percentages of faculty and students who agree that females are not as dedicated as males, by religious conservatism, sex, and field context (weighted totals in parentheses)

	Students Males	Females	Faculty Males	Females
Female minority				
Conservative	26.5 (24,212)	19.7 (21,509)	29.5 (3,653)	12.5 (2,742)
Not conservative	23.9 (25,598)	18.1 (28,058)	23.0 (7,166)	10.4 (4,566)
Gamma	+.070	+.053	+.167	+.102
Equalitarian				
Conservative	31.9 (27,291)	10.4 (11,724)	19.9 (3,709)	6.4 (2,830)
Not conservative	23.9 (33,318)	21.2 (21,645)	21.9 (9,637)	7.5 (3,614)
Gamma	+.199	−.397	−.061	−.087
Female majority				
Conservative	18.2 (24,688)	6.3 (51,728)	18.3 (3,247)	7.8 (7,502)
Not conservative	18.2 (29,995)	14.1 (43,795)	22.1 (8,899)	11.7 (9,721)
Gamma	.000	−.422	−.119	−.221

it sharply reverses in female fields. In those fields it is the less religiously conservative who view women as undedicated. We are at a loss to explain the contextual effect, but we speculate that religious conservatives in the hard sciences (masculine fields) may be different from religious conservatives in the humanities (feminine fields).

In Chapter 4 we compared men and women in connection with the factors that influence their choices of academic careers. Women were more likely to enter junior college teaching, the least prestigious academic career. Therefore, men who plan junior college teaching careers have as a reference group women planning similar careers and thus may have more sympathetic views of their dedication. Table 43 looks at graduate students choosing an academic career and compares those entering junior colleges with those entering colleges or universities.

Our hypothesis is upheld in all fields. Men who plan to enter junior college teaching are less likely to feel females are not dedicated. Junior college teaching may not indicate to them a lack of dedication. Since they get "less of the pie," they are less apt to be critical of their female colleagues. Although the percentage dif-

TABLE 43 Percentage of graduate students who agree that females are not as dedicated as males, by academic career choice, sex, and field context (weighted totals in parentheses)	Males	Females
Female minority		
College or university teaching	27.4 (13,514)	18.5 (14,896)
Junior college teaching	20.7 (458)	27.3 (3,378)
Gamma	+.182	−.246
Equalitarian		
College or university teaching	29.1 (34,506)	13.1 (12,147)
Junior college teaching	12.3 (4,673)	20.1 (2,344)
Gamma	+.493	−.250
Female majority		
College or university teaching	22.8 (20,952)	9.9 (16,759)
Junior college teaching	13.6 (2,972)	7.6 (6,565)
Gamma	+.303	+.143

	Males	Females
TABLE 44 *Percentage of graduate students who agree that females are not as dedicated as males, by likelihood of dropping out for lack of interest, sex, and field context (weighted totals in parentheses)* *Female minority*		
Definitely yes	15.3 (2,886)	44.6 (3,983)
Maybe	18.6 (8,010)	24.0 (9,862)
Will not	27.4 (39,193)	14.1 (35,812)
Gamma	−.267	+.444
Equalitarian		
Definitely yes	25.1 (2,058)	18.2 (2,704)
Maybe	21.6 (7,245)	25.2 (5,882)
Will not	28.5 (51,600)	14.9 (25,909)
Gamma	−.155	+.229
Female majority		
Definitely yes	17.6 (2,771)	28.2 (5,745)
Maybe	14.9 (8,976)	19.8 (13,900)
Will not	18.2 (44,400)	6.6 (78,807)
Gamma	−.087	+.567

ferences among women are minimal in female-dominated fields, they are fairly large among women in equalitarian and male-dominated fields. Women in these fields who plan to enter junior college teaching are more likely to believe females are not as dedicated. Women who enter the better jobs show by doing so that they are as dedicated as men. A woman has to be more dedicated (and ambitious) to think of attaining such a position, especially considering the low representation of females on faculties. Hence these individuals are less likely to agree that women are not as dedicated.

A fairly obvious indicator of lack of dedication among women would be their feeling that they may drop out because of lack of interest in the subject matter. In Table 44 we examine attitudes of both men and women toward female dedication, in both cases by the probability that the respondent will drop out because of lack of interest. Among women, the pattern is very strong. Women who feel that their lack of interest will cause them to drop out are the most likely to feel that females are not as dedicated. These women appear to project their own lack of interest onto their sex as a whole. Among men, the relationship runs in the opposite direction. Those who do not feel a lack of interest in their field are the most likely to feel that women are not as dedicated. Those individuals who exhibit dedication may more readily point an accusing finger at those who do not manifest similar interest. We suspect that these men would also agree that other men are not as dedicated as they themselves are.

If one believes that females are not as dedicated as males, it does not follow that one is politically conservative, antiminority, or religiously conservative. Attitudes toward women are independent, although the perceptions of our respondents are influenced by their own dedication or lack of it.

When we examine fields in which a high percentage of respondents feel that women are not as dedicated as men, we find some surface evidence for this belief. We shall therefore examine more closely the behavior of men and women in five such fields: chemistry, biochemistry, bacteriology, botany, and physiology. We selected from our sample all 1,779 graduate students in these fields: chemistry, 785 males and 121 females; bacteriology, 205 males and 85 females; biochemistry, 196 males and 39 females; botany, 105 males and 35 females; and physiology, 164 males and 44 females.

Table 45 examines the percentages in these fields of persons who strongly agree or agree with reservations that females are not as dedicated as males. As is generally the case, women in these fields

TABLE 45
Percentages of faculty and students who agree that females are not as dedicated as males, by sex and field (weighted totals in parentheses)

	Students			Faculty		
	Males	Females	Total	Males	Females	Total
Chemistry	37.2 (19,031)	24.7 (3,069)	35.5 (22,228)	39.9 (13,789)	19.8 (1,412)	39.7 (15,529)
Biochemistry	27.5 (3,920)	24.8 (850)	27.0 (4,770)	43.8 (2,123)	8.6 (150)	41.7 (2,291)
Bacteriology	34.3 (4,530)	31.4 (1,841)	33.5 (6,382)	35.2 (2,155)	15.2 (428)	32.3 (2,261)
Botany	39.0 (2,370)	21.2 (695)	35.2 (3,084)	35.6 (1,297)	21.5 (129)	34.7 (1,455)
Physiology	32.3 (3,651)	19.9 (997)	29.9 (4,658)	32.3 (2,699)	14.3 (300)	30.8 (3,089)

are less likely to agree with this item than men, and, again, the feeling that females are not as dedicated is a minority opinion. We find in some fields, however, that as many as a third of the women themselves feel that females are not as dedicated.

Although men and women may study within the same discipline, they do not necessarily enter with equal inputs. Commenting on studies of professional socialization that disregard the inputs of the students, Olesen and Whittaker wrote that these studies:

> . . . begin with the student arriving at the door of the institution as pristine and virginal as though untouched by Original Sin: no hint of being male or female, no taint of social class membership, no attributes of brilliance, stupidity, or simple ability. . . . The faceless, ahistorical student, having forsaken or never having considered private interests, the possibilities of marriage, or activities as a citizen, looks to life only as a professional person in the institutional years. . . . Our sketch terminates with the day of graduation when like the dolls in nurse-doctor kits, young professionals move as equally substitutable units from the school assembly line into a world where no further change can be brought upon or with them, they are now fully garbed with the indisputable trappings of the professional (Olesen & Whittaker, 1968, pp. 5–6).

The inputs with which women enter the fields listed in Table 45 may include a history of being a visible minority in undergraduate courses or of receiving "static" for majoring in a technical field and a self-concept different from that of their female counterparts who majored in, say, French or elementary education. Women also enter these five fields with a higher undergraduate grade-point average than men (Table 46).

There are many ways of measuring "dedication" to a field. Probably the most extreme form of dedication is career primacy—placing the graduate-student role above everything else. Career primacy was measured by, "I tend to subordinate all aspects of my life to

TABLE 46 Percentage of graduate students whose undergraduate GPA was B+ or better, by sex and field	Males	Females	Gamma
Chemistry	44.4	62.9	.288
Biochemistry	48.3	60.0	.200
Bacteriology	36.5	66.3	.456
Botany	35.6	52.7	.467
Physiology	42.9	70.8	.428

TABLE 47 Responses to, "I tend to subordinate all aspects of my life to my work," by sex and field (in percentages)	Strongly agree	Agree with reservations	Disagree with reservations	Strongly disagree
Chemistry				
Males	5.3	27.2	28.8	38.7
Females	6.3	26.4	27.9	39.4
Gamma = .001				
Biochemistry				
Males	6.9	21.9	35.9	35.3
Females	8.1	15.2	31.1	45.6
Gamma = .148				
Bacteriology				
Males	4.5	22.1	32.0	41.4
Females	4.1	22.2	32.7	40.9
Gamma = .003				
Botany				
Males	6.2	18.3	33.1	42.5
Females	11.6	23.2	43.6	21.5
Gamma = .316				
Physiology				
Males	7.0	28.5	35.5	29.0
Females	12.3	25.9	31.1	30.6
Gamma = .036				

my work." We find in Table 47 that about a third of the students in each field subordinate all to their work and that, in general, this dedication is no less common among women than among men. In chemistry, bacteriology, and physiology there are no significant differences between men and women in career primacy. In botany, however, women are more likely than men to subordinate all to their career, while the pattern reverses in biochemistry.

Field dedication could be measured in another way. If women are less dedicated to a particular field than men, then they should be more indifferent toward remaining in that field than their male counterparts. We asked our student sample, "If you were to begin your academic training again, would you still choose your present discipline for specialization?" Table 48 compares the responses of men and women to this item.

If women are thought to be less dedicated than men because they lack discipline loyalty, there seems to be little basis for that belief.

TABLE 48		Definitely yes	Probably yes	Probably no	Definitely no
Responses to, "Would you choose the same discipline?" by sex and field (in percentages)	Chemistry				
	Males	36.0	46.0	13.4	4.5
	Females	34.6	39.3	23.3	2.8
	Gamma = .086				
	Biochemistry				
	Males	35.8	47.9	12.9	3.4
	Females	44.0	31.2	18.3	6.4
	Gamma = .019				
	Bacteriology				
	Males	36.1	48.0	12.2	3.6
	Females	55.8	25.3	13.8	5.2
	Gamma = .219				
	Botany				
	Males	46.6	41.7	11.7	0.0
	Females	30.3	52.1	15.5	2.0
	Gamma = .285				
	Physiology				
	Males	38.2	46.3	11.4	4.1
	Females	35.4	42.0	21.1	1.6
	Gamma = .094				

In no field does a vast majority of students hold strong loyalties. In general only about 35 to 40 percent state that they would definitely choose the same field. As in the previous table, three fields have no significant differences by sex, while in bacteriology women are more loyal than men and in botany women are less loyal.

Another indicator of field dedication is actual productivity, e.g., the publication of articles. In the five fields we are examining, publication is rarely a solitary endeavor. Articles are usually published in teams—generally one or two professors and their chosen graduate students. As in most fields, the majority of students in these disciplines have not published an article (Table 49). There is no consistent pattern of publication by sex. In chemistry, botany, and bacteriology, men are more likely than women to have published, but in the other two fields they are about equally likely to have done so.

Once they receive their final degree, many graduate students in

TABLE 49
Percentage
of graduate
students who
have published
an article, by
sex and field

	Males	*Females*	*Gamma*
Chemistry	38.7	24.6	.319
Biochemistry	47.0	49.3	.046
Bacteriology	42.1	26.4	.339
Botany	26.8	22.7	.110
Physiology	43.2	46.5	.065

these fields will enter academic positions; women, however, are much more likely to enter academic positions in colleges than in universities. For example, according to our faculty data, women constitute 3 percent of the chemistry faculty in universities, compared to 12 percent in colleges and 18 percent in junior colleges. Similar patterns are found in the biological sciences, where women constitute 7 percent of the botany faculty in universities, compared to 19 percent in colleges. Studies have shown (e.g., Budner &

TABLE 50
Responses to,
"I hope to make
significant
contributions to
knowledge in
my field," by
sex and field
(in percentages)

	Strongly agree	*Agree with reservations*	*Disagree with reservations*	*Strongly disagree*
Chemistry				
Males	52.6	37.2	7.7	2.6
Females	30.5	44.1	20.9	4.5
Gamma = .407				
Biochemistry				
Males	59.2	37.5	2.9	0.5
Females	45.5	36.6	11.1	6.7
Gamma = .327				
Bacteriology				
Males	51.8	43.2	4.9	0.0
Females	41.3	43.0	13.1	2.6
Gamma = .259				
Botany				
Males	50.9	38.5	10.6	0.0
Females	26.9	50.4	17.6	5.2
Gamma = .430				
Physiology				
Males	60.4	34.2	4.9	0.5
Females	31.2	61.1	5.1	2.6
Gamma = .477				

Meyer, 1961) that, wherever they are placed, women more than men are expected to engage in teaching functions (and colleges emphasize teaching to a greater extent than do universities). The pattern that we see in Table 50 is thus not really surprising.

Few graduate students reject the idea of making significant contributions to knowledge in their fields. There is, however, a strong difference between men and women in all five fields: men are much more likely than women to strongly endorse the idea of making significant contributions. If professors and students feel that contributing to the acquisition of knowledge in a field can be equated with dedication to that field, then the differences between men and women graduate students—as reflected in Tables 49 and 50—may support the belief that women are not as dedicated as their male counterparts. The differences in publication are not as great as the differences in the desire to make significant contributions, but few women reject the notion of making such contributions—they are just less likely to strongly agree with it than are men.

In all five fields, entering graduate women are much less likely eventually to attain a doctorate than men. For example, Table 2 showed that in the 1969–70 academic year women received 23 percent of the master's degrees in chemistry and only 8 percent of the doctorates. Women do drop out of graduate school to a greater degree than men. Note in Table 51 that in every field except botany, women are more likely than men to state that inability to do the academic work will or may cause them to drop out of graduate school. Additionally, in all fields women are more likely than men to feel that emotional strain may lead to their dropping out. What is especially interesting is the high proportion of both men and women who feel the emotional strain of graduate education. At least a third of the graduate students in all fields believe that graduate education is affecting their emotional well-being.

TABLE 51 Percentage of graduate students who cite inability to do academic work or emotional strain as reasons for possibly dropping out, by sex and field		Inability			Emotional strain		
		Males	Females	Gamma	Males	Females	Gamma
	Chemistry	24.4	26.0	.148	28.2	33.1	.095
	Biochemistry	16.1	22.4	.187	27.1	56.9	.552
	Bacteriology	15.1	20.4	.164	38.0	39.9	.269
	Botany	19.0	9.2	.381	33.5	41.9	.178
	Physiology	12.8	23.0	.331	20.9	45.1	.482

Examining Table 51, one would be tempted to state that these grounds for dropping out are good indicators that women are not as dedicated. Women are more likely than men to feel unable to do the work and thus to drop out. However, it should be remembered that, among other things, women enter with a higher GPA in their subject matter than men. Advanced chemistry or biology courses are not very much different from undergraduate courses. The real differences begin in the laboratory, where graduate students work under the guidance of professors and do original work leading toward both publication and their degrees. It is our contention that what appears to be inability or lack of motivation is instead a lack of confidence and a less positive self-image. Men and women differ not only in the perception of their ability; they differ in their self-conceptions. Table 52 shows that women have less confidence in their ability to do original work.

TABLE 52 Responses to, "How satisfied are you with your ability to do original work?" by sex and field (in percentages)	Very satisfied	Satisfied	Dissatisfied	Very dissatisfied
Chemistry				
Males	21.6	54.3	21.3	2.9
Females	8.2	42.8	40.0	9.0
Gamma = .459				
Biochemistry				
Males	24.1	50.1	21.3	4.5
Females	17.7	40.2	27.7	14.4
Gamma = .275				
Bacteriology				
Males	25.0	41.5	29.1	4.5
Females	16.8	42.9	30.2	10.0
Gamma = .175				
Botany				
Males	18.5	52.3	25.0	4.2
Females	16.8	41.1	34.3	7.8
Gamma = .185				
Physiology				
Males	24.0	46.0	27.5	2.4
Females	19.4	27.4	46.3	7.0
Gamma = .310				

In no field is the majority of students very satisfied with their ability to do original work. This is not surprising, since so much of laboratory work is done under the supervision of a professor or full-time researcher. Women, however, are much more dissatisfied with their ability to do original work than are men. This is most true in chemistry, where half the women show dissatisfaction, compared to about a quarter of the men.

Since so much of the graduate work in these fields depends on professors, relationships with professors should be an important factor in the graduate-student careers of both men and women. Table 53 examines how students believe their closest professor perceives them.

From the standpoint of professional socialization, it is advantageous for graduate students to have a collegial or an apprenticeship relationship with their major professors. A close working relation-

	Colleague	Apprentice	Employee	Student	No contact
TABLE 53 Relationship between graduate students and closest professor, by sex and field (in percentages)					
Chemistry					
Males	28.0	25.9	4.1	32.6	9.5
Females	11.9	19.7	1.3	56.3	11.6
Gamma = .366					
Biochemistry					
Males	36.3	25.3	3.2	29.0	6.2
Females	19.4	11.9	0.0	50.3	18.4
Gamma = .459					
Bacteriology					
Males	31.5	27.9	3.4	32.8	4.4
Females	24.4	23.9	6.2	38.5	6.9
Gamma = .160					
Botany					
Males	39.5	26.0	2.8	27.9	3.8
Females	13.3	23.7	0.0	55.8	7.1
Gamma = .495					
Physiology					
Males	35.3	21.9	1.8	37.3	3.6
Females	21.9	33.6	0.0	39.3	5.2
Gamma = .144					

ship with a professor should facilitate research and aid the building of a professional self-image. Few men or women claim that they have no contact with professors outside the classroom, but women are much less likely to have the benefits of a close working relationship. In the five fields listed in the table, professors usually choose the students who join their research groups, and those who believe women are not as dedicated would probably be less likely to choose them for their research teams. Recent discussions between the author and graduate students in these fields revealed incidents of professors who avoided choosing women because "they will just get married," "they are just spending time in graduate school until something else comes along," and so forth.

Because women have less confidence in their ability and more distant relationships with their professors, it is not surprising that the pattern we see in Table 54 appears. Women are less likely to state that they are among the best students in their department, and they are more likely to retain a student (rather than a scholar or scientist) self-image.

In all five fields about half the men do not see themselves as students but rather as scholars or scientists. This is not surprising, since course work is less a part of these fields than of most others. Individuals who spend a lot of time in laboratories rather than classrooms would naturally gravitate toward a scholar or scientist self-image. Yet women are much less likely to see themselves as scholars or scientists even though the classroom plays as little part in their lives as in men's. Moreover, in all five fields they are less likely to state that they are among the best students in the department.

Differences in self-image are strong in all fields except bacteriology. Since self-image is shaped to a great extent by comparison with and reaction from significant others, it may be of importance

TABLE 54 Graduate students' self-image, by sex and field (in percentages)	Among the best			Scholar-scientist		
	Males	*Females*	*Gamma*	*Males*	*Females*	*Gamma*
Chemistry	23.0	12.0	.329	54.4	29.9	.445
Biochemistry	29.9	11.8	.346	57.7	38.1	.321
Bacteriology	22.1	17.9	.077	45.4	42.9	.029
Botany	37.7	14.6	.270	55.3	20.4	.555
Physiology	44.3	33.3	.268	49.7	28.2	.329

that bacteriology is the only one of the five fields that grants about the same percentage of bachelor's degrees to women as to men. Because the majority of undergraduate women in bacteriology do not go on to graduate school, those who do may consider themselves part of an elite. By comparing themselves with their undergraduate colleagues who left bacteriology after the B.S. to become lab technicians or high school teachers, graduate women in this field reinforce their scholar-scientist self-image. On the other hand, more women undergraduates in chemistry go on to graduate school than is the case in bacteriology. There are fewer women "left behind" for graduate women in chemistry to compare themselves with.

Evidence does seem to point to women and men being unequal in dedication. Respondents who believe women to be less dedicated are not inaccurate in their perceptions; we should, however, pursue the factors that create this lack of dedication. The two factors that seem to us to have the greatest effect on graduate school performance are self-image and relationship with professors. It is our contention that those students who have favorable self-images and those who have a close relationship with professors are the more successful students and thus appear dedicated.

In the discussion that follows, we would have liked to present four-way tables by field, but even our large body of data has its limits, and we will restrict our discussion to a summary analysis of all five fields.

Having a close relationship with a professor does have a positive academic effect on both men and women graduate students. Among those having a close (apprentice or collegial) relationship, 43.7 percent of the men and 42.0 percent of the women have published an article; however, among those having a student-teacher, employer-employee, or no-contact relationship with professors, 34.7 percent of the men have published, compared to 24.3 percent of the women. If they have a close relationship with a professor, women are just as likely as men to be productive; among students having a less close professorial relationship, however, men are more likely to publish than women.

Having a close relationship with a professor seems to be more reassuring for women than for men. Among students having such a relationship, 17.6 percent of the men and 20.3 percent of the women feel that inability will (or may) force them to drop out of graduate school. Among those with an employee, student, or no-contact relationship with professors about the same percentage of the men (18.6 percent) feel inability may force them to drop out, while 35 percent of the women feel this way. We interpret this to mean that women feel less secure than men, but that a close relationship with professors lessens their insecurity.[4]

To extend our argument that women are handicapped more by a poor self-image than by a real lack of dedication, we examined other items pertaining to self-confidence. For example, among students who have published an article, 24.1 percent of the men, compared to 39.1 percent of the women, are dissatisfied with their ability to do original work. Doing original work (which we assume article publishing is) is less likely to convince women of their ability than men. Among those not having published, 28.2 percent of the men, compared to 49.4 percent of the women, are dissatisfied with their ability to do original work. Not having published has little effect on the self-images of men, while it has a much greater effect on those of women. Women publishers are less confident than men, but non-publishing women are almost twice as likely as their male counterparts to be dissatisfied with their ability to do original work.[5]

When students rate themselves, men are more likely than women to state that they are among the best students in their department. Among these self-rated best students, 67.1 percent of the men, compared to 44.9 percent of the women, state that they hope to make significant contributions to knowledge in their fields. Among those who call themselves average or below average students, 40.8 percent of the men, compared to 31.9 percent of the women, hope to make significant contributions. Thus, those who have a positive self-image are more likely to hope to make significant contributions; yet, even among the "best" students, women are less likely than men to hope to make such contributions.

[4] It is possible that the relationship could be reversed. That is, the more able female students are selected by professors for close contact. In these five disciplines, professorial contact begins early (before the end of the first year), when students are still engaged in classroom work. It should be remembered, however, that women in general are more able than men when measured by GPA.

[5] A similar pattern obtains when we look at those students engaged and those not engaged in scholarly work (that they expect to lead to publication under their own names). Among those engaged in scholarly work, 26.4 percent of the men and 42.6 percent of the women are dissatisfied with their ability to do original work. Among those not engaged in scholarly work, 37.8 percent of the men and 54.0 percent of the women state dissatisfaction with their abilities.

Having published articles increases the likelihood that students will view themselves as scholars or scientists (rather than students). Among those who have published, 62.2 percent of the men and 44.0 percent of the women have this self-image. Among those who have not published, 47.3 percent of the men and 33.5 percent of the women have a scholar-scientist self-image. Again, men are more likely to exhibit this self-image whether or not they publish.

It is true, then, that women *appear* to be not as dedicated as men. However, given a close relationship with a professor or given a more positive self-image, women are just as likely as men to manifest signs of dedication. Women and men enter their disciplines with fairly equal academic inputs, but they differ in their self-confidence. If given encouragement by professors, women appear as dedicated as their male counterparts. Given less encouragement, their self-images suffer, their performance suffers, and they appear less dedicated to their fields.

We cannot establish that believing females to be less dedicated is an indication of blind prejudice. The belief becomes part of a cycle — a professor sees that women are not as dedicated as men and pays less attention to them. Paying less attention to them results in women becoming less dedicated; hence, the belief is upheld. The reasons for women having a less positive self-image are many, but as part of the input with which women enter graduate school, they are beyond the scope of our data. Once women enter graduate education, they may be faced with problems external to their graduate study that men may not have to face. One of these external pressures — conflict between the spouse role and the student role — will be dealt with in the next chapter.

6. External Constraints: Marital Status and Graduate Education

We have, so far, been looking at the problems that women encounter within graduate education; however, their life outside of graduate school may have a strong effect on life within it. The role of graduate student generally requires a lot of time, not only for class work but also for original research, studying for examinations, general reading, and so on. Whether or not they have other duties, married women in our society are expected to engage in those tasks (such as housekeeping and cooking) associated with their traditional sex role. Since the spouse and student roles are both major encompassing roles, the two may conflict. This conflict may have a strong effect on both roles.

We have found that for women, marriage has a deleterious effect on the role of student and that the least successful female students are those who attempt to combine the student and spouse roles. The most successful women are those who are divorced—they have experienced the conflict and have settled the problem by abandoning one major role. For men, on the other hand, marriage has an entirely different impact and is complementary to the student role. Married men have someone to care for their needs—from domestic to emotional to sexual. Losing this support through divorce has a negative effect on men's performance in graduate school.

Some feminists at the turn of the century questioned the utility of marriage for educated women, either because of the increased effort it took to maintain both a marriage and a career ("She should be sure that the man is of such a disposition as to be worth her effort" [Miller, 1899, p. 39]) or because they felt that educated women had the ability and the obligation to be self-supporting (". . . a woman must not ask a man to support her. It is economic beggary" [Stetson, 1898, p. 89]).

A contrary view is that the educated woman can make her greatest contribution by accepting what Philip Slater (1970, p. 62) has called the "Spockian challenge." This challenge posits that child rearing is the most important task for any woman.[1] A guide on college life for women advises potential coeds that "the educated woman may make a profound contribution in the direction of home and family living, and *in addition* [emphasis mine] extend her influence outside the home into the community" (Muller & Muller, 1960, p. 198). Many college undergraduates accept this Spockian challenge. In a 1968 national study (Cross, 1968, p. 10), 55 percent of the college women stated that they expected their life-long satisfactions to come from marriage and the family, while only 18 percent stated that their major satisfactions would come from a career. In another study of over 1,400 female Los Angeles high school seniors, 4 percent opted for a lifetime career and 48 percent stated that they planned only to be homemakers, while another 48 percent stated that they would try to combine both a career and homemaking (Turner, 1964, p. 280).

Attempting to combine a career and homemaking appears to be a considerable source of strain for many women (Coser & Rokoff, 1971). Marriage may enable or force (depending on the woman's viewpoint) a woman to drop out of a career (Ginzberg, 1966, p. 82). Married women who do remain employed may feel what one writer described as "self-conscious gratitude toward their husbands for helping them to maintain a career" (Lopate, 1968, p. 148) and for giving them the emotional support needed for maintaining two diverse and potentially conflicting roles. A consistent finding, in studies of married professional women, is that women view their careers as second to their husbands and children and their own careers as subordinate to their husbands' (see Arreger, 1966; Hubback, 1957; Lopate, 1968; Poloma & Garland, 1970; Sommerkorn, 1966).

As we previously observed (Table 9), women in graduate education are less likely to be married than their male counterparts. Our data, however, were gathered at one period of time, and we are not able to ascertain motivations for remaining single or obtaining a divorce. We are only able to control for marital status and

---

[1] Also illustrative is Bruno Bettelheim's statement: "We must start with the realization that as much as women want to be good scientists or engineers, they want first and foremost to be womanly companions of men" (Bettelheim, 1965, p. 15).

infer from differential behavior possible effects of marriage and divorce.

As Table 55 illustrates, if graduate women do marry, they are much more likely than men to have a spouse with graduate education. Traditionally, it has been deemed unacceptable in our society for a woman to dominate her husband in any way—from height (Feldman, 1971c) to education. Married women are thus freer to pursue postgraduate education if their spouses have attended graduate school. No such limitations exist for married men. Less than a quarter of married male students have spouses with graduate education, compared to over half the married graduate women. This marked difference obtains for all age groups. Even women who return to graduate school after the age of 40 are more likely to have spouses with graduate education than men of a similar age.

One of the major limitations brought about by marriage concerns enrollment status. Whatever their marital status, women are less likely to be enrolled full time than men (Table 56). Although marriage affects the full-time enrollment status of both men and

		Males	*Females*	*Ratio—percentage females/percentage males*
	22 or younger	13.7 (13,707)	63.0 (9,396)	4.60
	23	20.1 (25,432)	53.8 (12,431)	2.68
	24	21.5 (39,484)	68.7 (13,224)	3.20
	25	32.6 (43,573)	62.8 (12,517)	1.93
	26–27	27.3 (83,078)	64.0 (19,693)	2.34
	28–29	28.9 (57,300)	69.9 (12,734)	2.42
	30–34	22.0 (98,340)	57.7 (20,185)	2.62
	35–39	19.8 (46,640)	64.0 (20,977)	3.23
	40+	23.7 (56,969)	41.1 (52,633)	1.73
	TOTAL	24.2 (467,765)	55.4 (174,507)	2.29

TABLE 55 *Percentage of graduate students whose spouses have attended graduate school, by age and sex (weighted totals in parentheses)*

TABLE 56
Enrollment status of graduate students, by sex and marital status (in percentages)

	Full time	Part time	Weighted total
Single males	75.5	24.5	206,832
Single females	62.0	38.0	118,201
Married males	50.9	49.1	467,765
Married females	29.0	71.0	174,507
Divorced or separated males	63.6	36.4	9,627
Divorced or separated females	52.0	48.0	12,880

women, it is more likely to affect women than men. About half the married men are enrolled full time, compared to less than one-third of the married women. Divorce, too, affects enrollment status, although not so severely as marriage.

Since nationality may have a strong effect on attitudes toward the role of spouse and since part-time student status may have strong effects on orientation toward graduate education, a special subsample was selected of only full-time students who are United States citizens.[2] Subsequent analysis is based on this subsample.

Marital status of graduate students varies significantly by age (Table 57). As we might expect, single graduate students tend to

[2] This sample of full-time students who are United States citizens consists of a 1-in-3 sample of single men ($N = 1,704$), a 1-in-4 sample of married men ($N = 1,821$), all single ($N = 2,301$) and married women ($N = 1,382$), and all divorced or separated men ($N = 161$) and women ($N = 227$).

TABLE 57 *Age distribution of graduate students, by sex and marital status (in percentages; absolute numbers in parentheses)*

	22 or younger	23–25	26–29	30–34	35 or older	Weighted total
Single males	24.4	52.8	18.4	3.4	1.1	100.1 (38,730)
Single females	29.8	46.2	13.4	5.4	5.3	100.1 (57,543)
Married males	5.9	38.5	32.6	13.6	9.5	100.1 (47,111)
Married females	11.6	29.9	20.2	10.1	28.3	100.1 (37,605)
Divorced or separated males	1.9	13.8	28.6	38.0	17.7	100.0 (4,778)
Divorced or separated females	1.3	15.1	29.8	20.0	33.8	100.0 (5,502)

be younger than married or divorced students, and married students tend to be younger than divorced students. Married or divorced female students tend to be older than male students of the same marital status. Of the married women 28 percent are over 35, compared to 10 percent of the married men; similarly, 34 percent of the divorced or separated women are over 35, compared to 18 percent of the men. The tendency of married or divorced women to be older than men of similar status reflects the fact that women are more constrained by the role of spouse. Unlike women, men do not have to wait until their children are raised or until their spouses have an established career to continue in graduate school.

Table 58 examines students' motivations for attending graduate school by two measurements of intellectual motivation and one measurement of financial motivation. Intellectual and financial motivations appear to be independent. There is little relationship between agreement with "I am in graduate school in order to continue my intellectual growth" and agreement with "I am in graduate school to increase my earning power." (Among men, the gamma $= -.093$, while among women, the gamma $= +.073$.)

At all levels of marital status, women are more likely than men to express intellectual motivations for attending graduate school. Since the traditional role of women has not been one of principal provider, it would seem that they would be freer to attend graduate school for intellectual reasons. Our data indicate that this is true for married women, who may be partially supported by their spouses and who reveal less financial motivation than married

TABLE 58 *Motivations for attending graduate school, by sex and marital status (in percentages; weighted totals in parentheses)*

	(A) Continue intellectual growth*			(B) Study field for intrinsic interest†			(C) Increase earning power†		
	Males	Females	Gamma	Males	Females	Gamma	Males	Females	Gamma
Single	56.0	69.6	.285	28.6	39.3	.235	32.2 (38,730)	33.0 (57,543)	.017
Married	60.5	81.2	.475	32.5	47.6	.307	43.1 (47,111)	37.0 (37,605)	.127
Divorced or separated	61.6	78.4	.388	27.8	58.5	.570	48.2 (4,778)	49.5 (5,502)	.025

*Percentage who "strongly agree."
† Percentage who "strongly agree" or "agree with reservations."

men. In their less dependent single and divorced states, however, women are just as likely as male students to express more pragmatic financial motivations for attending graduate school. Financial motivations are most frequently expressed by divorced students. Men may be under pressure to pay child support or alimony, and some women may be striving for a more independent financial state.

Marital status has an effect on the intellectual motivations of women but not of men. At all levels of marital status, men show similar percentages in their motivations of continuing intellectual growth or studying a field for its intrinsic interests; among women, however, these motivations are lowest among single students and noticeably higher among married and divorced or separated students. We interpret these differences as reactions against some of the constraints of the marital role. Few of the duties of the housewife require intellectual prowess. Boredom and restlessness may enhance a desire for more intellectual stimulation, especially among college-educated housewives.[3]

Just as sex and marital status influence motivations for entering graduate school, so they give rise to differences in pressures and attitudes toward dropping out of graduate school. Section *A* of Table 59 shows that among students who are single or married, men are more likely than women to state that they have never

[3] The problem of the bored college-graduate housewife is amplified by Friedan (1963).

TABLE 59 *Pressure and attitudes toward dropping out of graduate school, by sex and marital status (weighted totals in parentheses)*

	(A) Percentage who never considered (in the past year) quitting graduate school for good			(B) Percentage who strongly disagree that they would be happier if they had not entered graduate school			(C) Percentage who state that emotional strain will or may force them to drop out of graduate school		
	Males	*Females*	*Gamma*	*Males*	*Females*	*Gamma*	*Males*	*Females*	*Gamma*
Single	61.0	43.4	.250	60.2	57.4	.046	24.4 (38,730)	33.5 (57,543)	.221
Married	65.3	53.9	.191	66.6	65.9	.022	18.8 (47,111)	29.0 (37,605)	.275
Divorced or separated	37.7	57.3	.378	43.6	72.9	.472	56.9 (4,778)	41.9 (5,502)	.295

considered quitting graduate school for good; among divorced graduate students, however, women are much more likely than men to express a commitment to remain in school. We see in section *B* that among single or married graduate students, sex has little effect on agreement with, "I think I would have been happier if I had not entered graduate school." Among divorced students, women are much more likely than men to disagree with this item. Divorced men are less committed to remain in graduate school, and they are unhappier with the graduate-student role than single or married men. Of all students, divorced women are most content with the graduate-student role.

In our sample of graduate students, sex or marital status has no bearing on students' belief that such things as a job offer or inability to do the work will cause them to drop out. However, among married students, 21 percent of the women, compared to 9 percent of the men (gamma of sex difference = +.44), state that pressure from their spouses may cause them to drop out of school. Observe in section *C* of Table 59 that single or married women are more likely than single or married men to feel that emotional strain may be a force causing them to quit their graduate education. As we might expect, emotional strain is highest among divorced students but, a reversal in the pattern occurs, as women are less likely than men to state that this strain may cause them to drop out. In all three sections of Table 59, divorced women show a higher degree of commitment to remain in graduate school than do divorced men, while the situation is reversed among single and married students.

A large proportion of our sample of full-time graduate students plan a career in college or university teaching. Once they enter this occupation, many of these students will be involved in publishing articles or presenting papers at professional meetings. Table 60 looks at these activities among graduate students who plan university or college teaching careers. We find that the greatest percentage differences between men and women pertain to married students. Married men are the most productive and married women are the least. It takes a fair amount of time to write a paper or an article, and the job cannot be done in a hit-or-miss fashion; rather, it takes specific blocks of time for research and writing. This time cannot be budgeted as easily by married women as by divorced or single women.

In the previous chapter we noted the importance of informal interaction with professors for success in graduate school. Women

	(A) Presented paper			(B) Published article		
TABLE 60 Percentage of graduate students who have presented a paper before a professional meeting or have published a journal article, by sex and marital status* (weighted totals in parentheses)	*Males*	*Females*	*Gamma*	*Males*	*Females*	*Gamma*
Single	12.0	11.6	.021	16.0 (11,401)	11.8 (17,592)	.175
Married	19.4	9.5	.395	23.1 (17,745)	12.8 (14,095)	.343
Divorced or separated	14.3	13.3	.040	20.3 (2,634)	18.1 (2,265)	.069

*Future college or university faculty only.

are less likely to engage in such interaction, but those who do differ little from men in "academic success." Many sociologists (e.g., Becker et al., 1961; Becker & Carper, 1956; Fox, 1957; and Kadushin, 1969), have also emphasized the importance of informal interaction among graduate students. Those who see their fellow students informally often help one another in the learning process and tend to be more professionalized. As we see in section *A* of Table 61, married women are denied this type of interaction to a large extent. Although women at all three marital statuses are less likely than men to see their fellow students socially, the greatest difference is found between married men and women. Even if a woman engages in the full-time student role, time must still be devoted to husband and family. This means that in many cases the majority of the people she sees socially will be friends of her husband's or mutual friends—not her fellow students. A married female graduate student may well find that the lifespace taken up by the formal activities of the student role and the demands of married life leave little time for additional involvement in the informal activities of graduate school. Unlike women, men are only slightly affected by marriage in how often they see their fellow students socially.

Total commitment to the student role involves subordinating all other roles. As we see in section *B* of Table 61, the majority of all graduate students do not make the student role the prime role. Although the differences between single and married men and women are minimal, men are slightly more likely than women to subordinate all to their graduate work. Among divorced or separated individuals, sex-based differences are much greater. Whereas divorced men are the least likely of all students to state that they tend to subordinate all to their work, divorced women are the most likely. We cannot establish causality, but the trend of the data indicates that divorced men are burdened with more responsibilities than their single or married male counterparts and thus must pay attention to other roles. Divorced women have shed some responsibilities and thus are freer to pursue the student role.

Komarovsky (1953, pp. 53–59) maintains that women are socialized to be family-oriented. Few graduate students place career ahead of family (Table 61, section C), but among both single and married graduate students, women are more family-oriented than men. This difference does not obtain between divorced or separated men and women. Divorced or separated women are more likely than their single or married female counterparts to place career ahead of family. This pattern leads us to speculate that in some instances the forced primacy of the family over career was a factor that led to divorce.

Marital status also has an effect on the future plans of graduate students, by affecting spatial mobility. Constraints on mobility may severely limit the range of job alternatives. Local students are much more likely than out-of-state students to plan to remain in the state

TABLE 61 Career primacy and informal peer interaction among graduate students, by sex and marital status (in percentages; weighted totals in parentheses)	*Males*	*Females*	*Gamma*
(A) *Almost none of the people I see socially are fellow students in my department*			
Single	17.8	25.3	.194
Married	22.8	43.8	.402
Divorced or separated	18.7	32.8	.283
(B) *I tend to subordinate all aspects of my life to my work*			
Single	27.9	25.4	.136
Married	29.2	23.7	.173
Divorced or separated	22.7	37.6	.344
(C) *My career will* not *take second place behind my family obligations*			
Single	32.5 (38,730)	27.4 (57,543)	.253
Married	29.9 (47,111)	17.5 (37,605)	.247
Divorced or separated	34.2 (4,778)	34.3 (5,502)	.013

after they complete their graduate education (Table 62). Among single graduate students, 60 percent of the local men and women plan to remain in the state, compared to 20 percent of out-of-state men and 27 percent of out-of-state women. Among out-of-state students, married men feel that they are just as free as single men to leave, but married women feel constrained to remain in the state of their graduate school. We see that marriage has no effect on the plans of spatial mobility of men but has a strong effect on those of women. Among divorced students, however, the male "locals" are more likely to plan to remain than the female locals. We previously noted a high degree of emotional strain and a questioning of commitment among divorced men. It may be that they are better able to find supportive relationships if they remain at home. Among out-of-state divorced students, women are much more likely to plan to remain in the state than are men. They and their children may be more constrained than men by the local attachments they have developed.

TABLE 62
Future plans of graduate students (weighted totals in parentheses)

(A) *Percentage intending to remain in state after completing graduate education, by sex, marital status, and whether raised in state of graduate school*

	Grew up in state of graduate school			Didn't grow up in state of graduate school		
	Males	*Females*	*Gamma*	*Males*	*Females*	*Gamma*
Single	59.0 (16,312)	60.6 (24,665)	.033	20.0 (22,145)	27.3 (32,444)	.201
Married	59.0 (18,373)	78.0 (14,542)	.305	21.8 (28,517)	52.3 (22,683)	.594
Divorced or separated	74.1* (2,069)	56.7 (2,367)	.395	27.6 (2,709)	51.6 (3,052)	.472

(B) *Percentage leaning heavily toward teaching rather than research, by sex and marital status†*

	Males	*Females*	*Gamma*
Single	20.2 (11,401)	32.7 (17,592)	.216
Married	18.0 (17,745)	34.6 (14,095)	.308
Divorced or separated	53.9 (2,634)	21.9 (2,265)	.489

*Smallest cell (divorced males who grew up in state) has 51 unweighted cases.
† Future college or university teachers only.

In American society, teaching has been deemed an expression of the female sex role (see Epstein, 1970, pp. 154–162). We find in section *B* of Table 62 that among single or married students who plan careers in college or university teaching, women are more likely than men to be strongly oriented toward teaching rather than research. The pattern reverses among divorced students, however. Divorced women are the least likely to be strongly teaching-oriented, while divorced men are most likely to be so. If divorce represents an escape for graduate women from the traditional family-oriented sex role, it may also serve to break the bonds of other aspects of the traditional female role. Divorced men are in a less secure position than married or single men. Under emotional and financial strain, they may find that teaching offers more security than research.

Although marriage may have deleterious effects on the student role for women, it has certain advantages. The stereotype of men being put through graduate school by their wives is true; 60 percent of married men state that their wives' jobs provide a source of income. But it is also true that married women are being put through graduate school by their husbands; 74 percent of married female graduate students state that their husbands' jobs are one source of their income.

TABLE 63
Finances and financial aid of graduate students, by sex and marital status (weighted totals in parentheses)

(A) Percentage stating their current finances are inadequate or very inadequate

	Males	Females	Gamma
Single	26.1	30.0	.096
Married	32.4	24.5	.188
Divorced or separated	57.6	32.4	.298

(B) Percentage receiving a fellowship during current (1968–69) academic year

Single	26.6	32.7	.147
Married	28.2	30.1	.047
Divorced or separated	22.6	29.1	.169

(C) Percentage receiving a teaching or research assistantship during current (1968–69) academic year

Single	30.5 (38,730)	27.2 (57,543)	.080
Married	34.7 (47,111)	29.2 (37,605)	.125
Divorced or separated	33.4 (4,778)	24.2 (5,502)	.221

Single men and women differ little in the perception of their finances (Table 63). Like single graduate students, few married men or women see their current financial situation as inadequate; however, women are slightly more likely to see themselves as having adequate finances than men. Stronger differences are found among divorced students. Divorced men may have to pay child support or alimony. We find that 58 percent of the divorced men, compared to 32 percent of the divorced women, view their current finances as inadequate or very inadequate.

Marital status has very little relationship with the receipt of financial aid. The general pattern is that men are more likely to receive teaching or research assistantships and women are more likely to receive fellowships. Decisions concerning financial aid may take sex into account but probably not marital status.

Our data imply that some women experience a sequence going from conflict between the spouse and the student roles to divorce to increased commitment to the student role. We have demonstrated that marital status has an effect on the student roles of both men and women, with the greatest academic "success" (that is, ability to adhere to a career primacy model) obtaining among married men and divorced women. Emile Durkheim (1951) wrote about the stabilizing effect marriage has for men, and our data are consistent with his observations. While marriage reduces conflicts for men, it increases them for women. Our data show that women who attempt to combine two full-time (and time-consuming) roles encounter problems, some of which may be solved by abandoning one of the two roles. Divorce is not the only way to lessen the conflict. Women may place less emphasis on the student role by becoming part-time students, and, indeed, more women are enrolled on a part-time basis than men.

The student and spouse roles are neither independent nor constant for women. In some instances they conflict and in other instances they complement each other. The effect of marital status on the student role is dependent on adherence to traditional sex roles. Less rigidity in adhering to these roles should ease some of the conflict between the spouse and student roles for women.

7. Observations on the Escape

It would have been satisfying to state, on the basis of this study, that a systematic pattern of discrimination is (or is not) leveled against women in graduate and professional school. Our data, however, do not substantiate either the presence or the absence of such discrimination. What has been borne out is that within graduate education there is a great deal of inequality based on sex. But inequality is not the same thing as discrimination.

Since the beginning of higher education in America, there has never been equality between men and women. Today, we find that although women constitute slightly over half of the college-age population, they are not equally represented in undergraduate education, let alone on the graduate or the faculty level. Women who do enroll in graduate school are less likely to attain graduate degrees than men. They are most likely to be enrolled in fields that are low in power, privilege, and prestige. Women who teach within higher education are less likely to aspire toward (and end up in) the more prestigious academic positions, although these lower aspirations do not appear to be based on inability or the lack of prerequisites.

Some people within graduate education believe that women are not as dedicated as men, and on the surface there appears some evidence for this belief. But we found that given equal opportunity, any differences in dedication between men and women disappear. We also found that women are constrained by their sex role when they attempt to balance marriage and life as a full-time student; such constraints do not affect married men.

We have utilized the perspectives of social science to demonstrate the presence of sex-based inequality in our system of higher education. But we cannot blame only American higher education for this inequality. Much of the inequality that we have uncovered is the result of the inputs that women bring with them to higher education. There are no immutable behavioral differences determined by sex. Behavioral differences appear to be the result of differential socialization, based largely on stereotypes of the sex roles of males and females. Not all women, however, are socialized to reject mathematics or to believe that they should serve as teachers. We have demonstrated that women who are in physics have the same basic world view and attitudes as men in physics. Just as all men are not alike, neither are all women. Women graduate students in physics are very unlike their female counterparts in French. Earlier socialization shaped their current interest in their field, and their field shaped many of their current behavioral characteristics.[1] Until differential socialization and stereotypes disappear, patterns of inequality will continue.

We do not wish to convey the idea that higher education is free of prejudice toward women, but the elimination of prejudicial rules is only one small step toward eliminating inequality. Setting up quotas on the basis of sex, while increasing female representation, is a token gesture and will not eliminate the different training that many women bring to colleges and universities. Education at all levels can respond by weakening the stereotyped conception of what each sex is suited for. Women should not be counseled out of (or counseled into) masculine fields simply because they are women. This counseling begins early—at the elementary school level or before. Higher education cannot magically create equality, because even as freshmen, many women do not enter with the same training and skills as men. Higher education, however, is just as guilty as other aspects of education in perpetuating the belief that women are naturally suited for some fields and men are naturally suited for others.

Although it is still present, inequality is less evident in equalitarian fields than in male-dominated or female-dominated fields. Fields that voluntarily admit women and men in equal numbers treat women more equally at all levels of education. If other fields

[1] Continuing analysis of the Carnegie graduate student data has revealed the impact of graduate school on professionalization. A major finding is that graduate school mainly serves to sharpen the preexisting skills and aptitudes of its students. What is most important for the development of professionalization is what students bring with them to graduate school, rather than what they learn there. Changes in attitudes toward and treatment of women, therefore, must take place in undergraduate education as well as in graduate school (Feldman & Noelker, 1973).

begin to keep a natural balance between women and men, it seems likely that sex-based inequality will lessen. But since few women are studying physics, electrical engineering, or economics as undergraduates, we cannot expect that women will suddenly be admitted in the same numbers as men at the graduate level. Change must come at all levels of education, and this is no simple matter or easy process. At present, bearing in mind current conceptions of the traditional roles of men and women and the current state of inequality based on sex, the mere presence of women in graduate school is no testimony that they have escaped the doll's house.

References

Abbott, Walter F., and Calvin F. Schmid: "Toward an Organizational Theory of Migration: University Prestige and First-Time Undergraduate Student Migration in the United States," paper presented before the 1969 meeting of the Population Association of America, Atlantic City, N.J.

Aiken, Wreathy: *Education of Women in Texas,* The Naylor Company, San Antonio, Tex., 1957.

Alexander, Anne: "Who's Come a Long Way, Baby?" *The Johns Hopkins Magazine,* vol. 21, pp. 11–15, April 1970.

Arreger, Constance: *Graduate Women at Work,* Oriel Press, Ltd., Newcastle upon Tyne, England, 1966.

Ashley-Montagu, M. F.: *The Natural Superiority of Women,* The Macmillan Company, New York, 1953.

Astin, Alexander, and Robert J. Panos: "A National Research Data Bank for Higher Education," *Educational Record,* vol. 47, pp. 5–17, Winter 1966.

Auvenen, Riita: "Women and Work: Social Attitudes and Women's Careers," *Impact of Science on Society,* vol. 20, pp. 73–80, January 1970.

Barker, Roger: "The Social Psychology of Physical Disability," *Journal of Social Issues,* vol. 4, pp. 28–38, Fall 1948.

Beach, Leland R.: "The Graduate Student," in Everett Walters (ed.), *Graduate Education Today,* pp. 118–128, American Council on Education, Washington, D.C., 1965.

Becker, Howard S., and James Carper: "The Development of Identification with an Occupation," *American Journal of Sociology,* vol. 61, pp. 289–298, 1956.

Becker, Howard S., Blanche Geer, Everett Hughes, and Anselm Strauss: *Boys in White,* The University of Chicago Press, Chicago, 1961.

Bennett, Helen M.: *Women and Work: The Economic Value of a College Education,* D. Appleton, New York, 1917.

Berelson, Bernard: *Graduate Education in the United States,* McGraw-Hill Book Company, New York, 1960.

Bernard, Jessie: *Academic Women,* The Pennsylvania State University Press, University Park, 1964.

Bettelheim, Bruno: "The Commitment Required of a Woman Entering a Scientific Profession in Present-Day American Society," in Jacquelyn A. Mattfeld and Carol E. Van Aken (eds.), *Women and the Scientific Professions,* pp. 3–19, The M.I.T. Press, Cambridge, Mass., 1965.

Bezdek, William, and Fred L. Strodtbeck: "Sex Role Identity and Pragmatic Action," *American Sociological Review,* vol. 35, pp. 491–502, June 1970.

Bierstedt, Robert: *The Social Order,* McGraw-Hill Book Company, New York, 1963.

Bird, Caroline: *Born Female,* David McKay Company, Inc., New York, 1968.

Bradburn, Norman O., et al.: *Women in the University of Chicago: Report of the Committee on University Women,* University of Chicago Academic Senate, Chicago, 1970.

Brown, Roger: *Social Psychology,* The Free Press, New York, 1965.

Bucher, Rue, Joan Stelling, and Paul Dommermuth: "Differential Prior Socialization: A Comparison of Four Professional Training Programs," *Social Forces,* vol. 48, pp. 213–223, 1969.

Budner, Stanley, and John Meyer: *Women Professors,* Columbia University Bureau of Applied Social Research, New York, 1961. (Mimeographed.)

Bureau of Vocational Information: *Women in Chemistry: A Study of Professional Opportunities,* Bureau of Vocational Information, New York, 1922.

Burton, John: *Lectures on Female Education and Manners,* J. Milliken, Dublin, 1794.

Caplow, Theodore: *The Sociology of Work,* The University of Minnesota Press, Minneapolis, 1954.

Caplow, Theodore, and Reece McGee: *The Academic Marketplace,* Anchor Books, Doubleday & Company, Inc., Garden City, N.Y., 1965.

Career Opportunities for Women, Department of Physics, University of Oklahoma, Norman, n.d.

Cartter, Allan: *An Assessment of Quality in Graduate Education,* American Council on Education, Washington, D.C., 1966.

Chandler, Marjorie O: *Opening Fall Enrollment in Higher Education, 1968: Part A — Summary Data,* Government Printing Office, Washington, D.C., 1969.

Chandler, Marjorie O., and Mary E. Hooper: *Students Enrolled for Advanced Degrees: Fall 1968 — Part B,* Government Printing Office, Washington, D.C., 1970.

College Blue Book, 1969-70, 13th ed., CCM Information Corporation, New York, 1969.

The College-Rater, College-Rater, Inc., Allentown, Pa., 1967.

Colson, Elizabeth, Elizabeth Scott, et al.: *Report of the Subcommittee on the Status of Women on the Berkeley Campus,* University of California Academic Senate, Berkeley, 1970.

Coser, Rose, and Gerald Rokoff: "Women in the Occupational World: Social Disruption and Conflict," *Social Problems,* vol. 18, pp. 535-554, Spring 1971.

Cross, K. Patricia: "College Women: A Research Description," paper presented before the 1968 annual meeting of the National Association of Women Deans and Counselors, Washington, D.C.

Currie, Ian, Henry Finney, Travis Hirschi, and Hanan Selvin: "Images of the Professor and Interest in the Academic Profession," *Sociology of Education,* vol. 39, pp. 301-323, Fall 1966.

Deutsch, Helene: *The Psychology of Women: A Psychoanalytic Interpretation,* Grune and Stratton, Inc., New York, 1945.

Durkheim, Emile: *Suicide,* The Free Press, New York, 1951.

Earnest, Ernest: *Academic Procession,* The Bobbs-Merrill Company, Inc., Indianapolis, 1953.

Eisenstadt, S. N.: *The Absorption of Immigrants,* Routledge & Keagan Paul, Ltd., London, 1954.

Emerick, Charles F.: "College Women and Race Suicide," *Political Science Quarterly,* vol. 24, pp. 269-283, 1909.

Epstein, Cynthia: *Woman's Place: The Options and Limits in Professional Careers,* University of California Press, Berkeley, 1970.

Erikson, Erik: "Inner and Outer Space: Reflections on Womanhood," *Daedalus,* vol. 93, pp. 582-606, Spring 1964.

Fancourt, Mary St. John: *They Dared to Be Doctors,* Longmans, Green & Co., Ltd., London, 1965.

Feldman, Saul D.: "Girls Stay Away from the Boys: Marital Status and Graduate Education," paper presented before the 1971 meeting of the Pacific Sociological Association, Honolulu, 1971a.

Feldman, Saul D.: *A Profile of Men and Women in Graduate Education,* Survey Research Center, Berkeley, Calif., 1971*b*. (Mimeographed.)

Feldman, Saul D.: "The Presentation of Shortness in Everyday Life: Height and Heightism in American Society: Toward a Sociology of Stature," paper presented before the 1971 meeting of the American Sociological Association, Denver, 1971*c*.

Feldman, Saul D. , and Frank J. Kohout: "Research Note: The Semantic Differential and Stereotype Research," revision of paper presented before the 1967 meeting of the Ohio Valley Sociological Society, South Bend, Ind.

Feldman, Saul D., and Linda S. Noelker: "Grasshoppers and Ants: Adaptive Strategies in Graduate Education," paper presented before the 1973 meeting of the Pacific Sociological Association, Phoenix.

Feldman, Saul D., and Gerald W. Thielbar: "Power, Privilege, and Prestige of Occupations," in Gerald Thielbar and Saul Feldman (eds.), *Issues in Social Inequality,* pp. 227–236, Little, Brown and Company, Boston, 1972.

Fischer, Ann, and Peggy Golde: "The Position of Women in Anthropology," *American Anthropologist,* vol. 70, pp. 337–343, 1968.

Fox, Renée C.: "Training for Uncertainty," in Robert K. Merton et al. (eds.), *The Student Physician,* pp. 207–241, Harvard University Press, Cambridge, Mass., 1957.

Franzblau, Abraham N.: *A Primer of Statistics for Non-Statisticians,* Harcourt, Brace & World, Inc., New York, 1958.

Frazier, E. Franklin: *Black Bourgeoisie,* The Free Press, New York, 1957.

Friedan, Betty: *The Feminine Mystique,* W. W. Norton & Company, Inc., New York, 1963.

Ginzberg, Eli: *Life Styles of Educated Women,* Columbia University Press, New York, 1966.

Goodsell, Willystine: *The Education of Women,* The Macmillan Company, New York, 1923.

Gourman, Jack: *The Gourman Report: Ratings of American Colleges,* The Continuing Education Institute, Phoenix, 1967.

Graham, Patricia A.: "Women in Academe," *Science,* vol. 169, pp. 1284–1290, Sept. 25, 1970.

Gross, Edward: "Plus ça change . . . ? The Sexual Structure of Occupations Over Time," *Social Problems,* vol. 16, pp. 198–208, Fall 1968.

Gross, Edward, and Paul V. Grambsch: *University Goals and Academic Power,* American Council on Education, Washington, D.C., 1968.

Gusfield, Joseph: *Symbolic Crusade,* The University of Illinois Press, Urbana, 1963.

Hacker, Helen: "Women as a Minority Group," *Social Forces,* vol. 30, pp. 60–69, 1951.

Harris, Ann S.: "The Second Sex in Academe," *AAUP Bulletin,* vol. 56, pp. 283–295, September 1970.

Hawtrey, Mabel: "Remarks before the International Conference of Women, 1899," in Countess of Aberdeen (ed.), *Transactions of the International Conference of Women,* pp. 169–171, T. Fisher Unwin, London, 1900.

Hirschi, Travis, and Joseph Zelan: *Student Activism,* Survey Research Center, Berkeley, Calif., 1971. (Mimeographed.)

Hodge, Robert W., Paul Siegel, and Peter Rossi: "Occupational Prestige in the United States, 1925–63," *American Journal of Sociology,* vol. 70, pp. 286–302, November 1964.

Hooper, Mary E.: *Earned Degrees Conferred: 1970–71, Summary Data,* U.S. Office of Education, Government Printing Office, Washington, D.C., 1973.

Hooper, Mary E., and Margaret O. Chandler: *Earned Degrees Conferred— 1968-69: Part B—Institutional Data,* U.S. Office of Education, Government Printing Office, Washington, D.C., 1971.

Hubback, Judith: *Wives Who Went to College,* Heinemann, London, 1957.

Hudson, Liam: *Frames of Mind,* Methuen & Co., Ltd., London, 1968.

Hutchinson, Emily J.: *Women and the Ph.D.,* North Carolina College for Women, Greensboro, 1930.

Ibsen, Henrik: *A Doll's House, The Wild Duck, The Lady from the Sea,* trans. R. Farquharson Sharp and Eleanor Marx-Aveling, E. P. Dutton & Co., Inc., New York, 1958.

Jencks, Christopher, and David Riesman: *The Academic Revolution,* Doubleday & Company, Inc., Garden City, N.Y., 1968.

Kadushin, Charles: "The Professional Self Concept of Music Students," *American Journal of Sociology,* vol. 75, pp. 389–405, 1969.

Kerlinger, Fred: *Foundations of Behavioral Research,* Holt, Rinehart and Winston, Inc., New York, 1964.

Kingsley, Florence: *Life of Henry F. Durant,* Century Company, New York, 1924.

Knudsen, Dean: "The Declining Status of Women: Popular Myths and the Failure of Functionalist Thought," *Social Forces,* vol. 48, pp. 183–193, December 1969.

Koch, Beverly: "Women Med Students—a Tough Road," *San Francisco Chronicle,* Feb. 23, 1971, p. 18.

Komarovsky, Mirra: *Women in the Modern World,* Little, Brown and Company, Boston, 1953.

Kraditor, Aileen (ed.): *Up from the Pedestal.* Quadrangle Books, Inc., Chicago, 1968.

Leland, Carole, and Marjorie Lozoff: *College Influences on the Role Development of Female Undergraduates,* Institute for the Study of Human Problems, Stanford, Calif., 1969.

Lerner, William (ed.): *Statistical Abstract of the United States—1970.* Government Printing Office, Washington, D.C., 1970.

Linn, Edwin L.: "Women Dentists: Career and Family," *Social Problems* vol. 18, pp. 393–404, Winter 1971.

Lopate, Carol: *Women in Medicine,* The Johns Hopkins Press, Baltimore, 1968.

Lundberg, George A.: "Some Neglected Aspects of the Minority Problem," *Modern Age,* vol. 2, pp. 285–297, Summer 1958.

Maccoby, Eleanor (ed.): *The Development of Sex Differences,* Stanford University Press, Stanford, Calif., 1966.

Maccoby, Eleanor: "Feminine Intellect and the Demands of Science," *Impact of Science on Society,* vol. 20, pp. 13–28, January 1970.

Maccoby, Herbert: "Occupational Image and Prestige among Teachers," paper presented before the 1963 Meeting of the American Sociological Association, Washington, D.C.

McClelland, Clarence P.: *The Education of Females in Early Illinois,* MacMurray College Bulletin, vol. 34, Jacksonville, Ill., April 1944.

McGuinan, Dorothy G.: *A Dangerous Experiment: 100 Years of Women at the University of Michigan,* Center for Continuing Education of Women, Ann Arbor, Mich., 1970.

Mencken, H. L.: *In Defense of Women,* Alfred A. Knopf, Inc., New York, 1924.

Miller, Mrs. Fenwick: "The Effect upon Domestic Life of Entry of Women into Professions," in Ishbell Aberdeen (ed.), *Women in Professions,* vol. 1, pp. 38–41, T. Fisher Unwin, London, 1899.

Millett, Kate: *Sexual Politics,* Doubleday & Company, Inc., Garden City, N.Y., 1970.

Mooney, Joseph D.: "Attrition among Ph.D. Candidates: An Analysis of a Cohort of Recent Woodrow Wilson Fellows," *Journal of Human Resources,* vol. 3, pp. 46–62, Winter 1968.

Mueller, John H., Karl F. Schuessler, and Herbert L. Costner: *Statistical Reasoning in Sociology,* 2d ed., Houghton Mifflin Company, Boston, 1970.

Muller, Leo C., and Ouida Gean Muller: *College for Coeds,* Pitman Publishing Corporation, New York, 1960.

Myrdal, Gunnar: *An American Dilemma,* Harper & Row, Publishers, Incorporated, New York, 1944.

Newcomer, Mabel: *A Century of Higher Education for Women,* Harper & Row, Publishers, Incorporated, New York, 1959.

O'Dowd, Donald, and David Beardslee: *College Student Images of a Selected Group of Professions and Occupations,* Wesleyan University Press, Middletown, Conn., 1960.

Olesen, Virginia, and Elvi Whittaker: *The Silent Dialogue,* Jossey-Bass, Inc., Publishers, San Francisco, 1968.

Oppenheimer, Valerie: "The Sex-Labelling of Jobs," *Industrial Relations,* vol. 7, pp. 219–234, May 1968.

Osgood, Charles, G. Suci, and Percy Tannenbaum: *The Measurement of Meaning,* The University of Illinois Press, Urbana, 1967.

Ouida: "The New Women," *North American Review,* vol. 158, pp. 610–619, 1894.

Perrucci, Carolyn C.: "Minority Status and the Pursuit of Professional Careers: Women in Science and Engineering," *Social Forces,* vol. 49, pp. 245–259, December 1970.

Poloma, Margaret M., and T. Neal Garland: "Role Conflict and the Married Professional Woman," paper presented before the 1970 meeting of the Ohio Valley Sociological Society, Cleveland.

Prothro, E. Jerry, and J. D. Keehn: "Stereotypes and Semantic Space," *Journal of Social Psychology,* vol. 45, pp. 197–209, 1957.

Riesman, David: Introduction to *Academic Women,* by Jessie Bernard, The Pennsylvania State University Press, University Park, 1964.

Robinson, W. S.: "Ecological Correlations and the Behavior of Individuals," *American Sociological Review,* vol. 15, pp. 351–357, June 1950.

Rossi, Alice: "Equality between the Sexes: An Immodest Proposal," *Daedalus,* vol. 93, pp. 607–652, Spring 1964.

Rossi, Alice: "Barriers to the Career Choice of Engineering, Science, and Medicine among American Women," in Jacquelyn A. Mattfeld and Carol E. Van Aken (eds.), *Women and the Scientific Professions,* pp. 51–127, The M.I.T. Press, Cambridge, Mass., 1965.

Rossi, Alice: "Status of Women in Graduate Departments of Sociology: 1968–1969," *American Sociologist,* vol. 5, pp. 1–12, February 1970.

Rudolph, Frederick: *The American College and University: A History,* Vintage Books, Random House, Inc., New York, 1962.

Ryan, W. Carson: *Studies in Early Graduate Education,* Carnegie Foundation for the Advancement of Teaching, New York, 1939.

Scarf, Maggie: "He and She: The Sex Hormones and Behavior," *The New York Times Magazine,* May 7, 1972, pp. 101–107.

Schoen, Kathryn T., et al.: "Report of the Ad Hoc Committee to Review the Status of Women at The Ohio State University," Ohio State University, Columbus, 1971.

Schuck, Victoria: "Femina studens rei publicae: Notes on Her Professional Achievement," *PS,* vol. 4, pp. 622–628, 1970.

Scully, Malcolm G.: "Women in Higher Education: Challenging the Status Quo," *The Chronicle of Higher Education,* vol. 4, pp. 2–5, Feb. 9, 1970.

Seward, Georgene, and Robert Williamson (eds.): *Sex Roles in a Changing Society,* Random House, Inc., New York, 1970.

Singletary, Otis (ed.): *American Universities and Colleges,* 10th ed., American Council on Education, Washington, D.C., 1968.

Slater, Philip: *The Pursuit of Loneliness,* Beacon Press, Boston, 1970.

Snider, James G.: "Profiles of Some Stereotypes Held by Ninth-Grade Pupils," *Alberta Journal of Educational Research,* vol. 8, pp. 147–156, 1962.

Sommerkorn, Ingrid: "On the Position of Women in the University Teaching Profession in England," unpublished doctoral dissertation, University of London, London, 1966.

Sprague, Robert J.: "Education and Race Suicide," *The Journal of Heredity,* vol. 6, pp. 158–162, 1915.

Stark, Rodney: *Graduate Study at Berkeley: A Study of Attrition and Duration,* Survey Research Center Monograph M32, Berkeley, Calif., 1967.

Stetson, Charlotte Perkins: *Women and Economics,* Small, Maynard, Boston, 1898.

Storr, Richard J.: *The Beginning of Graduate Education in America,* The University of Chicago Press, Chicago, 1953.

Talbot, Marion, and Lois Rosenberry: *The History of the American Association of University Women: 1881–1931,* Houghton Mifflin Company, Boston, 1931.

Talbot, Nell S.: "Why Not More Women Dental Students?" *Journal of Dental Education,* vol. 25, pp. 11–19, March 1961.

Thielbar, Gerald W., and Saul D. Feldman: "Occupational Stereotypes and Prestige," *Social Forces,* vol. 48, pp. 147–156, September 1969.

Thomas, Martha: "Present Tendencies in Women's College and University Education," *Educational Review,* vol. 35, pp. 64–85, January 1908.

Thompson, Eleanor: *Education for Ladies — 1830–1860: Ideas on Education in Magazines for Women,* King's Crown Press, New York, 1947.

Thwing, Charles F.: *The College Woman,* The Baker and Taylor Company, Hillside, N.J., 1894.

Thwing, Charles F.: *A History of Higher Education in America,* D. Appleton & Company, Inc., New York, 1906.

Trow, Martin A.: "Recruitment to College Teaching," in A. H. Halsey, Jean Floud, and C. Arnold Anderson (eds.), *Education, Economy, and Society,* pp. 602–620, The Free Press, New York, 1961.

Trow, Martin A., et al.: *Technical Report: National Survey of Higher Education,* Carnegie Commission on Higher Education, Berkeley, Calif., 1971. (Mimeographed.)

Turner, Ralph: "Some Aspects of Women's Ambition," *American Journal of Sociology,* vol. 70, pp. 271–285, November 1964.

Uesugi, Thomas, and W. Edgar Vinacke: "Strategy in a Feminine Game," *Sociometry,* vol. 26, pp. 75–78, March 1963.

Veysey, Laurence R.: *The Emergence of the American University,* The University of Chicago Press, Chicago, 1965.

Vollmer, Howard L., and Donald Mills: *Professionalization,* Prentice-Hall, Inc., Englewood Cliffs, N.J., 1966.

Weber, Max: *Essays in Sociology,* in Hans Gerth and C. Wright Mills (trans.), Oxford University Press, New York, 1946.

Wegner, Eldon E.: "Some Factors in Obtaining Postgraduate Education," *Sociology of Education,* vol. 42, pp. 154–169, Spring 1969.

Weisstein, Naomi: "Woman as Nigger," *Psychology Today,* vol. 3, pp. 20–22, 58, October 1969.

Wells, D. Collin: "Some Questions Concerning the Higher Education of Women," *American Journal of Sociology,* vol. 14, pp. 731–739, 1909.

White, Lynn, Jr.: *Educating Our Daughters,* Harper & Brothers, New York, 1950.

Winick, Charles: *The New People: Desexualization in American Life,* Pegasus, The Bobbs-Merrill Co, Inc., Indianapolis, 1968.

Women's Research Group: *Women at Wisconsin,* Women's Research Group, Madison, Wis., 1970.

Woodring, Paul: "Sexism on the Campus," *Saturday Review,* May 16, 1970, pp. 80, 88.

Woody, Thomas: *A History of Women's Education in the United States,* vol. 1, Science Press, New York, 1929*a*.

Woody, Thomas: *A History of Women's Education in the United States,* vol. 2, Science Press, New York, 1929*b*.

Young, Michael: *The Rise of the Meritocracy,* Thames and Hudson, London, 1958.

Appendix A: Methodology of the Carnegie Commission Study

The data for this study were derived from a national sample of faculty and students sponsored by the Carnegie Commission on Higher Education and the U.S. Office of Education and were gathered in cooperation with the Office of Research of the American Council on Education (ACE). Since 1966, ACE has been conducting national studies of undergraduate students in over 300 American institutions of higher education (universities, four-year colleges, and junior colleges); the data in this study utilize with some modifications the ACE sample institutions.

In 1966, 1,968 institutions were deemed eligible for the ACE national sample. The sample drew on the entire universe of American higher education, omitting only those institutions that were created since the *1965–66 Education Directory, Part Three* was published or those that had a freshman class of less than 30 individuals. The 1,968 institutions were stratified by institutional type (that is, two-year colleges, four-year colleges, and universities, enrollment (junior colleges only), and financial expenditures per student (universities and four-year colleges only). ACE deliberately oversampled universities as well as institutions with high enrollment or great affluence. The actual selection of the sample institutions is described by ACE.

The institutions were initially sorted into the appropriate stratification cells, the cell members shuffled, and 371 institutions randomly chosen for the contact sample. . . . The only departure from strict randomness was the deliberate inclusion in the 371 of 61 institutions that had been selected from a similar stratification design for [a] 1965 pilot study. . . . An additional 25 institutions, not included as part of the sample, were also selected either by their own request or because they were known to have educational programs of some special interest to the research staff (Astin & Panos, 1966, pp. 11–12).

Of the 371 institutions selected in this manner, 307 agreed to participate in ACE's research program.

The enumeration for the national Carnegie sample was begun in the fall of 1968. The original 1966 ACE sample had changed in several ways by this time: 25 institutions dropped out of the research program; 2 institutions were reclassified from universities to colleges, 4 colleges became universities, and 2 separate institutions were consolidated into one university; and, in 1967, ACE added 24 junior colleges. Because of the high withdrawal rates and underrepresentation of the junior colleges, the Carnegie sample included 24 more two-year colleges.

In the fall of 1968, the participating institutions were asked for lists of their faculty and graduate students. The letter requesting the faculty listing asked for:

. . . a list of the names and departmental addresses of the regular faculty of the academic departments and professional schools of your institution. This list should include any staff member who is in charge of courses: including visiting professors, visiting lecturers, and any lecturers, instructors, etc., whether "acting" or not, who are responsible for the teaching of any course during the '68–'69 academic year creditable toward a degree (associate, bachelor's, or higher). If possible, this list should not include graduate students acting as teaching assistants. If any question arises as to whether or not to include an individual, please include him.

The request for the list of graduate students asked for:

. . . a list of names and local, but not departmental, addresses of graduate and professional students enrolled in the departments and schools of your institution in degree programs beyond the undergraduate bachelor's degree. If the student is not in residence and does not have a local address, a home address would be appreciated.

Samples were drawn from the lists supplied by these institutions. On the list of graduate students, 3 out of 4 names were eliminated (systematic sample with a random start). A final 1-in-6 sample was derived by randomly removing one-third of the remaining cases. The faculty lists were reduced by systematically removing every seventh name, resulting in a 6-in-7 sample.

There were 303 institutions in the faculty sample. The total number of faculty in these schools was 116,115, of whom 100,290 were included in the sample. Of the 303 institutions 158 supplied lists of graduate students.[1] The total number of graduate and professional students in these institutions was 310,008, of whom 51,682 were sent questionnaires.

The questionnaires were machine-readable and self-administered.[2] Printing, mailing, and machine coding were handled by National Computer Systems in Minneapolis. Faculty questionnaires were mailed from Minneapolis in the second week of March 1969 over a period of five days. Graduate questionnaires were mailed during the third week in March over a three-day period. Follow-up reminder postcards were sent to all respondents one week after the initial questionnaire mailing. Two weeks after the mailing, a follow-up letter was sent to all respondents; six weeks later, a second questionnaire was sent to all who had not by that date returned their questionnaire. Approximately 8 percent of students and faculty receiving a second questionnaire returned it.

As a check of the NCS machine coding, 200 graduate-student and faculty questionnaires were also hand-coded. Comparisons were made column by column, through marginal distributions and through contingency checking. Only after there was full agreement between the hand-coded questionnaires and the machine-coded questionnaires were the bulk of the data machine-scored and machine-coded. Random coding error resulting from the use of the optical scanner was estimated at less than 0.5 percent.

To learn of biases due to nonresponse, after approximately 50 percent of both samples had responded, random samples of 2,000 faculty and 2,000 graduate students were selected for an intensive follow-up. Of the 2,000 students and 2,000 faculty, approximately half had already responded to the questionnaire. The rest were sent a third questionnaire and then telephoned. For the first call, telephone interviewers were instructed to encourage the respondent to complete and return the questionnaire. If the respondent agreed to do so, the interview was terminated. If the respondent indicated that he did not intend to complete the questionnaire, he was asked a brief list of questions identical to items on the questionnaire. After a lapse of some weeks, those respondents who had not completed the questionnaire but who had indicated willingness to complete it

[1] Most of the 303 institutions that supplied no graduate student list had no graduate students on roll. All participating universities, with one exception, sent graduate-student lists. Only a few four-year colleges did not send lists or sent them too late for inclusion in the sample.

[2] See Appendix C for copies of the questionnaires.

were called again. On the second call they were again encouraged to complete the questionnaire but were asked the brief list of questions whether or not they agreed to complete the questionnaire.

Because of disproportionate sampling and the failure to obtain graduate-student and faculty lists from some sample institutions, it was decided that the data would be more representative if they were weighted. As a first step, all sample institutions were placed into their 1966 ACE sampling cells. Tables A-1 and A-2 summarize this procedure. All but 228 of the 2,843 institutions of higher education listed by the U.S. Office of Education in the fall of 1968[3] were eligible for inclusion and could be located within the 1966 ACE sampling scheme. The 228 ineligible institutions contained slightly more than 2 percent of all the faculty and less than 4 percent of all the graduate students in American higher education. The bulk of ineligible faculty and graduate students are found in 123 autonomous theological seminaries[4] and in 31 autonomous graduate or professional schools.

[3] Institutions and enrollment listed on data tape (HEGIS II—Opening Fall Enrollment, 1968) supplied by the Office of Education.

[4] Seminaries attached to universities were included as part of the university.

TABLE A-1 *Assignment of institutions to 1966 ACE cells, with faculty institutional weights*

			Universe		Sample		
1966 ACE cell		Enrollment and affluence	Number of institutions*	Number of faculty	Number of institutions†	Number of faculty	Faculty weight
Public two-year colleges	1	Low enrollment	172	6,108	6	390	15.66
	2	•	182	10,621	7	447	23.76
	3	•	175	17,567	7	593	29.62
	4	•	54	9,068	5	645	14.06
	5	High	50	12,352	5	1,457	8.48
Private two-year colleges	6	Low enrollment	229	6,824	10	353	19.33
	7	•					19.33
	8	•	36	2,664	4	343	7.77
	9	High					7.77
Universities	10	Affluence unknown					
	11	Low	15	6,780	4	2,691	2.52

1966 ACE cell		Enrollment and affluence	Universe		Sample		Faculty weight
			Number of insti-tutions*	Number of faculty	Number of insti-tutions†	Number of faculty	
	12	•	10	3,715	5	2,418	1.54
	13	•	47	18,079	5	5,815	3.11
	14	•	52	20,306	12	9,401	2.16
	15	•	18	13,382	5	4,362	3.07
	16	•	69	36,638	13	19,060	1.92
	17	•	32	22,036	23	18,512	1.19
	18	•	44	19,177	8	8,146	2.35
	19	High	76	67,775	26	36,316	1.87
Four-year colleges	20	Affluence low					13.31
	21	•	449	37,497	30	2,818	13.31
	22	•	248	34,436	20	3,010	11.44
	23	•	250	34,435	22	2,241	15.37
	24	•	175	30,891	26	4,769	6.48
	25	•	84	11,747	19	2,091	5.62
	26	•	56	8,753	25	3,799	2.30
	27	•	29	5,078	12	2,401	2.11
	28	•	24	3,369	9	1,733	1.94
	29	High	39	6,998	18	3,160	2.21
Total eligible			2,615	446,296‡	326	136,971	3.26
Ineligible institutions							
No undergraduates	30		8	918	0		
Seminaries	31		123	3,137	0		
Professional schools	32		31	4,965	0		
Freshman class less than 30 students	33		66	1,302	0		
Total ineligible			228	10,322	0		
TOTAL			2,843	456,618			

* The number of institutions includes branch campuses counted as separate institutions by the U.S. Office of Education.
† This number includes 303 sample institutions.
‡ This figure constitutes 97.74 percent of total faculty.

TABLE A-2 *Assignment of institutions to 1966 ACE cells, with graduate-student institutional weights*

1966 ACE cell		Enrollment and affluence	Universe Number of institutions*	Universe Number of graduate students	Sample Number of institutions*	Sample Number of graduate students	Graduate-student weight
Public two-year colleges	1	Low enrollment	172				
	2	•	182				
	3	•	175				
	4	•	54				
	5	High	50				
Private two-year colleges	6	Low enrollment	229				
	7	•					
	8	•	36				
	9	High					
Universities	10	Affluence unknown					
	11	Low	15	27,447	4	9,403	2.92
	12	•	10	14,468	5	12,147	1.19
	13	•	47	43,664	5	15,202	2.87
	14	•	52	73,872	11	23,486	3.15
	15	•	18	42,569	5	12,320	3.46
	16	•	69	121,747	13	60,904	2.00
	17	•	32	71,985	18	57,486	1.25
	18	•	44	69,290	7	31,898	2.17
	19	High	76	187,622	18	93,878	2.00
Four-year colleges	20	Affluence low					18.60
	21	•	697	119,903	18	6,446	18.60
	22	•					18.60
	23	•	425	151,499	17	12,928	11.72
	24	•					11.72
	25	•	84	23,235	6	2,116	10.98
	26	•	56	20,119	15	4,932	4.08
	27	•	29	13,240	7	8,803	1.50
	28	•	24	8,178	6	3,794	2.16

1966 ACE cell		Enrollment and affluence	Number of insti- tutions*	Universe Number of graduate students	Sample Number of insti- tutions	Sample Number of graduate students	Graduate- student weight
	29	High	39	13,853	10	6,246	2.22
Total eligible			2,615	1,002,691†	165	361,989	2.77
Ineligible institutions							
No undergraduates	30		8	4,432	0		
Seminaries	31		123	17,813	0		
Professional schools	32		31	13,257	0		
Freshman class less than 30 students	33		66	2,976	0		
Total ineligible			228	38,478	0		
TOTAL			2,843	1,041,169			

* The number of institutions includes branch campuses counted as separate institutions by the U.S. Office of Education. This number includes 303 sample institutions.
† This figure constitutes 96.30 percent of total graduate students.

Branch or satellite campuses of institutions included in the ACE sampling frame were assigned to the sampling cell occupied by the main campus. Although in some cases branch-campus lists were provided, either directly or by the main campus, both faculty and graduate students at branch campuses are, in general, under-represented in the sample. Since we cannot distinguish between main and branch-campus respondents, we can neither exclude the latter from the sample nor adjust for their smaller likelihood of appearing in the sample by adjusting the magnitude of their weights. (The bias is not large. About 6 percent—61,000—of all graduate students are enrolled at such campuses. The names of 5,500 of these were on the lists sent to the Carnegie Commission.)

Initial assignment of institutions to the 1966 ACE cells revealed that the "unknown" categories of affluence for both universities and colleges were greatly undersampled. Rather than assign very large weights to these undersampled institutions, we attempted to distribute them over the other sampling cells on the basis of affluence information not available to ACE in 1966. All universities were easily reassigned on the basis of current information, but per-student expenditure information was still unavailable for many four-year colleges. Those colleges for which such information had become available were generally poor. We therefore combined the "unknown" category with the lowest category of affluence in the case of faculty and with the two lowest cells in the case of graduate students.

Finally, two faculty junior college cells and one graduate-student four-year college cell were sufficiently undersampled that we con-sidered it necessary for purposes of weighting to combine them with adjacent and much better sampled cells.

Once these operations were performed, we determined the total number of graduate students in each cell from enrollment infor-mation provided by the U.S. Office of Education; faculty numbers were obtained from the *College Blue Book* (1969), with missing information supplied from *The World Almanac: 1969* and ACE's *American Universities and Colleges* (Singletary, 1968). Tables A-1 and A-2 show the base institutional weights, created by divid-ing the number of individuals in the universe by the number in the sample.

We were now in a position to check for possible bias in the sam-ple. The first check was on institutional quality. The weights were first used to estimate the total number of faculty and of graduate students in each of several quality strata. These estimates were then compared with the actual numbers derived from published sources and from data tapes provided by the Office of Education. The Office of Education projected that 841,622 graduate students were registered in master's, doctoral, or first-professional degree pro-grams in 1968. The remaining graduate students were in nondegree or special programs. The projected total includes only graduate students in eligible institutions and does not include students in autonomous graduate institutions such as theological seminaries, independent medical or law schools, or graduate institutions that have no undergraduates. The results for graduate students are shown in Table A-3.

Table A-3 shows that high-quality institutions, both colleges and universities, were oversampled by ACE. After the extent of bias had been determined with respect to geographical location, size, and public or private control as well as quality, we adjusted the weights simultaneously for both quality and institutional con-

TABLE A-3
Actual populations of graduate students in quality strata and populations estimated from 1966 ACE cells

Quality ranking	Actual population	Estimate from ACE strata	Percentage estimate over or under actual population
Universities (total)	652,664	652,663	
High	172,330	226,983	(+) 31.7
Medium	258,232	231,134	(−) 10.5
Low	222,102	194,546	(−) 12.4
Colleges (total)	350,027	350,027	
High	60,791	78,190	(+) 28.6
Medium	120,682	114,927	(−) 4.8
Low	168,554	156,910	(−) 6.9

trol. The data were also adjusted for three other sources of variation: institutional nonresponse (that is, the relative completeness of the lists sent by the institutions), sampling of individuals from lists, and respondent nonresponse.

We reduced extreme graduate-student weights by combining no-response or incomplete-list institutions with institutions similar in quality, size, type of control, and geographical region. Seven small institutions in all were combined with other institutions for this purpose.

The final weights used for the tabulations in this study were thus an attempt to take into account the sampling of institutions, the bias with respect to quality and control, the sampling of individuals, and two types of nonresponse. These weights range in magnitude from 1.34 to 103.09 for faculty and from 0.82 to 1,314.94 for graduate students.

Of 51,682 questionnaires sent to graduate students enrolled in participating institutions, 32,963, or 64.0 percent, were eventually returned in usable form.[5] Of the 100,290 questionnaires sent to faculty, 60,028, or 59.8 percent, were returned.

The colleges and universities in the sample have been classified on the basis of quality into seven groups: high-, medium-, and low-

[5] An additional 650 (or 1.3 percent of the total) questionnaires were returned to the Commission. Of these, 378 were determined to be undergraduate responses and thus ineligible for the survey. Another 93 were returned with the identification number so defaced that institutional affiliation could not be determined. The remaining unusable questionnaires were duplicates of questionnaires already returned. Blank questionnaires were returned by 170 graduate students.

quality universities; high-, medium-, and low-quality colleges; and junior colleges. Our criterion for what constituted a university was determined by the classification scheme of the U.S. Office of Education. Universities are defined by OE as "institutions which give considerable stress to graduate instruction, which confer advanced degrees as well as bachelor's degrees in a variety of liberal arts fields, and which have at least two professional schools that are not exclusively technological." Institutions (except junior colleges) that did not meet these criteria were classified as colleges.[6]

The basic source of information on quality is *The Gourman Report,* which attempts to "provide a detailed rating of the undergraduate programs of nearly all of the colleges and universities in the United States" (Gourman, 1967, p. ix). Gourman lists three ratings for each institution: a rating of academic departments; a rating of nondepartmental aspects of the university, such as faculty morale, computer center, and counseling programs: and an overall rating which is the mean of departmental and nondepartmental ratings. Gourman's rating scheme is in some ways idiosyncratic — he does not really state how he evaluates or weights factors he includes such as athletic-academic balance, board of trustees, or commitment to excellence — and the justification for using Gourman's ratings is largely pragmatic. He does provide us with the most comprehensive rating of American colleges and universities available, and his method produces results similar to those obtained by other, less comprehensive rating systems.

Gross and Grambsch (1968, pp. 124–132), using information on graduate-department ratings supplied by Cartter (1966), rated major universities in terms of the overall quality of their doctoral training programs. Although the Gross-Grambsch index ranks graduate schools and Gourman ranks undergraduate education, Abbott and Schmid (1969) found that the correlation between the two rating systems (based on 79 universities) is $+.83$. They also provided (for 79 institutions) the following correlations with the Gourman rating: average compensation of faculty, 1963–64, $+.78$; number of library volumes, $+.74$; doctorates conferred, 1961–62,

---

[6] Certain institutions (e.g., Hamline University, Minnesota, and Saint Edward's University, Texas) call themselves "universities" without having any graduate or professional programs, while some schools (most notably California Institute of Technology) that are considered by many (see Berelson, 1960, pp. 280–281) to be universities are, on the basis of OE criteria, classified as four-year colleges.

+.71; and percentage of foreign students, +.66 (Abbott & Schmid, 1969, p. 21).

In short, then, the three categories we use for universities differ little from the gross categories of quality that might be obtained from other well-known quality rankings. Since the Gourman system applies to four-year colleges as well as universities, we have used it here.

At the time the data were gathered, we assured our cooperating institutions and our respondents of the confidentiality of our data. At no point would data be published concerning either individual institutions or individual departments. Since the original proposal stated that the data would be made public on September 1, 1971, we decided not to make public the names of the institutions sampled. The relevant information for the university sample is as follows:

High-quality universities

    Gourman score: 580+

    Number of universities sampled: 17

    Number of faculty, 1968–69: 35,118

    Number of faculty responding: 13,924

    Number of graduate students, 1968–69: 114,093

    Number of graduate students responding: 10,203

Medium-quality universities

    Gourman score: 477–579

    Number of universities sampled: 25

    Number of faculty, 1968–69: 21,050

    Number of faculty responding: 15,475

    Number of graduate students, 1968–69: 119,486

    Number of graduate students responding: 11,131

Low-quality universities

    Gourman score: Less than 477

    Number of universities sampled: 38

    Number of faculty, 1968–69: 30,407

    Number of faculty responding: 14,382

Number of graduate students, 1968–69: 90,863

Number of graduate students responding: 8,228

The number of institutions in each category reflects our desire to have the same number of faculty (and graduate students) in each category. That a larger number of institutions is required to produce the same number of faculty at the low end reflects the moderate correlation between quality and size found by most rating systems.

Grouping of the four-year colleges in our sample is based on a combination of Gourman rankings and rankings provided by *College-Rater* (an independent college and university rating system), with precedence given to the higher of the ratings available for each college. At first glance, *College-Rater* appears to base its rankings on a strategy very different from that employed by Gourman. In fact, it appears to have *The Gourman Report* in mind when it describes its own procedure.

COLLEGE-RATER does not attempt to evaluate the academic excellence of a college or university, the competency of its faculty and staff, or the scope and variety of its curricula. Neither does it profess to measure the efficacy of the operation of its various departments nor the size of its physical plant and endowment. Guidelines used do not take into account the quality of the academic program, the intellectual environment, educational techniques, facilities and other considerations. If such imponderables could be measured, the ratings would change considerably (*College-Rater,* 1967, p. 1).

In the end, however, Gourman and *College-Rater* come out with criteria that are much alike and with roughly similar rankings (the correlation between the two sets of scores is +.75). The four major criteria on which *College-Rater* scores are based are, in descending order, SAT/ACT scores of recently enrolled freshmen, proportion of faculty with doctorates, faculty salaries, and library collection. Three of these criteria, as we noted previously, were highly correlated with overall Gourman scores. College quality categories are as follows:

High-quality colleges

Gourman score: 445+

College-Rater score: 719+

Number of colleges sampled: 38

Number of faculty, 1968–69:   820

Number of faculty responding: 4,648

Number of graduate students, 1968–69:   20,733

Number of graduate students responding: 1,640

Medium-quality colleges

Gourman score: 378–444

College-Rater score: 550–718

Number of colleges sampled: 57

Number of faculty, 1968–69:   8,396

Number of faculty responding: 4,801

Number of graduate students, 1968–69:   14,809

Number of graduate students responding: 1,062

Low-quality colleges

Gourman score: 378 or less

College-Rater score: 550 or less

Number of colleges sampled: 84

Number of faculty, 1968–69:   8,952

Number of faculty responding: 4,658

Number of graduate students, 1968–69:   17,056

Number of graduate students responding: 699

All junior colleges were treated as one category.

Junior colleges

Number of junior colleges sampled: 41

Number of faculty, 1968–69:   4,228

Number of faculty responding: 2,140

Random samples of graduate students and faculty were drawn for intensive follow-up. From the original samples, 2,000 faculty members and 2,037 graduate students were selected. At the time the samples were drawn, over 50 percent of the individuals in the samples had returned the appropriate questionnaire. Thus, approximately 800 faculty members and 1,000 graduate students were left to follow up. The intention was to compare these special samples, both of which had a high rate of response, with the respective full samples to determine the extent of the bias, if any, that results from response rates of 64 percent for the graduate students and 60 percent for the faculty.

Intensive comparison of the samples revealed little bias among either graduate students or faculty. The entire faculty sample and the special follow-up faculty sample differed little in connection with sex, institutional quality, rank, field, age, or political self-identification. Among graduate students there were only minor (3 percent or less) differences on items such as sex, year entered graduate school, and degree working for and no differences on items such as discipline and politics.

There was special concern about possible political biases in our sample. Part of the questionnaire dealt with aspects of student activism, and we felt that individuals who were politically "left" would be less likely to answer. In a long editorial, the staff of the student newspaper at one institution urged their fellow students not to respond to the undergraduate portion of the Carnegie Commission–ACE study. The editorial stated in part:

As many have pointed out, the ACE questionnaire is a domestic counter-part to counter-insurgency, not meant to deal with the real problems in society but to develop techniques for weeding out malcontents and quelling revolt. There is only one way to respond to the ACE questionnaire: Don't cooperate. Throw it out.

However, our response rates appear to be unaffected by political considerations.[7]

---

[7] Full details on sampling, weighting, and nonresponse may be found in Trow et al. (1971).

Appendix B: Correlates from Chapter 3

	Correlation	Significance
Exciting developments		
Humanities orientation	—.62	.001
Things never understood by science	—.59	.001
Teaching orientation (graduate students)	—.51	.001
Faculty paid over $20,000	+.48	.001
Most respected		
Humanities orientation	—.48	.001
Mathematics orientation	+.53	.001
Teaching orientation (faculty)	—.52	.001
Faculty paid over $20,000	+.66	.001
Among best students	—.38	.05
Best students		
Humanities orientation	—.47	.01
Mathematics orientation	+.52	.001
Teaching orientation (faculty)	—.49	.001
Teaching orientation (graduate students)	—.43	.01
Faculty paid over $20,000	+.67	.001
Faculty paid consulting		
Principal duty of academics is to train graduate students	+.52	.001
Humanities orientation	—.34	.05
Graduate students planning teaching careers	—.66	.001
Field too research-oriented	—.36	.05
Faculty paid over $20,000		
Teaching orientation (faculty)	—.62	.001
Research activity	—.64	.001
Principal duty of academics is to train graduate students	—.46	.001

	Correlation	Significance
Teaching orientation		
Humanities orientation/teaching orientation (faculty)	+.46	.001
Humanities orientation/teaching orientation (graduate students)	+.58	.001
Mathematics orientation/teaching orientation (faculty)	−.47	.001
Mathematics orientation/teaching orientation (graduate students)	−.55	.001
Research activity (faculty)/teaching orientation (faculty)	+.75	.001
Research activity (faculty)/teaching orientation (graduate students)	+.89	.001
Consider self intellectual/teaching orientation (faculty)	−.59	.001
Consider self intellectual/teaching orientation (graduate students)	−.45	.01
Consider self scholar-scientist/teaching orientation (graduate students)	−.74	.001
Principal duty of academics is to train graduate students/teaching orientation (faculty)	−.35	.05
Graduate students planning college or university teaching careers/teaching orientation (graduate students)	−.12	n.s.*
Faculty research activity		
Mathematics orientation	+.40	.05
Humanities orientation	−.42	.05
Humanities and mathematics orientation		
Things never understood by science/ humanities	+.70	.001
Things never understood by science/ mathematics	−.36	.05
Faculty left or liberal/humanities	+.50	.001
Graduate students left or liberal/humanities	+.40	.01
Faculty left or liberal/mathematics	−.41	.01
Graduate students left or liberal/mathematics	−.25	n.s.
Scholar-scientist self-image/humanities	−.65	.001
Scholar-scientist self-image/mathematics	+.72	.001
Faculty intellectual self-image/humanities	+.17	n.s.

	Correlation	Significance
Graduate student intellectual self-image/ humanities	+.08	n.s.
Faculty intellectual self-image/mathematics	+.09	n.s.
Graduate student intellectual self-image/ mathematics	+.07	n.s.
Attitudes toward women		
Females not as dedicated (faculty)/humanities orientation	−.45	.01
Females not as dedicated (graduate students))/ humanities orientation	−.21	n.s.
Females not as dedicated (faculty)/ mathematics orientation	+.50	.001
Females not as dedicated (graduate students)/mathematics orientation	+.31	.05
Professors don't take women seriously/ females enrolled part time	−.42	.01
Professors don't take women seriously/ faculty low on research activities	−.66	.001

* n.s. = no significance

Appendix C: Questionnaires Used in this Study

STEREOTYPED IMAGERY QUESTIONNAIRE OF ACADEMIC DISCIPLINES

(1) (2) (3) (4)

Instructions

The purpose of this study is to measure the impressions people have about various subjects by having you rate them against a series of descriptive scales. In taking this test, please make your judgments on the basis of *your own* impressions. You will find different academic disciplines to be rated and beneath a set of scales. You are to do each page and each scale in order.

Here is how you are to use these scales:

If you feel that the academic discipline named is *very closely related* to one or the other end of the scale, you should place your check mark (or X) as follows:

Masculine <u>X</u>: __: __: __: __: __: __ Feminine

or

Masculine __: __: __: __: __: __: <u>X</u> Feminine

If you feel that the academic discipline is *quite closely related* to one or the other end of the scale (but not extremely), you should place your check mark as follows:

Masculine __: <u>X</u>: __: __: __: __: __ Feminine

or

Masculine __: __: __: __: __: <u>X</u>: __ Feminine

If the academic discipline seems *only slightly related* to one side as opposed to the other side (but is not really neutral), then you should check as follows:

Masculine __:__: **X**:__:__:__:__ Feminine

or

Masculine __:__:__:__: **X**:__:__ Feminine

The direction toward which you check, of course, depends upon which of the two ends of the scale seem most characteristic of what you're judging.

If you consider what you're judging to be *neutral* on the scale, both sides of the scale *equally associated* with the concept, then you should place your check mark in the middle space:

Masculine __:__:__: **X**:__:__:__ Feminine

Important

(1) Be sure to check every scale for every concept — *Do not omit any.*
(2) Never put more than one check mark on a single space.

Sometimes you may feel as though you've had the same item before. This will not be the case so *do not look back and forth* through the items. Do not try to remember how you checked similar items earlier. *Make each item a separate and independent judgment.* Work at fairly high speed. Do not worry or puzzle over individual items. It is your first impressions, the immediate "feelings" you get, that we want. On the other hand, please do not be careless, because we want your true impressions.

Please turn the page and begin.

		1	2	3	4	5	6	7	
15	Masculine	__ :	__	__ :	__ :	__ :	__ :	__	Feminine

(25) Educational administration

		1	2	3	4	5	6	7	
48	Masculine	__ :	__ :	__ :	__ :	__ :	__ :	__	Feminine

(26) Law

		1	2	3	4	5	6	7	
53	Masculine	__ :	__ :	__ :	__ :	__ :	__ :	__	Feminine

(27) Chemistry

		1	2	3	4	5	6	7	
19	Masculine	__ :	__ :	__ :	__ :	__ :	__ :	__	Feminine

(28) Civil engineering

18   Masculine — : — : — : — : — : — : — Feminine
(29) Chemical engineering

35   Masculine — : — : — : — : — : — : — Feminine
(30) Home economics

64   Masculine — : — : — : — : — : — : — Feminine
(31) Anthropology

66   Masculine — : — : — : — : — : — : — Feminine
(32) Political science

20   Masculine — : — : — : — : — : — : — Feminine
(33) Electrical engineering

71   Masculine — : — : — : — : — : — : — Feminine
(34) Architecture

69   Masculine — : — : — : — : — : — : — Feminine
(35) Social work

44   Masculine — : — : — : — : — : — : — Feminine
(36) Philosophy

75   Masculine — : — : — : — : — : — : — Feminine
(37) Botany

27   Masculine — : — : — : — : — : — : — Feminine
(38) Music

26   Masculine — : — : — : — : — : — : — Feminine
(39) Speech

25   Masculine — : — : — : — : — : — : — Feminine
(40) Dramatics

77   Masculine — : — : — : — : — : — : — Feminine
(41) Zoology

24   Masculine — : — : — : — : — : — : — Feminine
(42) Art

70   Masculine — : — : — : — : — : — : — Feminine
(43) Agriculture or forestry

54   Masculine — : — : — : — : — : — : — Feminine
(44) Geology

73   Masculine — : — : — : — : — : — : — Feminine
(45) Bacteriology

31   Masculine — : — : — : — : — : — : .... Feminine
(46) Dentistry

57   Masculine — : — : — : — : — : — : — Feminine
(6) Psychology

12   Masculine   __ : __ : __ : __ : __ : __ : __   Feminine
(7) Secondary education

37   Masculine   __ : __ : __ : __ : __ : __ : __   Feminine
(8) English

33   Masculine   __ : __ : __ : __ : __ : __ : __   Feminine
(9) Nursing

14   Masculine   __ : __ : __ : __ : __ : __ : __   Feminine
(10) Educational psychology

74   Masculine   __ : __ : __ : __ : __ : __ : __   Feminine
(11) Biochemistry

11   Masculine   __ : __ : __ : __ : __ : __ : __   Feminine
(12) Elementary education

79   Masculine   __ : __ : __ : __ : __ : __ : __   Feminine
(13) Business, commerce and management

32   Masculine   __ : __ : __ : __ : __ : __ : __   Feminine
(14) Medicine

43   Masculine   __ : __ : __ : __ : __ : __ : __   Feminine
(15) History

65   Masculine   __ : __ : __ : __ : __ : __ : __   Feminine
(16) Economics

51   Masculine   __ : __ : __ : __ : __ : __ : __   Feminine
(17) Physical and health education

47   Masculine   __ : __ : __ : __ : __ : __ : __   Feminine
(18) Journalism

49   Masculine   __ : __ : __ : __ : __ : __ : __   Feminine
(19) Library science

39   Masculine   __ : __ : __ : __ : __ : __ : __   Feminine
(20) French

40   Masculine   __ : __ : __ : __ : __ : __ : __   Feminine
(21) German

67   Masculine   __ : __ : __ : __ : __ : __ : __   Feminine
(22) Sociology

29   Masculine   __ : __ : __ : __ : __ : __ : __   Feminine
(23) Geography

50   Masculine   __ : __ : __ : __ : __ : __ : __   Feminine
(24) Mathematics

55   Masculine   __ : __ : __ : __ : __ : __ : __   Feminine
(47) Physics

41   Masculine __ : __ : __ : __ : __ : __ : __ Feminine
(48) Spanish

76   Masculine __ : __ : __ : __ : __ : __ : __ Feminine
(49) Physiology

21   Masculine __ : __ : __ : __ : __ : __ : __ Feminine
(50) Mechanical engineering

For statistical purposes, we would like some information about yourself. All answers are for tabulation purposes and remain strictly confidential.

1. Your sex: Male   _____
(51-1)

Female   _____
(51-2)

2. Your age: _____
(52-53)

3. Your religion: Protestant   _____
(54-1)

Catholic   _____
(54-2)

Jewish   _____
(54-3)

Other   _____
(54-4)

None   _____
(54-5)

4. Your year in school: Freshman   _____
(55-1)

Sophomore   _____
(55-2)

Junior   _____
(55-3)

Senior   _____
(55-4)

Graduate   _____
(55-5)

5. What is the highest level of formal education reached by your parents?

	Father	Mother
a. 8th grade or less	(56-1)	(57-1)
b. Some high school	(56-2)	(57-2)
c. Completed high school	(56-3)	(57-3)
d. Some college	(56-4)	(57-4)
e. Graduated from college	(56-5)	(57-5)
f. Attended graduate or professional school	(56-6)	(57-6)
g. Attained advanced degree	(56-7)	(57-7)

6. How old do you expect to be when you get married?
    a. I am married   _____
                              (58-1)

    b. Age 20 or younger   _____
                                 (58-2)

    c. Age 21–22   _____
                         (58-3)

    d. Age 23–24   _____
                         (58-4)

    e. Age 25–29   _____
                         (58-5)

    f. Age 30–35   _____
                         (58-6)

    g. Over age 35   _____
                           (58-7)

    h. I do not expect to marry   _____
                                        (58-8)

7. What do you think of the recent emergence of women's liberation?
    a. Unreservedly approve   _____
                                    (59-1)

    b. Approve with reservations   _____
                                         (59-2)

c. Disapprove with reservations $\underline{\qquad}$
(59-3)

d. Unreservedly disapprove $\underline{\qquad}$
(59-4)

8. From the list of academic disciplines that you rated, write in the number most closely corresponding to your major field (or intended major field). Use the number on the left-hand side of the page, not the number in parentheses.

$\underline{\qquad}$
(60-61)

Graduate Student Questionnaire

THE CARNEGIE COMMISSION ON HIGHER EDUCATION
THE AMERICAN COUNCIL ON EDUCATION

Dear Colleague:

American higher education is currently faced with grave problems. While we can see the broad outlines of these problems in over-crowded classrooms, rising costs, student rebellions, and threats to academic freedom, there is very little detailed information on the form they take in different institutions, or in different disciplines and professions. Nor do we have firm knowledge of how the people most directly affected, the students and the faculty, feel about them.

To provide such knowledge, the Carnegie Commission on the Future of Higher Education, in cooperation with the American Council on Education, is conducting a national survey of students and faculty in a broad sample of colleges and universities. The information we are gathering will be of help to the Carnegie Commission and to other bodies concerned with public policy in this area, as well as to scholars who are studying current problems and developments in American higher education.

We have no illusion that even a broad survey such as this will answer all our questions. We know the limits of questionnaires, and are conducting other studies, in other ways, to supplement this survey. Nevertheless, this survey will provide information that can be obtained in no other way. We know that you have much to do, and we know also that other surveys may have made similar demands on your time. But the present survey is unique in its scope and purposes: it is the first to ask similar questions of students and faculty in the same institutions, and it is the first to explore a variety of these issues on a national scale. The accuracy of the survey and the worth of its findings are dependent on your willingness to answer our questions. We believe the importance of the study will justify the time you give it.

One other matter. It is impossible to frame questions all of which are equally relevant to students in different fields and institutions; you may find some that seem inappropriate to your situation. We urge you to answer all the questions as well as you can; in our analysis we will be able to take into account the special circumstances that affect replies to some questions.

Finally, we assure you that your answers will be held in strictest confidence. We are interested only in statistical relationships and will under no circumstances report responses on an individual or departmental basis. Any special markings on your form are used solely for internal data processing.

We hope you will find the questionnaire interesting to answer, and that you will complete and return it to us while you have it at hand.

With our thanks for your cooperation.

Sincerely,

Logan Wilson

Clark Kerr

Logan Wilson
President
American Council
on Education

Clark Kerr
Chairman
Carnegie Commission on
Higher Education

1. **Your sex:**
   Male.......O   Female ....O

2. **What is your marital status?**
   Engaged.............................O
   Married (once only) ....O
   Married (remarried).....................O
   Separated ....O
   Single (never married) ....O
   Single (divorced) ....O
   Single (widowed) ....O

3. **Number of children:**
   None.......O   Two ....O
   One........O   Three or more .....O

4. **On the following list, please mark (1) all
   the degrees you now hold, (2) the degree(s)
   you are now working for, (3) the highest
   degree you expect to obtain.**
   (Mark each column)
   ┌─── 1. Now Hold
   ┌─── 2. Working For
   ①②③ ─ 3. Highest Expect to Obtain

   Less than Bachelor's (A.A., etc.)....①②③
   Undergraduate Bachelor's...........①②③
   First professional law degree ....①②③
   First professional medical degree
   (e.g., M.D., D.D.S.)...............①②③
   M.A.T............................①②③
   Other first professional beyond
   undergraduate bachelor's ....①②③
   Master's (except first professional)..①②③
   Doctor of Arts or equivalent for doc-
   torate degree without dissertation...①②③
   Ph.D...........................①②③
   Ed.D. ....①②③
   Other doctorate (except first profes-
   sional)........................①②③
   None............................①②③

5. **When do you expect to get the degree you are
   now working for?**
   This year.............................O
   Within two years.......................O
   Within three years ....O
   Within four years ....O
   Within five years ....O
   Six or more years ....O
   I don't expect to get the degree.........O

6. **Are you now thinking about a job after finishing
   graduate school?** *
   I already have a job....................O
   Yes, I am now looking.................O
   Yes, I'm thinking seriously about where to
   go....................................O
   Yes, but not seriously.................O
   No....................................O
   * "Graduate school" means any program of
   instruction beyond the undergraduate bach-
   elor's, including professional schools such as
   law and medicine.

7. **In what year did you (1) obtain your bachelor's
   degree, (2) first enter graduate school, (3)
   first enter this department** * **as a graduate
   student? (Mark one in each column)**
   ┌─── 1. Bachelor's Degree
   ┌─── 2. Entered Graduate School
   ①②③ ─ 3. Entered Department

   1955 or before.....................①②③
   1956-57 ....①②③
   1958-59 ....①②③
   1960-61 ....①②③
   1962-63 ....①②③
   1964.............................①②③
   1965.............................①②③
   1966.............................①②③
   1967 ....①②③
   1968-69 ....①②③
   * "Department" includes professional
   schools such as law, medicine, and social
   work.

7A. **Are you currently enrolled as a student?**
   Yes, full time.........................O
   Yes, part time ....O
   No, I am not enrolled.................O

8. **How many colleges and universities have
   you attended?**

	As an Undergraduate	As A Graduate Student
One	O	O
Two	O	O
Three	O	O
Four	O	O
Five or more	O	O

9. Mark institutions attended in following list of large institutions; or if your institution does not appear, mark appropriate "other" category. (Mark one in each column)

┌── 1. Institution Entered as Freshman
├─ 2. Bachelor's Degree
├─ 3. Institution (other than your present one) last attended as graduate student
①②③

None or not Applicable .... ①②③
Alabama, University of .... ①②③
Boston University.................. ①②③
Brigham Young University, Utah .... ①②③
Brooklyn College .... ①②③
California Institute of Technology.... ①②③
California, University of, at Berkeley.①②③
California, University of, at Los Angeles .... ①②③
Carnegie Institute of Technology, Pa.①②③
Catholic University of America, D.C. .①②③
Chicago, University of.............. ①②③
City College of New York .... ①②③
Colorado, University of .... ①②③
Columbia University, New York ..... ①②③
Cornell University .... ①②③
Dartmouth College, New Hampshire..①②③
Florida, University of .... ①②③
Georgia, University of .... ①②③
Harvard University .... ①②③
Hunter College, New York .... ①②③
Illinois, University of´............. ①②③
Indiana University, Bloomington ...①②③
Iowa State University.............. ①②③
Iowa, University of................ ①②③
Kansas, University of .... ①②③
Kentucky, University of............ ①②③
Louisiana State University .... ①②③
Maryland, University of .... ①②③
Massachusetts Institute of Technology.①②③
Michigan State University .... ①②③
Michigan, University of .... ①②③
Minnesota, University of .... ①②③
Missouri, University of, Columbia ...①②③
Nebraska, University of............ ①②③
New York University .... ①②③
North Carolina, University of .... ①②③
Northwestern University, Illinois..... ①②③
Notre Dame, University of, Indiana ..①②③
Oberlin College, Ohio .... ①②③
Ohio State University.............. ①②③
Oklahoma State University .... ①②③
Oklahoma, University of .... ①②③
Oregon State University............ ①②③
Pennsylvania State University ...... ①②③
Pennsylvania, University of .... ①②③
Pittsburgh, University of........... ①②③
Princeton University .... ①②③
Purdue University................. ①②③
Rensselaer Poly, New York .... ①②③

9 (Continued)

Rochester, University of........... ①②③
Rutgers, The State University, New Jersey .... ①②③
Southern California, University of... ①②③
Stanford University, California ..... ①②③
Swarthmore College, Pennsylvania ..①②③
Syracuse University................ ①②③
Temple University, Pennsylvania ....①②③
Tennessee, University of .... ①②③
Texas, University of .... ①②③
Utah, University of .... ①②③
Washington, University of, Seattle.......................... ①②③
Wayne State University, Michigan ....①②③
Wisconsin, University of........... ①②③
Yale University .... ①②③

Other private Ph.D.-granting university .... ①②③
Other public Ph.D.-granting university .... ①②③
Other private college (no Ph.D. program)....................... ①②③
Other public college (no Ph.D. program)....................... ①②③
A junior or community college .... ①
A foreign institution .... ①②③

10. Is the institution in which you are now enrolled the institution in which you took (a) your bachelor's (b) your master's degree (if any)?

	Bachelor's	Master's
Yes	○	○
No	○	○
Not applicable	○	○

11. In general, how do you feel about this institution?

It is a very good place for me .... ○
It is fairly good for me .... ○
It is not the place for me .... ○

12. In my department, the academic standards for (a) admission to graduate work (b) advanced degrees should be--

	Graduate Admissions	Advanced Degrees
Much higher	○	○
Somewhat higher	○	○
Left as they are	○	○
Somewhat lower	○	○
Much lower	○	○

13. From the following list, mark <u>one</u> subject in each column; mark the most appropriate <u>fine</u> categories, if applicable; where your precise field does not appear, mark the most similar category.

    1. Intended Undergraduate Major as Entering Freshman
    2. Actual Undergraduate Major
    3. Department in which you are studying *
    4. Intended or Actual Master's Degree
①②③④⑤ — 5. Intended Doctor's Degree

NONE OR NOT APPLICABLE . ①②③④⑤
Agriculture and/or Forestry . . . ①②③④⑤
Architecture and/or Design . . . . ①②③④⑤
Biological Sciences (General Biology) . . . . ①②③④⑤
  Bacteriology, Molecular Biology, Virology, Microbiology . . ①②③④⑤
  Biochemistry . . . . ①②③④⑤
  General Botany . . . . ①②③④⑤
  Physiology, Anatomy . . . . ①②③④⑤
  General Zoology . . . . ①②③④⑤
  Other Biological Sciences . . . . ①②③④⑤
Business, Commerce and Management . . . . ①②③④⑤
Education . . . . ①②③④⑤
  Elementary and/or Secondary . . ①②③④⑤
  Foundations . . . . ①②③④⑤
  Educational Psychology and Counseling . . . . ①②③④⑤
  Educational Administration . . . ①②③④⑤
  Other Education fields . . . . ①②③④⑤
Engineering . . . . ①②③④⑤
  Chemical . . . . ①②③④⑤
  Civil . . . . ①②③④⑤
  Electrical . . . . ①②③④⑤
  Mechanical . . . . ①②③④⑤
  Other Engineering fields . . . . . . ①②③④⑤
Fine Arts . . . . ①②③④⑤
  Art . . . . ①②③④⑤
  Dramatics . . . . ①②③④⑤
  Speech . . . . ①②③④⑤
  Music . . . . ①②③④⑤
  Other Fine Arts . . . . ①②③④⑤
Geography . . . . ①②③④⑤
Health Fields . . . . ①②③④⑤
  Dentistry . . . . ①②③④⑤
  Medicine . . . . ①②③④⑤
  Nursing . . . . ①②③④⑤
  Other Health fields . . . . ①②③④⑤
Home Economics . . . . ①②③④⑤

  * Mark main department, if you are studying in more than one.

13 Continued.
  Humanities . . . . ①②③④⑤
  English language & literature . ①②③④⑤
  Foreign languages & literature ①②③④⑤
  French . . . . ①②③④⑤
  German . . . . ①②③④⑤
  Spanish . . . . ①②③④⑤
  Other foreign languages (including linguistics) . . . . ①②③④⑤
  History . . . . ①②③④⑤
  Philosophy . . . . ①②③④⑤
  Religion & Theology . . . . ①②③④⑤
  Other Humanities fields . . . . . ①②③④⑤
  Journalism . . . . ①②③④⑤
  Law . . . . ①②③④⑤
  Library Science . . . . ①②③④⑤
  Mathematics and Statistics . . . . ①②③④⑤
  Physical & Health Education . . . ①②③④⑤
  Physical Sciences . . . . ①②③④⑤
  Chemistry . . . . ①②③④⑤
  Earth Sciences (incl. Geology) . ①②③④⑤
  Physics . . . . ①②③④⑤
  Other Physical Sciences . . . . . . ①②③④⑤
  Psychology . . . . ①②③④⑤
  Clinical . . . . ①②③④⑤
  Experimental . . . . ①②③④⑤
  Social . . . . ①②③④⑤
  Counseling and Guidance . . . . . ①②③④⑤
  Other Psychology fields . . . . . ①②③④⑤
  Social Sciences . . . . ①②③④⑤
  Anthropology . . . . ①②③④⑤
  Economics . . . . ①②③④⑤
  Political Science, Government . ①②③④⑤
  Sociology . . . . ①②③④⑤
  Other Social Sciences . . . . ①②③④⑤
  Social Work, Social Welfare . . . ①②③④⑤
  ALL OTHER FIELDS . . . . ①②③④⑤

14. Please indicate the extent of your agreement or disagreement with each of the following statements. Mark one circle for each item.

    1. Strongly Agree
    2. Agree With Reservations
    3. Disagree With Reservations
①②③④ — 4. Strongly Disagree

Opportunities for higher education should be available to all high school graduates who want it . . . . ①②③④
Most American colleges and universities are racist whether they mean to be or not . . . . ①②③④
American colleges and universities must be destroyed before they can be reformed . . . . ①②③④
The normal academic requirements should be relaxed in appointing members of minority groups to the faculty here . . . . ①②③④

14 Continued.

More minority group undergraduates should be admitted here
even if it means relaxing normal
academic standards of admission .①②③④

Student demonstrations have no
place on a college campus........①②③④

Students who disrupt the functioning of a college should be
expelled or suspended...........①②③④

Most college officials have been
too lax in dealing with student
protests on campus ....①②③④

College officials have the right
to regulate student behavior off
campus........................①②③④

Faculty unions have a divisive
effect on academic life.........①②③④

Teaching assistants' unions have
a divisive effect on academic
life..........................①②③④

College professors deserve more
respect from the public than they
now receive...................①②③④

**15. Do you subscribe to any academic or profes-
sional journals?**

None.......○   Three ....○
One........○   Four or more ....○
Two ....○

16. Have you:

Attended a meeting of an academic $\quad$ Yes $\quad$ No
or professional society ?..........○ $\quad$ ○
Presented a paper at a meeting of an
academic or professional society? ..○ $\quad$ ○
Published an article in an academic
or professional journal? ....○ $\quad$ ○

**17. Are you currently engaged in any scholarly or
research work which you expect to lead to
publication under your name?**

Yes..........○ $\qquad$ No ....○

**18. Have you decided on an area or areas of spec-
ialization within your field?**

I don't intend to specialize ....○
No, not yet ....○
Yes, tentatively ....○
Yes, definitely ....○

**19. How do you rate yourself among the graduate
students in your department?**

Among the best....................○
Above average ....○
About average......................○
Below average ....○

**20. How would you describe the following in your
department?** (Mark one in each row)

```
                          ┌──── 1. Excellent
                        ┌─── 2. Good
                      ┌── 3. Fair
                    ┌─ 4. Poor
①②③④⑤── 5. Don't Know
```

The academic ability of your
fellow graduate students ....①②③④⑤

The academic achievements of
the faculty ....①②③④⑤

The variety of graduate level
course offerings............①②③④⑤

The availability of faculty to
graduate students ....①②③④⑤

The quality of classroom instruction...................①②③④⑤

The relevance of course content to your future occupation .①②③④⑤

The intellectual environment...①②③④⑤

The academic reputation of
your department outside your
institution.................①②③④⑤

Your personal relations with
other graduate students ......①②③④⑤

**21. Please mark the extent of your agreement or
disagreement with each of the following
statements. Mark one circle for each item.**

```
              ┌──── 1. Strongly Agree
            ┌─── 2. Agree With Reservations
          ┌── 3. Disagree With Reservations
①②③④── 4. Strongly Disagree
```

I am in graduate school in order to:

Satisfy job requirements........①②③④

Continue my intellectual
growth.....................①②③④

Avoid the draft...............①②③④

Obtain an occupation with
high prestige...............①②③④

Increase my earning power......①②③④

Prepare for an academic
career ....①②③④

Find myself ....①②③④

See whether I really like a
particular field of study ....①②③④

Contribute to my ability to
change society..............①②③④

Get a teaching credential.......①②③④

Study my field for its intrinsic
interest....................①②③④

Better serve mankind ....①②③④

Engage in political activities ...①②③④

22. Please indicate the extent of your agreement or disagreement with each of the following statements. Mark one circle for each item.

1. Strongly Agree
2. Agree With Reservations
3. Disagree With Reservations
① ② ③ ④ — 4. Strongly Disagree

My field is too research oriented. .① ② ③ ④
I consider myself an intellectual. .① ② ③ ④
Much of what is taught in my department is irrelevant to what is going on in the outside world. . . .① ② ③ ④
I hope to make significant contributions to knowledge in my field . . . . .① ② ③ ④
My department has taken steps to increase graduate student participation in its decisions. . . . . . .① ② ③ ④
I am basically satisfied with the education I am getting. . . . . .① ② ③ ④
Most Ph.D. holders in my field get their degrees without showing much real scholarly ability . .① ② ③ ④
The typical undergraduate curriculum has suffered from the specialization of faculty members . .① ② ③ ④
Any institution with a substantial number of black students should offer a program of Black Studies if they wish it. . . . . .① ② ③ ④
Any special academic program for black students should be administered and controlled by black people . . . . .① ② ③ ④
Professors in my department don't really take female graduate students seriously. . . . . .① ② ③ ④
I see professors outside the classroom about as often as I would like. . . . . .① ② ③ ④
Professors here don't pay much attention to the graduate students . . . . .① ② ③ ④
The female graduate students in my department are not as dedicated to the field as the males . .① ② ③ ④
Teaching effectiveness, not publications, should be the primary criterion for the promotion of faculty . . . . .① ② ③ ④
In my department it is very difficult for a man to achieve tenure if he does not publish . . . . .① ② ③ ④
I tend to subordinate all aspects of my life to my work. . . . . .① ② ③ ④
Classified weapons research is a legitimate activity on college and university campuses. . . . . . . .① ② ③ ④

22 Continued.
Big contract research has become more a source of money and prestige for researchers than an effective way of advancing knowledge.① ② ③ ④
Many of the highest-paid university professors get where they are by being "operators," rather than by their scholarly or scientific contributions . . . . .① ② ③ ④
Genuine scholarship is threatened in universities by the proliferation of big research centers . . . . .① ② ③ ④
Part of my graduate education has been essentially a wasteful repetition of what I had already covered at the undergraduate level. . . .① ② ③ ④
Scientists should publish their findings regardless of the possible consequences. . . . . .① ② ③ ④
My career will take second place behind my family obligations . . . .① ② ③ ④
Exciting developments are taking place in my field . . . . .① ② ③ ④
My field is among the most respected academic disciplines. . . . . . . .① ② ③ ④
My field gets a good share of the best students . . . . .① ② ③ ④
Graduate students should be more militant in defending their interests . . . . .① ② ③ ④
Faculty members should be free on campus to advocate violent resistance to public authority. . . . . . . .① ② ③ ④
Faculty members should be free to present in class any idea they consider relevant . . . . .① ② ③ ④
One should attempt to insulate one's academic work from one's personal values . . . . .① ② ③ ④
Some of the best graduate students in my department drop out because they do not want to "play the game" or "beat the system." . . .① ② ③ ④
The doctorate is mainly a "union card," enabling one to get the kind of job he wants . . . . .① ② ③ ④
The graduate program in my department favors the bright, imaginative student. . . . . .① ② ③ ④

23. Do you find yourself bored in class these days?

Almost all the time . . . . O
Fairly often. . . . . O
Occasionally. . . . . O
Almost never. . . . . O
I don't take classes. . . . . O

24. How important to you are each of the following? (Mark one in each row)

- 1. Very Important
- 2. Fairly Important
- ①②③ — 3. Not Important

Recognition as a good student by my professors......①②③
Respect for my academic abilities from my fellow students..........①②③
Approval by my parents of what I am studying ....①②③

25. Do you think the following are likely to prevent you from completing your graduate work? (Mark one in each row)

Yes Maybe No

Lack of interest ....OOO
Lack of finances.................OOO
A job offer ....OOO
Inability to do the academic work....OOO
Too much emotional strain.........OOO
The draft.......................OOO
Pressure from my wife or husband ...OOO

26. On the average, how often do you meet informally (that is, for meals, parties, etc.) either on or off campus with graduate students in your department? With professors in your department? With people not connected with the university? (Mark one in each column)

- 1. Students
- 2. Professors
- ①②③ 3. People Not Connected With University

Once a week or more...............①②③
Two or three times a month.........①②③
About once a month................①②③
A few times a year ....①②③
Once a year or less...............①②③

27. About how many of the people you see socially are also graduate students in your department?

Almost all.......O   Some............O
Most...........O   Almost none ......O
About half.......O

28. Is there a professor in your department

Yes No
You feel free to turn to for advice on personal matters? ....O O
Who is taking or will take a special interest in helping you get a job when you finish graduate school?...O O

29. Does the professor with whom you have most academic contact outside the classroom regard you primarily as
A colleague..........................O
An apprentice ....O
An employee ....O
A student...........................O
No contact outside the classroom........O

30. As a graduate student, have there been times when you felt you did not know where you stood, i.e., how far along you really were or how well you were doing?
Yes, very often.......................O
Yes, often...........................O
Yes, occasionally ....O
No...................................O

31. At present how much attention are you giving to each of the following? (Mark one in each row)

- 1. Have Completed
- 2. Very Much
- 3. Some
- 4. Not Much
- ①②③④⑤ — 5. None

Required courses ....①②③④⑤
Preparation for preliminary exams (master's or doctoral) ....①②③④⑤
Preparation for language exams.①②③④⑤
Dissertation research ....①②③④⑤
Dissertation writing...........①②③④⑤

32. If you were to begin your academic training again, would you still choose your present discipline for specialization?
Definitely yes....O   Probably no.....O
Probably yes.....O   Definitely no....O

33. If no, would you choose another field
Very close to your own ....O
Not close, but related ....O
Quite different ....O

34. During the past year have you considered changing to another institution to finish your graduate training? Have you considered changing your field of study?

Institution Field of Study

I am changing ....OO
I have considered it seriously ....OO
I have considered it, but not seriously ....OO
I haven't considered it ....OO

35. During the past year have you considered quitting graduate school for good?
    Yes, and I have definitely decided to quit. .○
    Yes, I have given it serious consideration .○
    Yes, I have considered it, but not seriously .... ○
    No. .... ○

36. What was your undergraduate grade point average?
    A or A+ ..○   B.......○   C or below ..○
    A-.......○   B-......○
    B+.......○   C+.....○

37. As an undergraduate were you ever a member of a social fraternity or sorority?
    No. .... ○
    One year .... ○
    Two years .... ○
    Three years......................... ○
    Four or more years.................. ○

38. How important do you think it is that a student in your field get a firm grounding in the following during his <u>undergraduate</u> years?
    (Mark one in each row)
    ┌──────── 1. Extremely Important
    │ ┌────── 2. Fairly Important
    │ │ ┌──── 3. Fairly Unimportant
    ①②③④ — 4. Extremely Unimportant
    English ....①②③④
    Mathematics ....①②③④
    Physical science ....①②③④
    Life science ....①②③④
    Social science ....①②③④
    The humanities.................①②③④
    Art and music.................①②③④
    A foreign language.............①②③④

39. How satisfied are you with each of the following aspects of your <u>under</u>graduate education?
    (Mark one in each row).
    ┌──────── 1. Very Satisfied
    │ ┌────── 2. Satisfied
    │ │ ┌──── 3. Dissatisfied
    ①②③④ — 4. Very Dissatisfied
    Foreign languages ....①②③④
    Ability to write and organize
    material ....①②③④
    Preparation in my subject field ....①②③④
    General background of liberal education. ....①②③④
    Ability to work on my own ....①②③④
    Ability to do original work ....①②③④
    General preparation for graduate
    school ....①②③④

40. a. What role do you believe <u>undergraduates</u> should play in decisions on the following?
    (Mark one in each row)
    ┌──────── 1. Control
    │ ┌────── 2. Voting Power On
    │ │   Committees
    │ │ ┌──── 3. Formal Consultation
    │ │ │ ┌── 4. Informal Consultation
    ①②③④⑤ — 5. Little or no Role

    Faculty appointment and promotion.....................①②③④⑤
    Undergraduate admissions
    policy ....①②③④⑤
    Provision and content of
    courses.....................①②③④⑤
    Student discipline............①②③④⑤
    Bachelor's degree requirements .①②③④⑤

    b. What role do you believe <u>graduate</u> students should play in decisions on the following?
    Faculty appointment and promotion.....................①②③④⑤
    Departmental graduate admissions policy..............①②③④⑤
    Provision and content of graduate courses ....①②③④⑤
    Student discipline............①②③④⑤
    Advanced degree requirements ..①②③④⑤

41. Has your campus experienced any student protests or demonstrations during the current academic year?
    Yes .....○   No ....○
    (If no, skip to No. 44 on page 9)

42. How would you characterize your attitude toward the <u>most</u> <u>recent</u> demonstration?
    Approved of the demonstrators' aims and methods ....○
    Approved of their aims but not their methods ....○
    Disapproved of their aims ....○
    Uncertain or mixed feelings ....○
    Indifferent ....○

43. What was your role in this demonstration?
    (Mark <u>all</u> that apply)
    Helped to plan, organize, or lead the protest...................................○
    Joined in active protest with the demonstrators................................○
    Openly supported the goals of the protestors.................................○
    Openly opposed the goals of the protestors○
    Tried to mediate in the protest...........○
    Was not involved actively in any way .....○

44. (a) **Are you now employed (b) have you ever been employed for a term* or more while a graduate student as**

Am Now
Have Been

Part-time Research Assistant .... OO
Full-time Research position .... OO
Part-time Teaching Assistant .... OO
Full-time position as Teaching Associate or Teaching Fellow .... OO
Full or part-time faculty position as lecturer, instructor, acting assistant professor, etc. .... OO
Other academic position. .... OO
None of these. .... OO

* Quarter, semester, trimester, etc.

45. **Would you yourself be inclined to join a union for employed graduate students if one were organized?**

There is one; I am a member. .... O
There is one; I am not a member .... O
There isn't one; I almost certainly would join. .... O
There isn't one; I probably would join .... O
There isn't one; I probably would not join. O
There isn't one; I almost certainly would not join. .... O

46. **If a large group of employed graduate students were to call for a strike over a campus issue, and you agreed with their position on the issue, do you think you would participate in the strike?**

Definitely yes ... O   Probably not. ...... O
Probably yes .... O   Definitely not. ..... O

47. **Do you feel that there are circumstances in which a strike would be a legitimate means of collective action**

1. Definitely yes
2. Probably yes
3. Probably not
①②③④ — 4. Definitely not

For faculty members .... ①②③④
For teaching assistants .... ①②③④

48. **What do you think of the emergence of radical student activism in recent years?**

Unreservedly approve .... O
Approve with reservations .... O
Disapprove with reservations .... O
Unreservedly disapprove .... O

49. **About how many hours a week do you devote to each of the following?**
(Mark one in each row)

None 1-4 5-8 9-12 13-20 21-30 31-40 Over 40

Studying .... OOOOOOOO
Hours in class or required laboratories (Give actual, not credit hours and exclude teaching, if any) ..... OOOOOOOO
Employment connected with your field of study. .... OOOOOOOO
Employment not connected with your field of study. .... OOOOOOOO

50. **Which of the following occupations* have you engaged in continously for six months or more? Which one do you realistically expect to enter when you complete your graduate training?**

* Do not include apprenticeship, internship, or teaching/research assistantship.

1. **Have Done**
①② — 2. **Expect to enter**

Teaching at the elementary or secondary level. .... ①②
Teaching at the junior college level. ... ①②
Teaching at the college or university level. .... ①②
Full-time research at a university ...... ①②
Research with a non-profit organization or institute not affiliated with a university. .... ①②
Research in industry .... ①②
Self-employed professional practice alone. .... ①②
Self-employed professional practice with partner(s). .... ①②
Employed professional practice .... ①②
Self-employed, business .... ①②
Executive or administrator in government .... ①②
Executive or administrator in education. ①②
Executive or administrator in private industry .... ①②
Manual labor or factory work. .... ①②
Military service. .... ①②
Clerical or sales work .... ①②
Other. .... ①②

51. **Are you interested in an academic career?**
Very interested .... O
Fairly interested. .... O
Fairly uninterested. ..... O
Very uninterested .... O (Skip to No. 53)

52. Are you interested primarily in teaching or in research?

Very heavily in research . . . . O
In both, but leaning toward research. . . . . . . O
In both, but leaning toward teaching. . . . . . O
Very heavily in teaching. . . . . O

53. Have you ever spent any time in programs such as VISTA or the Peace Corps?

Yes. . . . . O
No, but I plan to. O
No, but I'd like to . . . . O
No, and I wouldn't like to. . . . . O

54. Please indicate the extent of your agreement or disagreement with each of the following statements. Mark one circle for each statement.

1. Strongly agree
2. Agree with reservations
3. Disagree with reservations
① ② ③ ④ — 4. Strongly disagree

There are many things that can never possibly be understood by the techniques of science. . . . . . . ① ② ③ ④
It is all right to get around the law if you don't actually break it.. . . . ① ② ③ ④
I am as strict about right and wrong as most people . . . . ① ② ③ ④
I enjoy reading poetry . . . . ① ② ③ ④
I enjoy classical music. . . . . ① ② ③ ④
I do a lot of serious reading outside my field of study . . . . ① ② ③ ④
Persons with a graduate education are no better than anyone else. . . ① ② ③ ④
There is too much concern in the courts for the rights of criminals. ① ② ③ ④
Most people who live in poverty could do something about their situation if they really wanted to ① ② ③ ④
I basically dislike large cities . . . ① ② ③ ④
I have a pretty good idea when I will finish my graduate education ① ② ③ ④
When I'm with other graduate students, we usually talk about our field of study . . . . ① ② ③ ④
I think I would be happier if I hadn't entered graduate school . ① ② ③ ④
I intend to remain in this state after I complete my graduate education. ① ② ③ ④
I am basically conservative in my religious beliefs. . . . . ① ② ③ ④
I think of myself primarily as a scholar or scientist and not as a student. . . . . ① ② ③ ④

54 Continued.

These days you hear too much about the rights of minorities and not enough about the rights of the majority . . . . ① ② ③ ④
Where de facto segregation exists, black people should be assured control over their own schools. . . . ① ② ③ ④
Racial integration of the public elementary schools should be achieved even if it requires busing . . . . ① ② ③ ④
Meaningful social change cannot be achieved through traditional American politics. . . . . ① ② ③ ④
The main cause of Negro riots in the cities is white racism. . . . . . . ① ② ③ ④
Communist China should be recognized immediately by the U.S. ① ② ③ ④
Hippies represent an important criticism of American culture. . . . ① ② ③ ④
Marijuana should be legalized . . . . ① ② ③ ④
Realistically, an individual person can do little to bring about changes in our society . . . . ① ② ③ ④
The decline in moral standards among youth is a major problem in America today . . . . ① ② ③ ④

55. How adequate are your finances to your present needs?

Very adequate. . . . . O
Adequate . . . . O
Inadequate. . . . . O
Very inadequate . . . . O

56. What was your total (family) income last year from all sources?

Less than $2,500. O $5,000 - $5,999. . . . O
$2,500 - $2,999. . . O $6,000 - $6,999. . . . O
$3,000 - $3,499. . . O $7,000 - $7,999. . . . O
$3,500 - $3,999. . . O $8,000 - $9,999. . . . O
$4,000 - $4,499. . . O $10,000 - $11,999. . O
$4,500 - $4,999. . . O $12,000 and over . . O

57. Apart from room and board, roughly what were your total educational expenses this term? (Include tuition, registration, other fees, books, lab supplies, etc.)

Under $50. . . . . . . O $400 - $499. . . . . . O
$50 - $99 . . . . O $500 - $699. . . . . . O
$100 - $199 . . . . . . O $700 - $999. . . . . . O
$200 - $299 . . . . . . O $1,000 or over . . . . O
$300 - $399 . . . . . . O

58. Which of the following have been sources of income for you during the current academic year? (Please check all that apply.) Which one of the following has been your <u>primary</u> source of income during the current year? Which has been your <u>primary</u> source of income since entering graduate school?

> ┌──── 1. A Source of Income This Year
> │ ┌── 2. Primary Source This Year
> │ │ ┌─ 3. Primary Source Since Entering
> ①②③   Graduate School

Fellowship .... ①②③
Teaching/research assistantship, internship .... ①②③
Non-academic job .... ①②③
Spouse's job .... ①②③
Savings .... ①②③
Investments .... ①②③
Aid from family .... ①②③
Loans from family or friends .... ①②③
Government or institutional loans .... ①②③
Other .... ①②③

59. How interested are you in local and national politics? How interested would you be in politics as a career? (Mark one in each column)

	Local	National	Career
Extremely interested	○	○	○
Moderately interested	○	○	○
Only slightly interested	○	○	○
Not interested at all	○	○	○

60.
> ┌──── 1. Left
> │ ┌── 2. Liberal
> │ │ ┌─ 3. Middle-of-the-Road
> │ │ │ ┌─ 4. Moderately Conservative
> ①②③④⑤ 5. Strongly Conservative

a. How would you characterize yourself politically at the present time? .... ①②③④⑤

b. What were your father's politics while you were growing up? .... ①②③④⑤

61. Whom would you have favored
a. At the Republican convention?
Nixon .... ○   Rockefeller .... ○

b. At the Democratic convention?
Humphrey ...... ○   McCarthy .... ○

62. Whom did you vote for in November?
Nixon .... ○   Another candidate .. ○
Humphrey ...... ○   Did not vote .... ○
Wallace .... ○   No answer .... ○

63. In what religion were you raised? What is your present religious preference?

> ┌──── 1. Religion in which raised
> ①② ── 2. Present religion

Baptist .... ①②
Baptist (Southern) .... ①②
Congregational (United Church of Christ) .... ①②
Episcopal .... ①②
Jewish .... ①②
Latter Day Saints (Mormon) .... ①②
Lutheran .... ①②
Lutheran (Missouri Synod) .... ①②
Methodist .... ①②
Presbyterian .... ①②
Quaker (Society of Friends) .... ①②
Roman Catholic .... ①②
Unitarian-Universalist .... ①②
Other Protestant .... ①②
Other religions .... ①②
None .... ①②
No answer .... ①②

64. Do you consider yourself
Deeply religious .... ○
Moderately religious .... ○
Largely indifferent to religion .... ○
Basically opposed to religion .... ○

65. Where did you live for most of the time while you were growing up? Where would you prefer to live after finishing graduate school?

	Lived	Would Prefer
On a farm	○	○
In a small town	○	○
In a moderate size town or city	○	○
In a suburb of a large city	○	○
In a large city	○	○

66. Do any of the following statements apply to you?

	Yes	No
I grew up in this state	○	○
I first came to this state as an undergraduate	○	○
I first came to this state as a graduate student	○	○

67. Since first entering graduate school, how many <u>academic years</u> have you <u>not</u> been enrolled in a college or university? (Do not count summer vacations.)
None .... ○   Three years .... ○
Less than one year . ○   Four years ..... ○
About 1 year .... ○   Five or more
Two years .... ○   years .... ○

68. What is the <u>highest</u> level of formal education reached by your spouse? Your father? Your mother? (Mark one in each column)

	Spouse	Father	Mother
No spouse	O		
8th grade or less	O	O	O
Some high school	O	O	O
Completed high school	O	O	O
Some college	O	O	O
Graduated from college	O	O	O
Attended graduate or professional school	O	O	O
Attained advanced degree	O	O	O

69. What is (was) your father's principal occupation? (Mark one)

College or university teaching, research or administration .... O
Elementary or secondary school teaching, administration .... O
Physician .... O
Lawyer .... O
Other professional .... O
Managerial, administrative, semiprofessional .... O
Owner, large business .... O
Owner, small business .... O
Other white collar: clerical or retail sales. O
Skilled wage worker .... O
Semi- and unskilled wage worker, farm laborer .... O
Armed forces .... O
Farm owner or manager .... O
Other .... O

70. In general, I would characterize my parents as: Mark one circle for each item.

1. Strongly Agree
2. Agree
3. Disagree
① ② ③ ④ — 4. Strongly Disagree

Interested in intellectual pursuits .... ① ② ③ ④
Interested in cultural pursuits .... ① ② ③ ④
Deeply religious .... ① ② ③ ④
Interested in politics .... ① ② ③ ④
Deeply concerned about their children .... ① ② ③ ④
Financially comfortable .... ① ② ③ ④
Having high aspirations for me ... ① ② ③ ④

71. How often do you now have contacts with your parents either through letters, phone calls, or personal visits?

Both parents deceased .... O
Am living with parents .... O
Once a week or more .... O
Two or three times a month .... O
About once a month .... O
A few times a year .... O
Once a year or less .... O

72. How often, on the average, do you attend: (Mark one in each row)

1. Once a week or more
2. Two or three times a month
3. About once a month
4. A few times a year
① ② ③ ④ ⑤ — 5. Once a year or less

A religious service .... ① ② ③ ④ ⑤
A concert .... ① ② ③ ④ ⑤
An "art" film .... ① ② ③ ④ ⑤
A play .... ① ② ③ ④ ⑤
An art exhibition .... ① ② ③ ④ ⑤
An athletic event .... ① ② ③ ④ ⑤

73. How many hours a day, on the average, do you spend watching television?

None .... O	About 2 .... O
About ½ or less .. O	About 3 .... O
About 1 .... O	Four or more ...... O
About 1½ .... O	

74. Your race:

Caucasian ...... O   Oriental .... O
Negro .... O   Other .... O

75. Your age:

21 or younger .... O   26-27 .... O
22 .... O   28-29 .... O
23 .... O   30-34 .... O
24 .... O   35-39 .... O
25 .... O   40 or older ...... O

	Yes	No
76. a. Are you a United States citizen?	O	O

	Yes	No
b. (If yes) Have you ever been a citizen of another country?	O	O

Faculty Questionnaire

THE CARNEGIE COMMISSION ON HIGHER EDUCATION

THE AMERICAN COUNCIL ON EDUCATION

Dear Colleague:

American higher education is currently undergoing its greatest changes in a hundred years. The extent and rapidity of these changes are causing severe strains and grave problems in our colleges and universities. But while we can see the broad outlines of these problems in over-crowded classrooms, rising costs, student rebellions, and threats to academic feeeedom from several quarters, there is very little detailed information on the form they take in different kinds of institutions, or in different disciplines and professions. Nor do we have firm knowledge of how the people most directly affected, the students and faculty, feel about these problems and issues.

To meet this need for more and better knowledge, the Carnegie Commission on Higher Education, in cooperation with the American Council on Education, is conducting a national survey of students and faculty in a broad sample of colleges and universities. The information we are gathering will be of help to the Carnegie Commission and to other bodies concerned with public policy in this area, as well as to scholars who are studying current problems and developments in American higher education. Our findings will be published in books and reports; the data we collect will be made available in an anonymous form to other scholars and students of higher education.

We have no illusion that even a broad survey of this kind will answer all our questions. We know the limits of questionnaires, and are conducting other studies, in other ways, to supplement this survey. Nevertheless, a broad survey such as this provides information that can be obtained in no other way. We know how busy faculty members and administrators are. And we know also that other surveys may have made similar demands on your time. But the present survey is unique in its scope and purposes: it is the first to ask similar questions of students and faculty in the same institutions, and it is the first to explore a variety of these issues on a national scale. The accuracy of the survey and the worth of its findings are dependent on your willingness to answer our questions. We believe the importance of the study will justify the time you give it.

One other matter. It is impossible to frame questions all of which are equally relevant to faculty members in many different fields and kinds of institutions; you may find some that seem inappropriate to your situation. We urge you to answer all the questions as well as you can; in our analysis we will be able to take into account special circumstances that affect replies to some questions.

Finally, we assure you that your answers will be held in strictest confidence. We are interested only in statistical relationships and will under no circumstances report responses on an individual or departmental basis. Any special markings on your form are used solely for internal data processing.

We hope you will find the questionnaire interesting to answer, and that you will complete and return it to us while you have it at hand.

With our thanks for your cooperation.

Sincerely,

Logan Wilson   *Clark Kerr*

Logan Wilson   Clark Kerr
President   Chairman
American Council   Carnegie Commission
  on Education   on Higher Education

1. What is your present rank?
   Instructor .... O
   Assistant Professor .... O
   Associate Professor .... O
   Professor .... O
   Lecturer .... O
   No ranks designated .... O
   Other .... O

2. What kind of appointment do you have here?
   Regular with tenure..................... O
   Regular without tenure .... O
   Acting .... O
   Visiting............................... O

3. During the spring term *, how many hours per week are you spending in formal instruction in class? (Give actual, not credit hours)
   None.. O   7-8 .... O   13-16........ O
   1-4 ... O   9-10 ...... O   17-20 .... O
   5-6 ... O   11-12 ..... O   21 or more... O

4. Are your teaching responsibilities this academic year
   Entirely undergraduate .... O
   Some undergraduate, some graduate .. O ⎤ Skip to
   Entirely graduate.................. O ⎦ No. 7
   Not teaching this year .... O → Skip to
                                            No. 8

5. How much do you control the content of your undergraduate courses?
   Almost completely.. O   Somewhat ..... O
   Substantially ...... O   Hardly at all... O

6. In about how many of the undergraduate courses you teach do you use the following?

	Most	Some	None
Term papers	O	O	O
Frequent quizzes.............	O	O	O
Graduate teaching assistants ..	O	O	O
Closed-circuit television	O	O	O
Computer or machine-aided instruction	O	O	O

7. About how many students, at all levels, are enrolled in your courses this term?
   None.... O   Under 25 .. O   100-249 ..... O
                 25-49 ..... O   250-399 ..... O
                 50-99 ..... O   400 or more .. O

*Quarter, semester, trimester, etc.

8. Do you discourage undergraduates from seeing you outside your regular office hours?
   Yes, almost always .... O
   Yes, but with many exceptions............ O
   No .... O

9. Please indicate your agreement or disagreement with each of the following statements.
   1. Strongly Agree
   2. Agree With Reservations
   3. Disagree With Reservations
   4. Strongly Disagree
   ① ② ③ ④

   Most undergraduates are mature enough to be given more responsibility for their own education ..... ① ② ③ ④
   Graduate students in my subject do best if their undergraduate major was in the same general field..... ① ② ③ ④
   Most graduate students in my department*are basically satisfied with the education they are getting .... ① ② ③ ④
   Most Ph.D. holders in my field get their degrees without showing much real scholarly ability .... ① ② ③ ④
   My department*has taken steps to increase graduate student participation in its decisions........... ① ② ③ ④
   The graduate program in my department*favors the bright, imaginative student .... ① ② ③ ④
   Many of the best graduate students can no longer find meaning in science and scholarship .... ① ② ③ ④
   Graduate education in my subject is doing a good job of training students .... ① ② ③ ④
   Some of the best graduate students drop out because they do not want to "play the game" or "beat the system" .... ① ② ③ ④
   The female graduate students in my department*are not as dedicated as the males...................... ① ② ③ ④
   The typical undergraduate curriculum has suffered from the specialization of faculty members .... ① ② ③ ④
   This institution should be as concerned about students' personal values as it is with their intellectual development .... ① ② ③ ④

*If no graduate program in your department, leave blank.

9 Continued.

Most undergraduates here are basically satisfied with the education they are getting .... ①②③④

A man can be an effective teacher without personally involving himself with his students .... ①②③④

Most faculty here are strongly interested in the academic problems of undergraduates .... ①②③④

Most American colleges reward conformity and crush student creativity .... ①②③④

This institution should be actively engaged in solving social problems .... ①②③④

More minority group undergraduates should be admitted here even if it means relaxing normal academic standards of admission .... ①②③④

Any institution with a substantial number of black students should offer a program of Black Studies if they wish it .... ①②③④

Any special academic program for black students should be administered and controlled by black people .... ①②③④

Undergraduate education in America would be improved if:
a) All courses were elective ..... ①②③④
b) Grades were abolished .... ①②③④
c) Course work were more relevant to contemporary life and problems .... ①②③④
d) More attention were paid to the emotional growth of students .. ①②③④
e) Students were required to spend a year in community service at home or abroad .... ①②③④
f) Colleges and universities were governed completely by their faculty and students .... ①②③④
g) There were less emphasis on specialized training and more on broad liberal education ..... ①②③④

10. For each of these areas, should present academic standards in your institution (a,b) and your graduate department (c,d) be--
(Mark one in each row)

— 1. Much higher
— 2. Somewhat higher
— 3. Left as they are
— 4. Somewhat lower
— 5. Much lower
①②③④⑤⑥— 6. No graduate department
a) Undergraduate admissions .. ①②③④⑤
b) Bachelor's degrees .... ①②③④⑤
c) Graduate admissions....... ①②③④⑤⑥
d) Advanced degrees .... ①②③④⑤⑥

11. Do you feel that the administration of your department*is:
Very autocratic .... O
Somewhat autocratic.................... O
Somewhat democratic .... O
Very democratic .... O

*Here and hereafter, if you have a joint appointment, answer for your main department. If your institution has no departments, answer for the equivalent administrative unit (e.g., division for junior colleges).

12. Is the chairman of your department appointed for a fixed short term (3 years or less) or for a long or indefinite period?
Long/Indefinite... O   Short term...... O

13. Roughly how many regular members (at the rank of instructor or above) does your department have this year?
3 or fewer........ O   16 - 20 .... O
4 - 5 .... O   21 - 25 .... O
6 - 7 .... O   26 - 30 .... O
8 - 10 .... O   31 - 40 .... O
11 - 15 .... O   41 or more ..... O

14. How much has your department changed in size in the last 3 years? Is it:
Much larger .... O
Somewhat larger .... O
About the same .... O
Smaller .... O

15a Do you think your department is now
Too big............................. O
About right.......................... O
Too small............................ O
b Do you think your institution is now
Too big............................. O
About right.......................... O
Too small............................ O

16. How active are you (a) in your own department's affairs? (b) in the faculty government of your institution (committee memberships, etc,) (Mark one in each column)

	Department	Institution
Much more than average......	O	O
Somewhat more than average..	O	O
About average	O	O
Somewhat less than average .	O	O
Much less than average	O	O

17. How much opportunity do you feel you have to influence the policies (a) of your department? (b) of your institution?

(Mark one in each column)

	Department	Institution
A great deal	O	O
Quite a bit	O	O
Some	O	O
None	O	O

18. How many of the people you see socially are: (a) members of the faculty here?

Almost all ...... O   Some .... O
Most .... O   Almost none .. O
About half ...... O

(b) members of your department?

Almost all ...... O   Some .... O
Most .... O   Almost none .. O
About half ...... O

19. What do you think of the emergence of radical student activism in recent years?

Unreservedly approve .... O
Approve with reservations .... O
Disapprove with reservations .... O
Unreservedly disapprove .... O

20. With respect to the student revolt at Columbia last year, were you in sympathy with

the students' aims and their methods .... O
their aims but not their methods .... O
neither their aims nor their methods ..... O
I don't know enough about it to judge .... O

21. Have any of your children been active in civil rights, anti-Vietnam, or other demonstrations?

Yes .... O
None active .... O
None of that age .... O

22. Has your campus experienced any student protests or demonstrations during the current academic year?

Yes ... O   No .... O (if no, skip to No. 25)

23. How would you characterize your attitude toward the most recent demonstration?

Approved of the demonstrators' aims and methods .... O
Approved of their aims but not their methods .... O
Disapproved of their aims .... O
Uncertain or mixed feelings .... O
Indifferent .... O

24. What was your role in this demonstration? (Mark all that apply)

Helped to plan, organize, or lead the protest .... O
Joined in active protest with the demonstrators .... O
Openly supported the goals of the protestors .... O
Openly opposed the goals of the protestors .. O
Tried to mediate in the protest .... O
Was not involved actively in any way ...... O

25. What effect have student demonstrations (on your campus or elsewhere) had on each of the following? (Mark one in each row)

1. Very favorable
2. Fairly favorable
3. Fairly harmful
4. Very harmful
① ② ③ ④ ⑤ — 5. No effect

Your research	① ② ③ ④ ⑤
Your teaching	① ② ③ ④ ⑤
Your relations with departmental colleagues	① ② ③ ④ ⑤
Your relations with other colleagues	① ② ③ ④ ⑤
Your relations with students	① ② ③ ④ ⑤
Your view of your campus administration	① ② ③ ④ ⑤
Your institution's relations with the local community	① ② ③ ④ ⑤

26a. What role do you believe undergraduates should play in decisions on the following?

1. Control
2. Voting power on committees
3. Formal consultation
4. Informal consultation
① ② ③ ④ ⑤ — 5. Little or no role

Faculty appointment and promotion	① ② ③ ④ ⑤
Undergraduate admissions policy	① ② ③ ④ ⑤
Provision and content of courses	① ② ③ ④ ⑤
Student discipline	① ② ③ ④ ⑤
Bachelor's degree requirements	① ② ③ ④ ⑤

b. What role do you believe graduate students should play in decisions on the following?

Faculty appointment and promotion	① ② ③ ④ ⑤
Departmental graduate admissions policy	① ② ③ ④ ⑤
Provision and content of graduate courses	① ② ③ ④ ⑤
Student discipline	① ② ③ ④ ⑤
Advanced degree requirements	① ② ③ ④ ⑤

27. Please indicate your agreement or disagreement with each of the following statements.

1. Strongly agree
2. Agree with reservations
3. Disagree with reservations
4. Strongly disagree

The normal academic requirements should be relaxed in appointing members of minority groups to the faculty here ①②③④

Opportunities for higher education should be available to all high school graduates who want it ①②③④

Most American colleges and universities are racist whether they mean to be or not ①②③④

Public colleges and universities must be more responsive to public demands than are private institutions ①②③④

Junior faculty members have too little say in the running of my department ①②③④

A small group of senior professors has disproportionate power in decision-making in this institution ①②③④

This institution would be better off with fewer administrators ①②③④

There should be faculty representation on the governing board of this institution ①②③④

Trustees' only responsibilities should be to raise money and gain community support ①②③④

The administration here has taken a clear stand in support of academic freedom ①②③④

Faculty unions have a divisive effect on academic life ①②③④

Teaching assistants' unions have a divisive effect on academic life ①②③④

Faculty members should be more militant in defending their interests ①②③④

Collective bargaining by faculty members has no place in a college or university ①②③④

Most rules governing student behavior here are sensible ①②③④

Campus rules here are generally administered in a reasonable way ①②③④

Undergraduates known to use marijuana regularly should be suspended or dismissed ①②③④

Political activities by students have no place on a college campus ①②③④

27 Continued.

Student demonstrations have no place on a college campus ①②③④

Students who disrupt the functioning of a college should be expelled or suspended ①②③④

Most campus demonstrations are created by far left groups trying to cause trouble ①②③④

College officials have the right to regulate student behavior off campus ①②③④

Respect for the academic profession has declined over the past 20 years ①②③④

A student's grades should not be revealed to anyone off campus without his consent ①②③④

Faculty members should be free on campus to advocate violent resistance to public authority ①②③④

Faculty members should be free to present in class any idea that they consider relevant ①②③④

Campus disruptions by militant students are a threat to academic freedom ①②③④

28. Have you known of a case here within the past two years in which a man's politics affected his chances for retention or promotion?

I know definitely of a case ○
I've heard of a case ○
I don't know of a case ○
I'm sure it hasn't happened ○

29. In recent years, have you ever felt intimidated in your classes by students with strong political or racial views?

Yes ○   No ○

30. In what year did you obtain your highest degree?

1928 or before ○
1929-1933 ○
1934-1938 ○
1939-1943 ○
1944-1948 ○
1949-1953 ○
1954-1958 ○
1959-1963 ○
1964-1966 ○
1967 or later ○

31. How many years elapsed between your obtaining your bachelor's degree and your highest degree?

No degree higher than bachelor's ○
I am still working for a higher degree ○
1 - 2 years ○
3 - 4 years ○
5 - 7 years ○
8 - 10 years ○
11 - 15 years ○
Over 15 years ○

32. On the following list, please mark
   1. (If any) the degree(s) for which you are currently working
   2. **All** degrees that you have earned
   3. **All** degrees you have earned at <u>this</u> institution

	Working Toward	Now hold	Earned here
Less than Bachelor's (A.A., etc.)	①	②	③
Undergraduate Bachelor's	①	②	③
First professional law degree	①	②	③
First professional medical degree (e.g. M.D., D.D.S.)	①	②	③
Other first professional beyond undergraduate bachelor's	①	②	③
Master's (except first professional) ...	①	②	③
Doctor of Arts or equivalent for doctorate degree without dissertation ...	①	②	③
Ph.D	①	②	③
Ed.D.............................	①	②	③
Other doctorate (except first professional)	①	②	③
None	①	②	③

33. From the following list, mark <u>one</u> subject in each column; mark the most appropriate <u>fine</u> categories, if applicable; where your precise field does not appear, mark the most similar category.

   1. Undergraduate major
   2. Highest postgraduate degree
   3. Present principal teaching field
   4. Present primary field of research, scholarship, creativity
   5. Department* of teaching appointment

① ② ③ ④ ⑤

	1	2	3	4	5
NONE	①	②	③	④	⑤
Agriculture and/or Forestry.....	①	②	③	④	⑤
Architecture and/or Design	①	②	③	④	⑤
Biological Sciences (General Biology)	①	②	③	④	⑤
Bacteriology, Molecular biology, Virology, Microbiology	①	②	③	④	⑤
Biochemistry	①	②	③	④	⑤
General Botany	①	②	③	④	⑤
Physiology, Anatomy	①	②	③	④	⑤
General Zoology	①	②	③	④	⑤
Other Biological Sciences	①	②	③	④	⑤
Business, Commerce and Management	①	②	③	④	⑤
Education....................	①	②	③	④	⑤
Elementary and/or Secondary ..	①	②	③	④	⑤
Foundations	①	②	③	④	⑤
Educational Psychology and Counseling	①	②	③	④	⑤
Educational Administration	①	②	③	④	⑤
Other Education fields	①	②	③	④	⑤

	1	2	3	4	5
Engineering	①	②	③	④	⑤
Chemical.....................	①	②	③	④	⑤
Civil	①	②	③	④	⑤
Electrical...................	①	②	③	④	⑤
Mechanical	①	②	③	④	⑤
Other Engineering fields	①	②	③	④	⑤
Fine Arts	①	②	③	④	⑤
Art..........................	①	②	③	④	⑤
Dramatics and Speech	①	②	③	④	⑤
Music........................	①	②	③	④	⑤
Other Fine Arts	①	②	③	④	⑤
Geography....................	①	②	③	④	⑤
Health Fields................	①	②	③	④	⑤
Medicine	①	②	③	④	⑤
Nursing	①	②	③	④	⑤
Other Health fields	①	②	③	④	⑤
Home Economics	①	②	③	④	⑤
Humanities	①	②	③	④	⑤
English language & literature..	①	②	③	④	⑤
Foreign languages & literature ..	①	②	③	④	⑤
French.......................	①	②	③	④	⑤
German	①	②	③	④	⑤
Spanish......................	①	②	③	④	⑤
Other foreign languages (including linguistics).........	①	②	③	④	⑤
History	①	②	③	④	⑤
Philosophy	①	②	③	④	⑤
Religion & Theology	①	②	③	④	⑤
Other Humanities fields	①	②	③	④	⑤
Industrial Arts	①	②	③	④	⑤
Journalism	①	②	③	④	⑤
Law	①	②	③	④	⑤
Library Science..............	①	②	③	④	⑤
Mathematics and Statistics	①	②	③	④	⑤
Physical & Health Education	①	②	③	④	⑤
Physical Sciences.............	①	②	③	④	⑤
Chemistry	①	②	③	④	⑤
Earth Sciences (incl. Geology)..	①	②	③	④	⑤
Physics......................	①	②	③	④	⑤
Other Physical Sciences	①	②	③	④	⑤
Psychology...................	①	②	③	④	⑤
Clinical.....................	①	②	③	④	⑤
Experimental	①	②	③	④	⑤
Social	①	②	③	④	⑤
Counseling and Guidance......	①	②	③	④	⑤
Other Psychology fields	①	②	③	④	⑤
Social Sciences..............	①	②	③	④	⑤
Anthropology & Archaeology	①	②	③	④	⑤
Economics	①	②	③	④	⑤
Political Science, Government ..	①	②	③	④	⑤
Sociology	①	②	③	④	⑤
Other Social Sciences.........	①	②	③	④	⑤
Social Work, Social Welfare.....	①	②	③	④	⑤
ALL OTHER FIELDS..........	①	②	③	④	⑤

* Mark main department, if you have a joint appointment.

34. On the following list of large American universities, mark one in each column; if the names
of your institutions do not appear, mark appropriate "other" categories.

　　　── 1. Bachelor's degree
　　　── 2. Highest degree
①②③ ── 3. First regular teaching job

NONE or not appropriate...........①②③
Boston University ....①②③
Brown University, R.I. ....①②③
California Institute of Technology ...①②③
California, University of, at Berkeley①②③
California, University of, at Los
　Angeles.......................①②③
Carnegie Institute of Technology, Pa.①②③
Catholic University of America, D.C.①②③
Chicago, University of ....①②③
Colorado, University of...........①②③
Columbia University Teachers'
　College, N.Y..................①②③
Columbia University, N.Y. ....①②③
Cornell University, N.Y. ....①②③
Duke University, N.C..............①②③
Florida, University of............①②③
Fordham University, N.Y..........①②③
Harvard University, Mass.........①②③
Illinois, University of............①②③
Indiana University at Bloomington ...①②③
Iowa State University ....①②③
Iowa, University of ....①②③
Johns Hopkins University..........①②③
Kansas, University of ....①②③
Louisiana State University.........①②③
Maryland, University of..........①②③
Massachusetts Instutute of Technology①②③
Michigan State University..........①②③
Michigan, University of...........①②③
Minnesota, University of..........①②③
Missouri, University of, at Columbia .①②③
Nebraska, University of ....①②③
New York University..............①②③
North Carolina, University of.......①②③
Northwestern University, Ill........①②③
Notre Dame University, Ind ....①②③
Ohio State University ....①②③
Oklahoma, University of..........①②③
Oregon State University ....①②③
Oregon, University of ....①②③
Pennsylvania State University......①②③
Pennsylvania, University of........①②③
Pittsburgh, University of ....①②③
Princeton University, N.J..........①②③
Purdue University ....①②③
Rochester, University of..........①②③
Rutgers University, N.J............①②③
Southern California, University of....①②③
Stanford University, Calif..........①②③

34 Continued
Syracuse University, N.Y............①②③
Texas, University of ....①②③
Utah, University of................①②③
Virginia, University of.............①②③
Washington University, Mo...........①②③
Washington, University of, Wash .....①②③
Western Reserve University, Ohio.....①②③
Wisconsin, University of ....①②③
Yale University, Conn ....①②③
Other private Ph.D.-granting univer-
　sity..........................①②③
Other state Ph.D.-granting university ..①②③
Other private college (no Ph.D.
　program).....................①②③
Other public college (no Ph.D.
　program).....................①②③
A foreign institution...............①②③
A junior or community college ....①②③

35. How long have you been employed (beyond
the level of teaching or research assistant):
a. in colleges or universities?

1 year or less..... ○	10-14 years ..... ○
2-3 years .... ○	15-19 years ..... ○
4-6 years........ ○	20-29 years ..... ○
7-9 years .... ○	30 years or more. .○

b. at this institution?

1 year or less..... ○	10-14 years ...... ○
2-3 years........ ○	15-19 years ...... ○
4-6 years........ ○	20-29 years ...... ○
7-9 years .... ○	30 years or more. ..○

36. At how many different colleges or universities
have you been employed full-time (beyond the
level of teaching or research assistant)?

None .... ○	Four .... ○
One .... ○	Five .... ○
Two............. ○	Six............. ○
Three .... ○	Seven or more ....○

37. Comparing yourself with other academic men of
your age and qualifications, how successful do
you consider yourself in your career?
　Very successful ... ○
　Fairly successful.. ○
　Fairly unsuccessful ○
　Very unsuccessful ..○

38. In general, how do you feel about this
institution?
　It is a very good place for me............. ○
　It is fairly good for me................... ○
　It is not the place for me................. ○

39. Do you think you could be equally or more satisfied with life in any other college or university?

Definitely yes .... O
Probably yes .... O
Probably no .... O
Definitely no .... O

40. If you were to begin your career again, would you still want to be a college professor?

Definitely yes .... O
Probably yes .... O
Probably no .... O
Definitely no .... O

41. (a) Mark **all** types of work that you have engaged in for a year or more since earning your bachelor's degree (not counting part-time work while in graduate school). (b) What were you doing immediately prior to taking a job at this institution? (Mark one)

	Have Done	Did Last
Teaching in a university	O	O
Teaching in a 4-year college........	O	O
Teaching in a junior or community college	O	O
Full-time non-teaching research position in a college or university ..	O	O
Post-doctoral fellowship or traineeship in a university...............	O	O
Full-time college or university administration	O	O
Teaching or administration in an elementary or secondary school	O	O
Research and development outside educational institutions	O	O
Executive or administrative post outside educational institutions	O	O
Other professional position	O	O
Student	O	O
Other...........................	O	O

42. Please indicate your agreement or disagreement with each of the following statements.

1. Strongly agree
2. Agree with reservations
3. Disagree with reservations
①②③④ — 4. Strongly disagree

My field is too research oriented . .①②③④
I prefer teaching courses which focus on limited specialties to those which cover wide varieties of material................... ①②③④

42 Continued
I consider myself an intellectual ..... ①②③④
I hardly ever get the time to give a piece of work the attention it deserves .... ①②③④
I tend to subordinate all aspects of my life to my work.................... ①②③④
A man's teaching and research inevitably reflect his political values ..... ①②③④
My commitments to different aspects of my job are the source of considerable personal strain .... ①②③④
I am in frequent communication with people in my own academic specialty in other institutions.......... ①②③④
Many of the highest-paid university professors get where they are by being "operators", rather than by their scholarly or scientific contributions .... ①②③④
By and large, full-time professional researchers in universities are people who couldn't quite make it on the faculty............................ ①②③④
Genuine scholarship is threatened in universities by the proliferation of big research centers .... ①②③④
The concentration of federal and foundation research grants in the big institutions (Mark each line)
1) is unfair to other institutions ..... ①②③④
2) is corrupting to the institutions and men that get them .... ①②③④
3) contributes substantially to the advancement of knowledge .... ①②③④
Many professors in graduate departments exploit their students to advance their own research .... ①②③④
In my department it is very difficult for a man to achieve tenure if he does not publish .... ①②③④
Teaching effectiveness, not publications, should be the primary criterion for promotion of faculty .... ①②③④
Faculty promotions should be based in part on formal student evaluations of their teachers...................... ①②③④
A professor at a junior college or state college ought to get the same pay as a university professor of equal seniority.......................... ①②③④
Classified weapons research is a legitimate activity on college and university campuses .... ①②③④
Big contract research has become more a source of money and prestige for researchers than an effective way of advancing knowledge .... ①②③④

43. Given the following four possible activities of academic men, please mark the first three in order:
    1. According to their importance to you personally
    2. According to your understanding of what your institution expects of you
    (Mark one in each column)

	Importance to Me			Institution's Expectation		
	First	Second	Third	First	Second	Third
Provide undergraduates with a broad liberal education	O	O	O	O	O	O
Prepare undergraduates for their chosen occupation	O	O	O	O	O	O
Train graduate or professional students	O	O	O	O	O	O
Engage in research	O	O	O	O	O	O

44. Within the past two years have you received an offer of another job or a serious inquiry about your availability for another position?
    An offer.............................O
    Not an offer, but a serious inquiry.........O
    Neither ....O

45. In a normal week, what proportion of your work time is devoted to the following activities:
    a. Administration (departmental or institutional, including committee work)

    None .....O 1-10% ...O 41-60% ......O
              11-20%...O 61-80% ......O
              21-40%...O 81-100% .....O

    b. Consulting (with or without pay)
    None .....O 1-10% ....O 41-60% ......O
              11-20%...O 61-80% ......O
              21-40%...O 81-100%.....O

    c. Outside professional practice
    None .....O 1-10% ....O 41-60% ......O
              11-20%...O 61-80% ......O
              21-40%...O 81-100% .....O

46. To how many academic or professional journals do you subscribe?
    None .....O 3-4 ......O 11-20........O
    1-2.......O 5-10 .....O More than 20 .O

47. How many articles have you published in academic or professional journals?
    None .....O 3-4 ......O 11-20........O
    1-2.......O 5-10 .....O More than 20 .O

48. How many books or monographs have you published or edited, alone or in collaboration?
    None ....O   3-4 ....O
    1-2............O   5 or more ....O

49. How many of your professional writings have been published or accepted for publication in the last two years?
    None ..O 3-4 ....O More than 10 .O
    1-2.....O 5-10 ......O

50. Do your interests lie primarily in teaching or in research?
    Very heavily in research.................O
    In both, but leaning toward research........O
    In both, but leaning toward teaching........O
    Very heavily in teaching.................O

51. Are you currently engaged in any scholarly or research work which you expect to lead to publication?
    Yes.....O   No.....O (If no, skip to No. 55)

52. Which of these statements applies to your current major piece of research or scholarship?
    I am essentially working alone ....O
    I am working with one or two colleagues....O
    I am a member of a larger group...........O

53. Are any of the following working with you on any research project? (Mark all that apply)
    Graduate research assistants..............O
    Post-doctoral fellows or trainees ....O
    Full-time professional level research personnel............................O

54. In the past 12 months, did you receive research support from: (Mark all sources that apply)
    Institutional or departmental funds ....O
    Federal agencies ....O
    State or local government agencies.........O
    Private foundations ....O
    Private industry ....O
    Other ....O
    None.................................O

55. During the past two years, have you served as a paid consultant to: (Mark all that apply)
    Local business, government or schools .....O
    A national corporation....................O
    A non-profit foundation...................O
    Federal or foreign government.............O
    A research project ....O
    Other ....O
    No paid consulting......................O

56. Are you a member of any of the following organisations? (Mark all that apply)

American Association of University Professors . . . . ◯

American Federation of Teachers . . . . ◯

A National Education Association affiliate . . . . ◯

A local or state association or union of college teachers . . . . ◯

A state, county or city employees' association or other association not confined to college teachers . . . . ◯

An association limited to teachers at your institution (other than the Academic Senate) . . . . ◯

57. Do you feel that there are circumstances in which a strike would be a legitimate means of collective action:

a. for faculty members

Definitely yes . . . . ◯
Probably yes . . . . ◯
Probably not . . . . ◯
Definitely not . . . . ◯

b. for teaching assistants

Definitely yes . . . . ◯
Probably yes . . . . ◯
Probably not . . . . ◯
Definitely not . . . . ◯

58. Please indicate your agreement or disagreement with each of the following statements.

1. Strongly agree
2. Agree with reservations
3. Disagree with reservations
①②③④ — 4. Strongly disagree

Where de facto segregation exists, black people should be assured control over their own schools . . ①②③④
Racial integration of the public elementary schools should be achieved even if it requires busing . . . . ①②③④
Meaningful social change cannot be achieved through traditional American politics . . . . ①②③④
With a few exceptions, the Chicago police acted reasonably in curbing the demonstrations at the Democratic National Convention . . . . . ①②③④
Hippies represent an important criticism of American culture . . . ①②③④
Marijuana should be legalized . . . ①②③④

58 Continued

Some form of Communist regime is probably necessary for progress in underdeveloped countries . . . . . . ①②③④
In the USA today there can be no justification for using violence to achieve political goals . . . . ①②③④
The main cause of Negro riots in the cities is white racism . . . . ①②③④

59. Which of these positions on Vietnam is closest to your own?

The U.S. should withdraw from Vietnam immediately . . . . ◯
The U.S. should reduce its involvement, and encourage the emergence of a coalition government in South Vietnam . . . . . . ◯
The U.S. should try to reduce its involvement, while being sure to prevent a Communist takeover in the South . . . . ◯
The U.S. should commit whatever forces are necessary to defeat the Communists ◯

60. How active were you in last year's political campaigns:

a. before the conventions?

Very active . . . . ◯
Fairly active . . . . ◯
Not very active . . . . ◯
Not active at all . . . . ◯

b. after the conventions?

Very active . . . . ◯
Fairly active . . . . ◯
Not very active . . . . ◯
Not active at all . . . . ◯

61.

1. Left
2. Liberal
3. Middle-of-the-road
4. Moderately conservative
①②③④⑤ — 5. Strongly conservative

a. How would you characterize yourself politically at the present time? . . . . ①②③④⑤

b. What were your politics as a college senior? . . . . ①②③④⑤

c. What were your father's politics while you were growing up? . . . . ①②③④⑤

d. How would you describe the prevailing political sentiments of undergraduates here? . . . . ①②③④⑤

62. Whom would you have favored:
   a. At the Republican convention:
   Nixon.........○   Rockefeller......○

   b. At the Democratic convention:
   Humphrey......○   McCarthy........○

63. Whom did you vote for in **November**?
   Humphrey...○   Another candidate.....○
   Nixon.......○   Did not vote..........○
   Wallace ....○   No answer ....○

64. Whom did you vote for in 1964?
   Johnson....○   Another candidate.....○
   Goldwater ..○   Did not vote..........○
                    No answer ....○

	Yes	No
65. a. Are you a United States citizen?...○	○	

   b. IF YES: Have you ever been a
   citizen of another country?........○   Yes ○   No ○

66. Have you ever been a member of a
   student political club or group?.......○   Yes ○   No ○

67. Have you ever attended a junior or
   community college as a student? ......○   Yes ○   No ○

68. During your career as a graduate student:
   Were you ever a teaching assis-
   tant? ....○   Yes ○   No ○
   Were you ever a research
   assistant?......................○   Yes ○   No ○
   Were you ever awarded a fellow-
   ship or scholarship worth $1,000
   per year or more?.................○   Yes ○   No ○
   Was there a faculty member who acted
   as your "sponsor" when you were
   looking for your first job? ....○   Yes ○   No ○

69. Do you have a working association
   with any research institute or center
   within your institution?.............○   Yes ○   No ○

70. In your department, are decisions other
   than personnel matters normally made
   by the vote of the whole department,
   including junior members?...........○   Yes ○   No ○

71. a. Are you now chairman or head of
   your department?................○   Yes ○   No ○
   b. IF NO: Have you ever been chair-
   man or head of a university or
   college department?.............○   Yes ○   No ○

72. a. Do you hold a full-time administrative position outside your own
   department?.....................○   Yes ○   No ○
   b. IF NO: Do you hold a part-time
   administrative position outside
   your own department?...........○   Yes ○   No ○

73. a. Are you now negotiating for, or
   have you already found or accepted, another position for
   the fall of 1969 ?...............   Yes ○   No ○
   b. IF NO: Are you looking for
   another position?...............   Yes ○   No ○
   c. IF NO: Would you seriously
   consider a reasonable offer of
   another position?...............   Yes ○   No ○

74. Would you describe yourself as conservative in your religious beliefs?....   Yes ○   No ○

75. How would you rate each of the following?
   ──── 1. Excellent
   ──── 2. Good
   ──── 3. Fair
   ①②③④ ─ 4. Poor

   Your own salary ....①②③④
   Your own graduate education .....①②③④
   The academic reputation of your de-
   partment outside your institution..①②③④
   At your institution--
   The intellectual environment ......①②③④
   Faculty salary levels.............①②③④
   Teaching load ....①②③④
   Ratio of teaching faculty to students①②③④
   The administration...............①②③④
   The effectiveness of your campus
   senate or faculty council ....①②③④
   General research resources (e.g.,
   library, labs, computers, space,
   etc.) ....①②③④
   Availability of research funds from
   all sources.....................①②③④
   Cultural resources ....①②③④
   In your department--
   The intellectual environment ......①②③④
   Personal relations among faculty...①②③④
   Faculty/student relations ....①②③④

76. How often, on average, do you
   ──── 1. Once a week or more
   ──── 2. Two or three times a month
   ──── 3. About once a month
   ──── 4. A few times a year
   ①②③④⑤ ─ 5. Once a year or less
   See undergraduates informally
   (for meals, parties, informal
   gatherings) ?...................①②③④⑤
   Spend 4 hours uninterruptedly on
   professional reading, writing or
   research?.....................①②③④⑤
   Attend:
   1. A religious service ....①②③④⑤
   2. A concert ....①②③④⑤
   3. An "art" film ....①②③④⑤
   4. A play ....①②③④⑤
   5. An art exhibition ....①②③④⑤
   6. An athletic event...........①②③④⑤

77. Do you consider yourself
    Deeply religious ....○
    Moderately religious ....○
    Largely indifferent to religion ....○
    Basically opposed to religion ....○

78. a. In what religion were you raised?
    Protestant.......○   Other............○
    Catholic ....○   None............○
    Jewish..........○   No answer ......○

    b. What is your present religion?
    Protestant.......○   Other............○
    Catholic ....○   None ....○
    Jewish..........○   No answer ....○

79. What is the highest level of formal education
    reached by your spouse? Your father? Your
    mother? (Mark one in each column)

    Spouse / Father / Mother

    No spouse.......................○
    8th grade or less ....○○○
    Some high school..................○○○
    Completed high school ....○○○
    Some college ....○○○
    Graduated from college............○○○
    Attended graduate or professional
      school ....○○○
    Attained advanced degree ....○○○

80. What is (was) your father's principal
    occupation? (Mark one)
    College or university teaching, research or
      administration ....○
    Elementary or secondary school teaching
      or administration ....○
    Other professional.....................○
    Managerial, administrative, semiprofes-
      sional ....○
    Owner, large business ....○
    Owner, small business ....○
    Other white collar: clerical, retail sales...○
    Skilled wage worker ....○
    Semi- and unskilled wage worker, farm
      laborer............................○
    Armed forces ....○
    Farm owner or manager................○

81. What is your basic institutional salary, before
    tax and deductions, for the current academic year?
    Below $7,000.....○ $17,000-$19,999..○
    $7,000-$9,999.....○ $20,000-$24,999..○
    $10,000-$11,999...○ $25,000-$29,999..○
    $12,000-$13,999...○ $30,000 and over .○
    $14,000-$16,999...○

82. Is this based on
    9/10 months.......○   11/12 months ......○

83. In recent years, roughly how much have you earned
    over and above your basic salary? (Please esti-
    mate as a percentage of your basic salary.)
    0%..... ○   Under 10%.○   30%-39% ....○
                 10%-19% ..○   40%-49% ....○
                 20%-29% ..○   50% and over ○

84. What are the two largest sources of your supple-
    mentary earnings? (Mark one in each   Second
    column)   Largest   Largest
    Summer teaching................○........○
    Teaching elsewhere (extension,
      etc.) other than summer teaching ○.......○
    Consulting ....○........○
    Private practice ....○........○
    Royalties (from publications,
      patents) ....○........○
    Fees for speeches and lectures ..○.......○
    Research salaries and payments .○.......○
    Other.........................○........○
    None ....○........○

85. What is your marital status?
    Married (once only)......................○
    Married (remarried) ....○
    Separated ....○
    Single (never married) ....○
    Single (divorced).......................○
    Single (widowed).......................○

86. How many dependent children do you have?
    None ....○   Two ....○
    One ....○   Three or more .....○

87. What is your date of birth?
    1903 or before .....○   1924-1928 ....○
    1904-1908........○   1929-1933........○
    1909-1913........○   1934-1938 ....○
    1914-1918........○   1939-1943 ....○
    1919-1923........○   1944 or later ......○

88. Your sex: Male ....○   Female ......○

89. Your race:
    White/Caucasian.......................○
    Black/Negro/Afro-American ....○
    Oriental ....○
    Other................................○

Index

Snider, James G., 40
Sommerkorn, Ingrid, 126
Southern Methodist University, 39
Soviet Union, 37
Sprague, Robert J., 23
Stark, Rodney, 9, 19
Stetson, Charlotte Perkins, 1, 22, 125
Storr, Richard J., 31*n.*
Strodtbeck, Fred L., 13
Switzerland, 35

Talbot, Marion, 33–34
Talbot, Nell S., 38
Texas, University of, 160*n.*
Thielbar, Gerald W., 40, 51
Thomas, Martha, 27
Thompson, Eleanor, 28
Thwing, Charles F., 26, 29
Trow, Martin A., 77*n.,* 164*n.*
Troy Seminary, 23
Tufts University, 28
Turner, Ralph, 13, 126

Uesugi, Thomas, 13
U.S. Office of Education, 14, 15*n.,* 151,
    154, 158, 160

Vassar, Matthew, 26
Vassar College, 26, 27, 28

Veysey, Laurence R., 31*n.*
Vinacke, W. Edgar, 13
Vollmer, Howard L., 38

Washington, University of, 28
Weber, Max, 37
Wegner, Eldon E., 9
Weisstein, Naomi, 12
Wellesley College, 26
Wells, D. Collin, 23
Western Reserve University, College for
    Women, 29
White, Lynn, Jr., 38
Whittaker, Elvi, 113
Willard, Emma, 23
Williamson, Robert, 13*n.*
Winick, Charles, 67*n.*
Wisconsin, University of, 28, 39
    Women's Research Group, 9
Women's Medical College of Pennsylvania,
    35
Woodring, Paul, 9
Woody, Thomas, 4, 22, 24, 25, 28, 29, 32,
    35

Yale University, 25, 26, 31, 32
    Graduate School, 28

Zelan, Joseph, 106